THE BANTAM SHAKESPEARE

THE EDITORS

OSCAR JAMES CAMPBELL established the text for this edition and served as the authority on all points of scholarship. Recognized as one of the leading Shakespearean scholars, he is editor of *The Living Shakespeare* and author of *Shakespeare's Satire, Comical Satyre, Shakespeare's Troilus and Cressida,* and numerous other books and articles on literary subjects. Dr. Campbell is now Professor Emeritus of Columbia University; he was formerly Chairman of the English Department.

ALFRED ROTHSCHILD, writer and lecturer, has an original and penetrating approach to many subjects. A life-long Shakespeare addict, he originated the unique features of the Bantam Shakespeare. He worked on every phase of the project in close contact with the other editors, and supervised the production of the final manuscript.

STUART VAUGHAN is one of the country's most prominent theatrical directors. Formerly Artistic Director of the Phoenix Theatre in New York, he is now at the head of the newly established Seattle Repertory Theatre. He staged the Phoenix's highly successful productions of *Hamlet* and *Henry IV, Parts I* and *II.* He was the first director of the New York Shakespeare Festival productions in Central Park, for which he staged *Romeo and Juliet, Macbeth, Two Gentlemen of Verona, Julius Caesar,* and *Othello.* At the Heckscher Theatre in New York, he also directed *Richard III* and *As You Like It.* Mr. Vaughan supervised in particular the stage directions in this edition, wrote the essay on the Elizabethan theatre, and contributed a number of notes.

HENRY IV, PART II

by

WILLIAM SHAKESPEARE

EDITED BY
OSCAR JAMES CAMPBELL
ALFRED ROTHSCHILD
STUART VAUGHAN

BANTAM BOOKS / NEW YORK

HENRY IV, PART II
A Bantam Classic / published June 1964

ACKNOWLEDGMENTS

BRADBROOK, M. C.: from *Shakespeare and Elizabethan Poetry.*
Oxford University Press, 1952; Chatto & Windus Ltd., 1951. Reprinted by permission of the Publishers.

BRADLEY, A. C.: from *Oxford Lectures on Poetry;* reprinted by
permission of Macmillan & Company Ltd. and St. Martin's
Press, Inc.

CHARLTON, H. B.: from *Shakespearian Comedy;* reprinted by permission of Methuen & Company Ltd.

TILLYARD, E. M. W.: from *Shakespeare's History Plays.* Copyright
1946 by The Macmillan Company. Reprinted by permission of
The Macmillan Company, Mr. Stephen Tillyard, and Chatto and
Windus Ltd.

WILSON, JOHN DOVER: from *The Fortunes of Falstaff;* reprinted
by permission of Cambridge University Press.

*Bantam Books are published by Bantam Books, Inc. Its trade-mark,
consisting of the words "Bantam Books" and the portrayal of a bantam, is registered in the United States Patent Office and in other
countries. Marca Registrada. Printed in the United States of Amer-
ica. Bantam Books, Inc., 271 Madison Ave., New York 16, N. Y.*

Foreword

BY ALFRED ROTHSCHILD

Still another Shakespeare! To be sure—but a Shakespeare "with a difference."

It all started years ago with a complaint from a high school student. He had seen a performance of *Julius Caesar*, and was intensely excited about it. Then he tried reading the play, and found he just couldn't make any progress. He was disappointed and puzzled. "What makes it so tough?" he asked.

He didn't know he was planting a seed. It was there and then that this edition began to take shape.

The Bantam Shakespeare seeks to provide in a convenient and easily comprehended form as much guidance and information for the student and general reader as is reasonably possible.

This is how we have tried to achieve our objective:

Text

By "text" we mean the words the characters actually speak. While it is true that this text, written in Elizabethan English, contains words and phrases no longer in common usage, allusions to matters and events no longer easily recognized, and various other obscurities, there was never any doubt about one rule: the basic text must not be violated.

So this is not a new text. There are no "improvements," no rewritten lines, no "corrections" of Elizabethan grammar—even though a change might make some lines more easily understood by modern readers. The editors of this edition are all purists—on fundamentals. But it cannot be repeated too often that there is no such thing as a "pure" Shakespeare text—no such thing even as agreement on whether some passages in the plays were written by Shakespeare himself.

There is, however, an authoritative consensus on the basis

of which the so-called "Cambridge Edition" was published about one hundred years ago. William Aldis Wright and William George Clark, the editors, were not, of course, trying to improve Shakespeare. What they did, with infinite care and learning, was to reconcile differences in the original quarto and folio texts, to correct printers' errors, and so on, with due regard to the research and opinions of scholars before them. This Cambridge Edition is now almost universally accepted as the standard reading text.

A special edition of the Cambridge Shakespeare, published under the auspices of the same Cambridge editors, is known as the "Globe" edition, and it is this text that for the purposes of the Bantam Shakespeare is regarded as basically sacrosanct. We have made some changes in punctuation, and also in spelling, particularly in substituting the letter "e" for the apostrophe in words like "aimed," in which the "e" is now always silent. Where we do deviate from the text, which is rarely, we explain why in a Note.

Glossary

Unfamiliar and obscure words in the text of the plays are customarily explained in a glossary at the back of the book, or at the foot of the text page. As a rule, there is no indication that a particular word is "glossed." This means that sometimes the reader will stop to hunt in vain, and sometimes fail to look for an explanation when he should—that is, when the modern meaning of a word differs from its Elizabethan meaning. Take the word "commodity," for example. It is certainly neither uncommon nor obscure. But as used by Shakespeare in *Henry IV, Part II* it means "profit"; and unless the reader is made aware of this he cannot properly understand the passage in which the word occurs.

Our method is to place an asterisk next to the word that requires clarification, and then to give the equivalent on the same line in the right-hand margin, so that the eye, particularly as it becomes accustomed to the arrangement, can take it in at a glance.

Obviously, these marginal glosses must be kept within certain limits of length, not only for typographical reasons, but also because excessive length would defeat our objective of having the reader absorb the explanation with the least possible interruption of his train of thought.

In some instances, the word in the glossary margin is not simply the modern equivalent of the word marked with an asterisk, as, for instance, on line 13 of the first scene of *Hamlet*. There "rivals" is easily and with reasonable accuracy translated into modern English as "partners." But now take the word "instrument" in the line "Give me the gown. Where is thy instrument?" (*Julius Caesar*, IV, 3, 239.) "Instrument'" is certainly not an unfamiliar word, nor is it used here in an unfamiliar sense. But there is nothing in the preceding lines to indicate that Brutus is referring to a musical instrument. On the stage, this presents no problem, and stage directors through the centuries have known how to convey the information to the audience. But it is different with the reader. He needs help if he is not to be confused and thus lose something of the atmosphere of one of the most charming and effective touches in the play. So we marked "instrument" with an asterisk and printed "*i.e.*, lute" in the margin, fully aware that "lute" is not a definition of "instrument."

It will be noticed that sometimes there is a slight break in the line in which an asterisk occurs. This signifies that the gloss covers more than one word and applies jointly to the two or more words from the break to the asterisk.

Occasionally, two asterisks will be found on one line. When this occurs, the two glosses are separated by a diagonal stroke.

It is interesting to note, incidentally, that very few glosses are needed for an understanding and appreciation of most of the great key passages. This is not an accident: it is part of the genius of Shakespeare. At his greatest, he is at his simplest —or perhaps we should say that he then achieves that simplicity of effect which hides the infinite complexity of perfection.

Stage Directions

Here we have a situation entirely different from that which applies to the text. Stage directions are simply not text at all. They are not part of the poetry, the characterization, the dramatic vigor of the lines, which are the glory of Shakespeare. The stage directions that have come down to us from the quartos and folios are almost certainly only the brief markings in the prompt books used in the early staging of the plays. It was not until nearly one hundred years after

Shakespeare's death that an edition, edited by Nicholas Rowe, was published, incorporating systematic division into acts and scenes, and many new stage directions.

The history of presenting Shakespeare in print is long. Progress has been difficult and slow. It took many years to change even such externals as Elizabethan spelling and typography. The time has come to take a further step forward by bringing other externals such as stage directions up to date.

The obvious function of stage directions in a reading edition is to help the reader follow the action of the play. There should be an adequate description of the scenes and of the way the characters move about. Our rule has been to follow the Globe edition directions, but to amplify them where necessary, to modernize the language, and also to paragraph speeches in accordance with their context. In the few instances where we have deemed it essential to go beyond this in order to help the reader understand what is going on, we have called attention to the change in a Note.

In all cases the stage directions are as simple and direct as we could make them. Mood-setting imagery has no place here, any more than a description of a character's state of mind. That would be tantamount to interpreting the character for the reader. Actually, every effort has been made to avoid interpretation. The purpose is not to get in the reader's way, but to illuminate it. The text must be allowed to speak for itself, so that the reader can make his own interpretation as he progresses with his reading. Not that the Bantam Shakespeare neglects interpretation—on the contrary, it makes a special feature of interpretative comment. But it does so where it belongs: in the appendix.

What must be made clear is the difference between a reading version of a Shakespeare play, where stage directions that interpret character are wrong, and a stage or acting version where they are not only right but also essential—and, indeed, inevitable.

Even though the standard division into scenes and acts admittedly leaves something to be desired, we have adhered to it. Nothing substantial is to be gained by changing or eliminating it, but much to be lost, since it is used in all the important reference works, such as Schmidt's Lexicon and Bartlett's Concordance.

The customary way of printing the passage beginning with

line 62 of the second scene of the first act, where Falstaff is on
a London street talking to his page, is this:

Enter the LORD CHIEF-JUSTICE *and* SERVANT.

PAGE.
Sir, here comes the nobleman that committed the prince
for striking him about Bardolph.
FALSTAFF.
Wait close; I will not see him.
CHIEF-JUSTICE.
What's he that goes there?
SERVANT.
Falstaff, an 't please your lordship.
CHIEF-JUSTICE.
He that was in question for the robbery?
SERVANT.
He, my lord: but he has since done good service at
Shrewsbury; and, as I hear, is now going with some
charge to the Lord John of Lancaster.
CHIEF-JUSTICE.
What, to York? Call him back again.
SERVANT.
Sir John Falstaff!
FALSTAFF.
Boy, tell him I am deaf.
PAGE.
You must speak louder; my master is deaf.
CHIEF-JUSTICE.
I am sure he is, to the hearing of anything good. Go,
pluck him by the elbow; I must speak with him.
SERVANT.
Sir John!

Now see what happens when the passage is printed the
Bantam way—how easy it is to follow the action step by step.

(*The* LORD CHIEF-JUSTICE, *accompanied by* SERVANT,
enters at a distance.)
PAGE (*aside to* FALSTAFF).
Sir, here comes the nobleman that committed the prince
for striking him about Bardolph.
FALSTAFF (*aside to* PAGE).
Wait close;* I will not see him.   conceal
(*Starts to walk away.*)   yourself
CHIEF-JUSTICE (*to* SERVANT).
What's he that goes there?
SERVANT.
Falstaff, an 't please your lordship.

CHIEF-JUSTICE.

He that was in question for* the robbery?   questioned
                                                                                                        about
SERVANT.

He, my lord: but he hath since done good service at Shrewsbury; and, as I hear, is now going with some charge* to the Lord John of Lancaster.   troops

CHIEF-JUSTICE.

What, to York? Call him back again.

SERVANT (*calling*).

Sir John Falstaff!

FALSTAFF (*aside to* PAGE).

Boy, tell him I am deaf.

PAGE (*to* SERVANT).

You must speak louder; my master is deaf.

CHIEF-JUSTICE.

I am sure he is, to the hearing of anything good.

    (*To* SERVANT.)

Go, pluck him by the elbow; I must speak with him.

SERVANT (*pulling at* FALSTAFF'S *sleeve*).

Sir John!

and so on, to the conclusion of the scene.

It should be noted that the additions and changes we have made are inherent in the text. Take the stage direction, "Starts to walk away." We derive this information from the next line, spoken by the Chief-Justice, "What's he that goes there?" which makes it clear that Falstaff is actually moving away.

Note, too, how the glosses function. "Conceal yourself," "questioned about," "troops"—these are all terms which must be understood in the sense in which Shakespeare used them if this characteristically so important passage, of which the excerpt given forms only the beginning, is to be fully appreciated. With the Bantam method of glossing, you do not interrupt your reading five times: the clarifying meaning, fitting into the grammatical construction of the line, is right there under your eye for your instant use. Thus the thread of your thinking is not broken: your mind, to quote from a particularly pregnant comment by Samuel Johnson, is not "refrigerated" by interruptions.

Notes

Here, too, the aim of the Bantam Shakespeare is maximum reader convenience. The words or passages requiring Notes are consecutively numbered. The Notes in the appendix are

numbered in rotation, and also identified by the number of
the line. Thus, the reader knows at once not only that there
is a Note, but where to find it conveniently and quickly.
All the Notes have been written to meet our special objec-
tives. We have tried to keep them succinct, without limiting
them in either length or number.

Commentaries

The inclusion of a wide range of commentaries in a paper-
back edition is another original Bantam feature. And we go
further: we tie the commentaries together by means of intro-
ductory paragraphs. This is important because comment
written in the eighteenth century, for example, should not
be viewed in the same light as comment written, say, one
hundred years later. Some of Voltaire's criticism sounds preposterous today, but the fact is that it cannot be properly
evaluated without consideration of the historical and literary
background against which it was written.

Format

A great deal of thought has been given to typographical
arrangement. The practice of abbreviating character names,
so that "Hamlet" becomes "Ham," and "Antony" "Ant," is
not only esthetically disturbing but often seriously confusing
—as when you have "Macd" for "Macduff" on one line, and
"Macb" for "Macbeth" on the next. In the Bantam Shakespeare, the name of the character speaking is printed in full
and on a separate line. This not only helps to open up the
printing in general, but also has the highly desirable effects
of reducing the number of run-over lines and always keeping
the first line of a speech in correct alignment. All other details, such as the placing of parenthetical stage directions, and
the numbering of the lines, have been handled so as to
achieve maximum reading ease.

Other Features

Preceding each play is an essay by Professor Campbell
written especially for this edition. It analyzes the play, and
gives details regarding the source of the plot, the date of
composition, and so on. We have also added an annotated
bibliography and a chronological table, both prepared by
Professor Campbell. The chronological table, bringing as it
does events in Shakespeare's life into relation with other

events of the time, makes enlightening and fascinating reading. Even a casual glance reveals that Galileo was born in the same year as Shakespeare; that Shakespeare was thirteen at the time of the publication of Holinshed's *Chronicles of England, Scotland and Ireland*, on which he drew so heavily for his historical plays; and twenty-four at the time of the defeat of the Spanish Armada.

It is important for the reader to know something about the difference between our modern stage and that for which Shakespeare wrote. An essay on the Elizabethan theatre, written by Mr. Stuart Vaughan, has therefore been included.

While the functions of the three editors are clearly defined on the title page, it should be said that the final manuscript emerged as the result of much reviewing of scripts and many conferences involving all the editors. Among these, we must in all fairness include Donald Reis of Bantam Books, whose help in every respect proved invaluable. In actual practice there was no sharp separation of function. So much is here as a result of a harmonious exchange of views and blending of ideas in the action and reaction of open-minded discussion, that it is impossible to tell where one contribution began and the other left off.

About two hundred years ago, Samuel Johnson wrote:

> Let him that is yet unacquainted with the powers of Shakespeare, and who desires to feel the greatest pleasure that the drama can give, read every play from the first scene to the last, with utter negligence of all his commentators. When his fancy is once on the wing, let it not stop at correction or explanation. When his attention is strongly engaged, let it disdain alike to turn aside to the name of Theobald and of Pope. Let him read on through the brightness and obscurity, through integrity and corruption; let him preserve his comprehension of the dialogue and his interest in the fable. And when the pleasures of novelty have ceased, let him attempt exactness and read the commentators. . . .

The advice is good. Countless commentators have written countless words on the precise meaning of countless terms and phrases, with countless varieties of interpretation. It has not been possible, if only because of space limitations, to do more than indicate some of the more prominent controversial issues.

If you want to venture further, you will do well to use our bibliography as a guide. But always remember that the Why and Wherefore of Shakespeare is part of the mystery of the universe. Learn to enjoy him as a poet and a dramatist. Regard him as you would a magnificent view of land and sea, comprehending an infinite variety of light and shade and color, to which you open up your heart and soul and mind, and let it work its wonders upon you.

Contents

Introduction

BY OSCAR JAMES CAMPBELL

From the moment he first planned his two plays on Henry IV, Shakespeare designed the two parts to form a single drama, the subject of which would be "The Reclamation of as Profligate Prince." At the end of *Part I*, Henry has killed in single combat the unmatched warrior Hotspur; this glorious achievement has enabled him to take the "crown of chivalry" from his antagonist's head and place it firmly on his own. The display of prowess on the battlefield, coupled with the deep respect he shows for his fallen foe, gives him the right to serve as the perfect example of a chivalric knight. But he has yet to show that respect for the law which is the most important attribute of an English sovereign. His painful realization that he must assume the duties and burdens of the crown is movingly dramatized in the scenes with his dying father, and throughout the second part of *Henry IV* by his gradual alienation from Falstaff and his climactic break with this, his official jester and comrade in profligacy.

The fortunes of Falstaff in *Part II* are a definite sequel to those dramatized in *Part I*. In the last scene of the first play he enters carrying on his back the body of Hotspur, whom he impudently announces he has slain by a stab in his victim's thigh. He throws the dead man down at the feet of Prince Hal, exclaiming, "If your father will do me any honor, so; if not, let him kill another Percy himself." Hal at once enters into the spirit of this extravagant joke. "For my part," he assures Sir John, "if a lie will do thee grace, I'll gild it with the happiest terms [that is, most favorable reports] at my command."

At the old rogue's first appearance in *Part II*, we see that Hal has kept his promise. Falstaff's false reputation for valor has gone to his head; he appears in the guise of a courtier and, if we are to believe Dover Wilson, ridiculously decked

out. And he has engaged a tiny little page to walk before him
to carry his sword and immense shield. He plays this courtier
part only intermittently, but enough to establish the fact that
he is a different person from the fat man who fled from the
hold-up at Gadshill roaring like a bull calf. He is, rather, the
professional old soldier who knows and employs all the tricks
of his trade.

Falstaff was so popular with the audiences that saw him in
the first part of *Henry IV* in the Globe Theatre that Shakespeare realized that he must give him a "fat part" in the
sequel. The spectators must have clamored for more of that
"good portly man," Sir John Falstaff. Many are the contemporary references to his popularity. Leonard Digges in some
verses prefixed to the First Folio edition of Shakespeare's
plays bears witness to Falstaff's appeal at the box office. Ben
Jonson's comedies, he admits, are fine drama,

> Yet these sometimes, even at a friend's desire
> Acted, have scarce defraid the sea-cole fire
> And doore-keepers.

Digges is referring to the fire which heated the indoor Blackfriars' Theatre. Jonson's comedies, he says, even when given
a request performance, seldom attracted a large enough audience to pay for the heat, light, and wages of the ticket takers.

> When, let but Falstaff come
> Hal, Poins, the rest, you scarce shall upon a room,
> All is so pester'd [that is, clogged up, overcrowded].

Another couplet proves that *Henry IV, Part 1* was a great
favorite with the crowds, for when Falstaff and his familiars
appeared, the groundlings would stop cracking nuts and hold
their jaws and hands in a state of suspended animation.

> I could praise Heywood now, or tell how long
> Falstaff from cracking nuts, has kept the throng.

To make the Prince's final banishment of the fat knight
acceptable to audiences so deeply in love with him, Shakespeare evidently decided that he would have to debase him.
It is true that by way of satisfying the playgoers' expectations,
the dramatist allows the old rogue to invent new versions of
the jests and the verbal adroitness that had most delighted the

audiences in *Part I.* Yet in most instances Falstaff's buffoonery is so involved with vulgarity and evil as to become, to modern audiences at least, almost repulsive. The difference between the two scenes in the Boar's Head Tavern is striking. Dover Wilson describes it in this succinct fashion: "Boar's Head in *Part I,* an elysium of frolic and good fellowship, has become a brothel." Yet this second scene is just as funny in its own fashion as is the earlier one. The two new characters who appear in this second scene, Pistol and Doll Tearsheet, arouse immortal laughter. Doll displays that mixture of sentimentality and vulgarity which has always characterized ladies of her profession. It is she more than Falstaff who becomes in this scene a source of mirth.

This process of debasing Falstaff continues until the play is almost half over. But Shakespeare's heart clearly was not in his task. The degradation of the old knight, dramatically necessary though it might be, did not stimulate his creator's imagination to its best achievement. Accordingly, Shakespeare invented Justice Shallow, his cousin Justice Silence, and all the household of the witless country justice. These bumpkins, painted with the same shrewd realism with which Shakespeare had drawn the denizens of Eastcheap, served as a new whetstone for Falstaff's sense of the absurd. And he "devised matter enough" out of these quaffers of thin potations to keep the world in perpetual laughter for over three hundred years.

The follies of the new group of clowns raises the comedy again to the high plane it had reached in *Part I.* But they also interrupt and reverse the process of vulgarization which Shakespeare had begun, and re-establish Sir John so firmly in our good graces that many critics believe the result upset the author's plans for his finale. The new king's public repulse of his old companions seems more like a smug parade of virtue than triumphant proof of reclamation. But to criticize this is to forget that Shakespeare's play is not a moral tract but a work of art. The truth is that in spite of Falstaff's immorality, our aesthetic delight in him remains as strong as ever. To the very end of the double drama Shakespeare holds the artistic balance so evenly between Sir John and Prince Hal that it never occurs to us to pass moral judgment on either the rascal's vices or Hal's apparent disloyalty to his old crony.

With all this dramatic business to be developed around Falstaff and Prince Henry, Shakespeare found little space for the historical events which serve at least as a foundation for his dramatic structure. Only a few scenes are devoted to the new rebellion instigated by Northumberland and the Archbishop and to its suppression through the Machiavellian cunning of Prince John. In such a small compass, however, the dramatist is able to make this second rebellion in the reign of Henry IV resemble the revolt which the Catholic lords of the northern counties raised against Queen Elizabeth in 1569. The likeness between the two rebellions quickened the interest of Elizabethan audiences in the events of a far-off time, for they had all been taught to seek in history guides to wise political action in current crises.

Shakespeare devotes most of the serious part of the play to showing the Prince's growing understanding of the burdens a king must assume. Throughout *Henry IV, Part II* the King is in a state of profound melancholy and foreboding, a just moral retribution for his sin in dethroning the anointed sovereign, Richard II. On his deathbed these fears assail him in aggravated form until at last he places his uneasy crown upon a pillow beside him and lapses into unconsciousness. The Prince, thinking his father dead, puts the symbol of kingship on his own head and walks into the next room in a state of mingled grief and misgiving. But the King, regaining consciousness, misconstrues the act as proof that the Prince is impatient to become ruler in order that he may "pluck the muzzle of restraint" from his conduct. Thus suspicion and dismay poison the King's last moments and inflict bitter punishment upon him even in his dying hour.

The monarch sends for his son, and the Prince succeeds in convincing his father of the sincerity of his resolve to abandon his present wild courses. Then it is that Henry IV utters a prophecy of great political and ethical import: the "indirect crooked ways" by which he won the crown have inevitably turned his reign into one long era of civil strife and personal unhappiness; but his son's reign, he announces, will be free of all such manifestations of God's wrath. Prince Hal's reformation is certain, for the good reason that his wildness was a form of divine punishment visited upon his father. After the King's death, it will no longer have cause for being. The erstwhile prodigal's unruly impulses will be buried deep in his father's grave. A spirit thus purified by the interposition of God will be ready to assume the role of the ideal English sovereign. In the process of his reform, the abandonment of his riotous companions is to be regarded as proof of a deep moral conversion.

More important evidence of Prince Hal's reclamation is to be found in his unswerving allegiance to the impartial administration of justice, which is symbolized in the figure of the Lord Chief-Justice. Some modern critics, believing that Shakespeare's central purpose in *Part II* was to show the victory of Justice over Profligacy or Misrule, think that in these scenes the author is taking pains to show the ineptitude of Vanity or Misrule when she fences with Justice. This is to overemphasize the influence of the technique of the morality play upon these encounters. A spectator intent only on what is happening before his eyes is moved to hearty laughter at Falstaff's success in thawing the Justice's severity into mirth. But the Justice awakens in Falstaff no respect for the law. When Sir John hears that Prince Hal has become King, his first words are, "The laws of England are at my commandment. . . . And woe to my lord chief-justice."

But the knight does not know that the "tide of blood" in Prince Hal which "flowed in vanity till now" has turned and now "doth . . . ebb back to the sea" to "mingle with the state of floods and flow henceforth in formal majesty." As an ideal king, Henry V must acknowledge his subjection to the common law of England no less than to natural law and to the laws of God. Therefore, one of the surest signs of his conversion is his expressed admiration of the Chief-Justice's daring in sending the heir apparent to prison for breaking the law. One of his first acts as King is to hand the Justice a sword, the symbol of his office, with the injunction that he use it

> With the like bold, just and impartial spirit
> As you have done 'gainst me.

In this dramatic fashion the young King declares his allegiance to the majesty of justice, then as now the first object of an English ruler's devotion.

Throughout these scenes Falstaff has too much of the breath of life in him to serve as a mere foil to the political virtues of the Prince. Shakespeare has provided his comic hero with an enlarged circle of familiars who are ridiculous in themselves but who also develop in Falstaff new powers of awakening laughter. Shakespeare's skill in comic characterization appears at its supreme best in his realistic pictures of these figures from low life. He begins by converting the lightly sketched hostess of *Part I* into the voluble Dame Quickly, the easy victim of Falstaff's blandishments and an expert in making fritters of the English tongue. Pistol, the swaggerer and empty braggart, is another fresh creation of Shakespeare's teeming imagination. A "humor figure," or caricature, fashioned in imitation of Jonson's comic manner, he talks "pure cannon fire and bounce" in a vocabulary gleaned from the most absurdly bombastic of contemporary dramas. In Pistol's garbled quotations Shakespeare is probably poking fun at the inflated verbiage of the old-fashioned plays with which the Lord Admiral's Men, the only London rivals of Shakespeare's company, used to regale their somewhat unintelligent audience.

The most immediately popular of the new cronies of Falstaff was the imbecile country Justice of the Peace, Master Shallow. His first comic function was to offer an exaggerated contrast to Falstaff in every particular of body and spirit. In the first place he is excessively thin—as Falstaff says, "the very genius of famine," so lean that "his dimensions to any thick sight were invincible." His mind and spirit match his starveling figure; they, too, seem to be the result of "thin potations." He meanders in his talk, mixing sententious utterance on the brevity of life with inquiries as to the current price of his ewes and bullocks in the market, all interspersed with fictitious reminiscences of his wild youth while a student at Clement's Inn. So lifelike is he that critics have thought that he was drawn from the model of some country squire known to Shakespeare in Warwickshire. It is more likely that he embodied a Londoner's idea of the typical rural justice—stupid, self-important, and corrupt, in every way absurd.

Shallow's close cooperation with Sir John in the method of recruiting is a telling picture of a flagrant Elizabethan scandal. England in the great Queen's day had no regular army. Soldiers were impressed or drafted, were inadequately and irregularly paid, and were never pensioned. These facts explain the soldier's insatiable appetite for plunder and the ordinary man's evasion of the draft by bribing either the local constable or the recruiting officer. It was inevitable that levies like those of Falstaff should be of "rogues, runagates, drunkards and all sorts of vagabonds and disorderly persons." We can readily understand that Falstaff's methods of recruiting would not have appealed to London audiences as very jolly fun. In this phase of his roguery he offered only too lifelike a portrait of a figure profoundly sinister to the Elizabethan mind—an object of hatred and of dread. Shakespeare could be sure that his audiences were in no danger of growing sentimental over the young King's eternal renunciation of his companionship with a recruiting officer.

Nevertheless, it was probably the popularity of Falstaff that led Shakespeare to entertain the notion of sending the rogue to France as one of the entourage of King Henry V. He planned this development for his next play. And in his Epilogue to *Henry IV, Part II*, he promises to "continue the story, with Sir John in it." But he soon changed his mind, perhaps realizing that, as King, Henry must be kept far away from Falstaff and that no memories of Eastcheap must be allowed to follow the ideal monarch upon the fields of Harfleur and Agincourt. A simpler reason for the dramatist's change of mind may lie in the departure of Will Kempe from the company. This would almost certainly have compelled Shakespear to cut the role which that great comedian seems to have played. Whatever the reason may be, Falstaff has no part in *Henry V* except as the subject of the immortal speech in which Dame Quickly reports his death. He appears, it is true, in *The Merry Wives of Windsor*, but there he is merely some other fat man who has appropriated Sir John's name. The real Falstaff died in the Boar's Head Tavern because, as Pistol puts it, his heart was "fracted and corroborate." The man in *The Merry Wives* is a usurper.

Shakespeare's Life and Times

BY OSCAR JAMES CAMPBELL

We have little information about the private life of William Shakespeare. The facts enumerated in the following Chronology seldom reveal any secrets of the poet's personality or of his dramatic achievements. None of his associates in the theatre have left any record of their friend, whom they knew, respected and admired. Nor did any of his contemporaries write even a brief account of his life. This is not strange. In sixteenth-century England only dignitaries of church or state were considered fit subjects for a biography.

The table below does make it clear that the poet was fortunate in the time of his birth, for, in the latter half of the sixteenth century, England basked in the full light of the Renaissance. He was equally fortunate in that the moment of his arrival on the scene coincided with new developments in the theatre. The first public playhouse was built in London when Shakespeare was in his early twenties. And when he began to write plays one company of actors had gained enough eminence and stability to provide a stage on which Shakespeare could bring to fruition all the elements of his genius.

The facts concerning his professional career, though more numerous, do not disclose any of the formative influences upon the design of the dramas or upon their distinctive character. However, these facts, joined with the meager records of the poet's personal life, have established the foundation upon which have been built all later biographies, interpretations and criticisms of Shakespeare and his works.

Chronology

HISTORIC AND LITERARY EVENTS	SHAKESPEARE AND HIS FAMILY
1558 Elizabeth I crowned Queen. Thomas Kyd born. Robert Greene born.	
1561 Francis Bacon born.	John Shakespeare elected Chamberlain of Stratford.
1564 Christopher Marlowe born. Galileo Galilei born.	Shakespeare born, April 23; baptized April 26.
1566	Gilbert, Shakespeare's brother, born; died 1612.

1567
Mary, Queen of Scots,
  dethroned. James VI (later
  James I of England) crowned.	

1572 Massacre of St. Bartholomew. Ben Jonson born.	
1573 John Donne born.	
1575 Earl of Leicester's entertainment of the Queen at Kenilworth.	
1576 Burbage builds the first public playhouse, The Theatre.	

1577
Drake begins circumnavigation
  of the earth; finished 1580.
Holinshed's *Chronicles of
  England, Scotland and
  Ireland*.	

1579 John Lyly's *Euphues: The Anatomy of Wit*.	

1581
Tenne Tragedies of Seneca.

1582

Shakespeare's marriage.

1583
Philip Massinger born.
The Queen's Company formed.

Shakespeare's daughter,
Susanna, born.

1584
Reginald Scot's *The
  Discovery of Witchcraft.*

1585

Shakespeare's twins,
  Hamnet and Judith, born.

1586
Sir Philip Sidney killed at
  Zutphen.
John Ford born.

1587
Mary, Queen of Scots, beheaded.
Marlowe's *Tamburlaine, I.*
Kyd's *Spanish Tragedy.*

1588
Defeat of the Spanish Armada.
Principal actors of Lord
  Leicester's Company join
  Lord Strange's Men.
Marlowe's *Tamburlaine, II.*
Lyly's *Endimion.*

1589
Henry of Navarre crowned
  King of France as Henry IV.
Greene's *Friar Bacon and
  Friar Bungay.*
Marlowe's *Jew of Malta.*

Comedy of Errors.

1590
Sidney's *Arcadia* published.
Spenser's *Faerie Queene (I-III).*

Titus Andronicus.
Henry VI, I.

1591

Henry VI, II.
Henry VI, III.

1592
Death of Greene.   *Two Gentlemen of Verona.*
Marlowe's *Doctor Faustus* and
    Edward II.

1593
Theatres closed by plague.   *Venus and Adonis.*
Death of Marlowe.   Sonnets begun.
                                           Richard III.

1594
Shakespeare's company becomes   *Rape of Lucrece.*
    the Lord Chamberlain's Men.   *Love's Labour's Lost.*
Death of Kyd.   *Taming of the Shrew.*
                                           King John.

1595
Raleigh's first expedition to   *Richard II.*
    Guiana.   *A Midsummer Night's Dream.*
Spenser's *Amoretti,*   *Merchant of Venice.*
    Epithalamium.
Sidney's *Defense of Poesy*
    published.

1596
Spenser's *The Faerie Queene*   *Romeo and Juliet.*
    (*IV-VI*), *Four Hymns,* and   Hamnet Shakespeare dies.
    Prothalamium.

1597
Bacon's *Essays* (first edition).   *Henry IV, I.*
King James's *Demonologie.*   *Merry Wives of Windsor.*
                                           Shakespeare buys and renovates
                                               New Place in Stratford.

1598
Edict of Nantes issued by   *Henry IV, II.*
    Henry IV, giving Huguenots   *Much Ado About Nothing.*
    political rights.
Jonson's *Every Man in His*
    Humour acted.
Seven books of Chapman's
    translation of the *Iliad.*

1599
Death of Spenser.   *Henry V.*
Globe Theatre built.   *Julius Caesar.*
Essex' expedition to Ireland.
Jonson's *Every Man out of His*
    Humour acted.
Dekker's *Shoemaker's Holiday.*

1600
Fortune Theatre built.
East India Company founded.
Children of The Chapel acquire
  a hall in Blackfriars'
  Monastery.

As You Like It.
Twelfth Night.

1601
Insurrection and execution of
  Essex.

Hamlet.
Troilus and Cressida.

1602
Sir Thos. Bodley's Library at
  Oxford opened.

All's Well That Ends Well.

1603
Death of Queen Elizabeth.
Accession of James I.
Shakespeare's company
  becomes the King's Men.
Heywood's *A Woman Killed
  with Kindness.*
Jonson's *Sejanus His Fall.*
Florio's translation of
  Montaigne's *Essays.*

1604
Treaty of Peace with Spain.

Measure for Measure.
Othello.

1605
The Gunpowder Plot.
Middleton's *A Trick to Catch
  the Old One.*

King Lear.

1606
Jonson's *Volpone.*

Macbeth.

1607
Settlement of Jamestown,
  Virginia.
Beaumont's *The Knight of the
  Burning Pestle.*

Antony and Cleopatra.
Timon of Athens.
Shakespeare's daughter Susanna
  married to Dr. John Hall.

1608
Burbage leases Blackfriars'
  Theatre for Shakespeare's
  company.
John Milton born.

Coriolanus.
Pericles, Prince of Tyre.

1609

Beaumont and Fletcher's
  Philaster.

Shakespeare's *Sonnets* published.

1610

Beaumont and Fletcher's
  Maid's Tragedy.

Cymbeline.

1611

Chapman completes translation
  of the *Iliad*.
Authorized version of
  The Bible.

The Winter's Tale.
The Tempest.

1612

Death of Prince Henry.
Beaumont retires from the
  theatre.
Webster's *The White Devil*.
Shelton's translation of
  Don Quixote, Part I.

1613

Globe Theatre burned.
Marriage of Princess Elizabeth
  to the Elector Palatine.

Henry VIII (with Fletcher).
The Two Noble Kinsmen (with
  Fletcher).
Buys a house in Blackfriars.

1614

Globe Theatre rebuilt.
Jonson's *Bartholomew Fair*.
Webster's *The Duchess of
  Malfi*.

1616

Death of Beaumont and
  Cervantes.
Jonson publishes his plays in a
  single volume entitled
  The Works of Ben Jonson.

Marriage of Judith Shakespeare
  to Thomas Quiney.
Death of Shakespeare, April 23.

1623

Publication of the Folio edition
  of Shakespeare's plays.

Death of Anne Hathaway.

Shakespeare's Theatre

BY STUART VAUGHAN

"The play in manuscript is only a blueprint for its performance in the theatre." This thought, whoever first gave voice to it, must have been one of Shakespeare's assumptions, for he took no care about the publishing of his work. He wrote plays to be acted, not to be read. These plays are as related to the theatre of Shakespeare's day as a shooting script is to modern film techniques. The structural evolution of that theatre, and the way it was used, profoundly influenced the nature of the plays themselves.

The simplest theatre of the Middle Ages was the platform of boards placed on trestles in the center of a town square. A frame at the back of the stage provided a place for the actors to be concealed and from which to make their entrances. Sometimes the sides of the platform were curtained off so that the area under the stage could be used for dressing space. The platform was about five feet high in order that the audience standing around on three sides of the stage could see with fair comfort. In such simple surroundings, the text of the play had to tell the audience where the action was placed, and the actors themselves moved the few pieces of furniture in full view of the audience, since there was no provision for a front curtain, nor had anyone yet thought of that idea. Here already are the basic elements of Shakespeare's stage.

When, instead of passing the hat among the gathered audience, admission was charged to the enclosed yard of an inn, the other elements of the Elizabethan theatre had come together. Members of the audience still stood around the stage; but all about the circular courtyard more comfortable places were available—seats placed at the various windows and balconies of the inn, providing more ease and better visibility. In touring, James Burbage, the leading manager of the day, had made enough money to build a real theatre for plays.

He had no precedent to follow but the shape of the inn yards he knew so well, and so he made his first building, The Theatre, in the circular shape which became the model for the subsequent public playhouses of this period.

Drawings and descriptions which have come down to us are not very definitive. Deductions from the plays themselves, along with such contemporary information as we do possess, have given us some notion of the form and use of this theatre. There were several tiers of galleries around the yard or "pit." These held the best places, and the occupants of these areas could sit and still see over the heads of the "groundlings" who gathered, standing in the pit, around the stage, which was still about five feet above ground level. The stage projected out into the pit, and was surrounded on at least three sides by audience. The galleries were roofed, and the stage was partially covered by a roof called "the shadow," but the standees in the pit were exposed to the open sky, which was the chief source of light for the plays. Performances took place at three in the afternoon.

There was some kind of permanent architectural background for the stage, with one large opening which revealed an area sometimes called "the inner stage." This opening was probably curtained, and most authorities conjecture that it was used for "discoveries," when the curtain could be drawn back to reveal a tableau, or a scene already set and in progress. It is doubtful that scenes of any length were played there, however, since, in order for the whole audience to see, the action would have been eventually brought down onto the projecting platform, or "forestage." There were at least two other doors, at the right and left of this large opening, which provided access to the stage. There was also an area above this main opening, probably some sort of gallery stretching along the back wall, where scenes could be played. Above that was a gallery for musicians.

Large properties, like beds or thrones, were probably discovered on the inner stage, but there was another means of moving furniture, dead bodies, or set pieces. "Mutes," or nonspeaking actors, were employed. They were probably masked and wore a conventional livery. They were the servants of the stage, and were either accepted as invisible by the audience, or functioned as servants, soldiers, or in similar capacities, carrying out necessary tasks like throne-moving or wine-pouring.

We are not sure what physical changes were made on the stage as the plays proceeded rapidly from, say, forest to castle to shipboard. We know that there were no intermissions or other interruptions in the performance. As actors for one scene left the stage, others for the next scene were already entering. Perhaps signs were hung denoting, for example, "The Boar's Head Tavern," but the dialogue is always so clear about change of locale that these seem hardly necessary. Certainly most objects needed on the stage had to be of a portable nature. Certainly the pattern of physical action must have been in constant flux, like the turning of a wheel, to permit all members of the audience to see. The stage thus presented a continual flow of movement, not a series of static framed pictures.

The actors and the audience were in close contact. Indeed, certain noblemen were permitted to sit on the stage itself, apparently within arm's reach of the action. The actors' costumes were elaborate and expensive, to bear such close and sophisticated scrutiny, but to our eyes they would have presented a strange mixture of attempted historical accuracy and contemporary elegance. Shakespeare's theatre did not try to ignore the problem of presenting Romans who looked like Romans, but apparently neither actors nor public had a very clear idea of what Romans looked like.

We are dealing, then, with an active, exciting spectacle, presented on a very flexible stage which can stimulate the audience's imagination. We go into a movie theatre and are transported by two-dimensional images flashed on a silvered fabric. The Elizabethan audience watched and listened around a wooden platform where as great a transformation was possible through the mind's activity.

The truly complete production of Shakespeare today should permit the same speed of presentation, the same kind of physical action, the same actor-audience intimacy, and a similar imaginative participation on the part of the audience. In the last century elaborate scenic productions became the rule, but great waits for scene changes and large theatres demanding slow elocution necessitated vastly cut versions of the plays. The modern theatre has tried various means of getting back to Shakespeare. The "space stage" technique involves a stage bare of all but steps and platforms. Flexible lighting is relied on for change of locale and emphasis. The "unit set" provides basic walls and other pieces which, by means of simple and rapid adjustments, can be converted into a somewhat differently shaped acting area for each of a number of scenes. Revolving stages change more realistic scenery rapidly. Structural stages have been built which provide simple doors and platforms, giving us Shakespeare's acting space without his décor. Reconstructions of Elizabethan stages have been built and used. Various combinations of all these methods have been tried. Each director will make his own personal choice of method in realizing the particular play he is working on. If he is doing his job well, he will be in search of the best way he can to achieve his author's impact and intention with the means at his disposal in today's theatre.

The Second Part of
King Henry the Fourth

CHARACTERS

RUMOR, *the Presenter*
KING HENRY *the Fourth*
HENRY, *Prince of Wales, afterward King Henry V*
THOMAS, *Duke of Clarence*
PRINCE JOHN *of Lancaster*
PRINCE HUMPHREY *of Gloucester*
} *sons of King Henry IV*

EARL OF WARWICK
EARL OF WESTMORELAND
EARL OF SURREY
GOWER
HARCOURT
BLUNT
LORD CHIEF-JUSTICE *of the King's Bench*
A SERVANT *of the Chief-Justice*
EARL OF NORTHUMBERLAND
SCROOP, *Archbishop of York*
LORD MOWBRAY
LORD HASTINGS
LORD BARDOLPH
SIR JOHN COLEVILE

TRAVERS *and* MORTON, *retainers of Northumberland*
SIR JOHN FALSTAFF
PAGE *to Sir John*
BARDOLPH
PISTOL
POINS
PETO
SHALLOW
SILENCE
} *country justices*
DAVY, *servant to Shallow*
MOULDY, SHADOW, WART, FEEBLE, *and* BULLCALF, *recruits*
FANG
SNARE
} *Sheriff's Officers*
LADY NORTHUMBERLAND
LADY PERCY
MISTRESS QUICKLY, *hostess of the Boar's Head Tavern in Eastcheap*
DOLL TEARSHEET
EPILOGUE, *a dancer*
LORDS, ATTENDANTS, PORTER, DRAWERS, BEADLES, GROOMS *and others*

SCENE: *England*

Note: Drawers drew and served liquor.

Henry IV was king of England from 1399 until his death in 1413, at the age of 46. He was succeeded by his oldest son Henry, Prince of Wales, who reigned as Henry V.

It must be understood that Shakespeare's plays should not be regarded as historically accurate in every detail.

INDUCTION

Warkworth. Before the EARL OF NORTHUMBERLAND'S castle.

(RUMOR *enters, dressed in a garment covered with painted tongues.*)

RUMOR.

Open your ears; for which of you will stop
The vent of hearing when loud Rumor speaks?
I, from the orient to the drooping west,
Making the wind my post-horse, still* unfold   continuously
The acts commencèd on this ball of earth:
Upon my tongues continual slanders ride,
The which in every language I pronounce,
Stuffing the ears of men with false reports.
I speak of peace, while covert enmity
Under the smile of safety wounds the world: 10
And who but Rumor, who but only I,
Make fearful musters and prepared defense,
Whiles the big year, swoln with some other grief,
Is thought with child by the stern tyrant war,
And no such matter? Rumor is a pipe*   *i.e.,* wind instrument
Blown by surmises, jealousies, conjectures,
And of so easy and so plain a stop
That the blunt* monster with uncounted heads,   stupid
The still-discordant wavering multitude,
Can play upon it.
              But what need I thus   20
My well-known body to anatomize*   analyze
Among my household? Why is Rumor here?
I run before King Harry's* victory;   *i.e.,* Henry IV

Who in a bloody field by Shrewsbury
Hath beaten down young Hotspur and his troops,
Quenching the flame of bold rebellion
Even with the rebels' blood. But what mean I
To speak so true at first? My office is
To noise abroad that Harry Monmouth* fell   *i.e.,* Prince
                                                          Henry
Under the wrath of noble Hotspur's sword,   30
And that the king before the Douglas' rage
Stooped his anointed head as low as death.
This have I rumored through the peasant* towns   provincial
Between that royal field of Shrewsbury
And this worm-eaten hold* of ragged stone,   stronghold
Where Hotspur's father, old Northumberland,
Lies crafty-sick: the posts come tiring on,[1]
And not a man of them brings other news
Than they have learned of me: from Rumor's
   tongues
They bring smooth comforts false, worse than
   true wrongs.   40
   (*He goes.*)

ACT I

SCENE 1. Before the gates of NORTHUMBERLAND's castle.

(LORD BARDOLPH *enters*.)

LORD BARDOLPH (*calls*).
Who keeps the gate here, ho?
(*A* PORTER *opens the gate*.)
                              Where is the earl?

PORTER.
What shall I say you are?

LORD BARDOLPH.   Tell thou the earl
That the Lord Bardolph doth attend* him here.   await

PORTER.
His lordship is walked forth into the orchard.*   garden
Please it your honor, knock but at the gate,
And he himself will answer.

LORD BARDOLPH. (*as he sees* NORTHUMBERLAND *approach*).   Here comes the earl.
(NORTHUMBERLAND *enters, walking with a
crutch, and wearing a kerchief bound round his
head. The* PORTER *goes*.)

NORTHUMBERLAND.
What news, Lord Bardolph? Every minute now
Should be the father of some stratagem:*   violence
The times are wild; contention, like a horse
Full of high feeding, madly hath broke loose   10
And bears down all before him.

LORD BARDOLPH.   Noble earl,
I bring you certain news from Shrewsbury.

NORTHUMBERLAND.
Good, an God will!

LORD BARDOLPH.   As good as heart can wish:
  The king is almost wounded to the death;
  And, in the* fortune of my lord your son,   to the good
  Prince Harry slain outright; and both the Blunts
  Killed by the hand of Douglas; young Prince John
  And Westmoreland and Stafford fled the field;
  And Harry Monmouth's brawn,* the hulk Sir   fattened
    John,*   boar
                                                 i.e., John Falstaff
  Is prisoner to your son. O, such a day,   20
  So fought, so followed* and so fairly won,   concluded
  Came not till now to dignify the times,
  Since Cæsar's fortunes!
NORTHUMBERLAND.   How is this derived?
  Saw you the field? Came you from Shrewsbury?
LORD BARDOLPH.
  I spake with one, my lord, that came from thence,
  A gentleman well bred and of good name,
  That freely rendered me these news for true.
NORTHUMBERLAND (*as he sees* TRAVERS *approach*).
  Here comes my servant Travers, whom I sent
  On Tuesday last to listen after news.
LORD BARDOLPH.
  My lord, I over-rode* him on the way;   overtook
  And he is furnished with no certainties   31
  More than he haply may retail from me.
    (TRAVERS *enters*.)
NORTHUMBERLAND.
  Now, Travers, what good tidings comes with
    you?
TRAVERS.
  My lord, Sir John Umfrevile turned me back
  With joyful tidings; and, being better horsed,
  Out-rode me. After him came spurring hard
  A gentleman, almost forspent* with speed,   exhausted
  That stopped by me to breathe his bloodied*   *i.e.*, by spurs
    horse.
  He asked the way to Chester; and of him
  I did demand what news from Shrewsbury.   40
  He told me that rebellion had bad luck

And that young Harry Percy's spur was cold.
With that, he gave his able horse the head,
And bending forward struck his armèd heels
Against the panting sides of his poor jade
Up to the rowel-head, and starting so
He seemed in running to devour the way,
Staying no longer question.*   to be
                                                    questioned
NORTHUMBERLAND.   Ha! Again:
Said he young Harry Percy's spur was cold?
Of Hotspur Coldspur—that rebellion   50
Had met ill luck?

LORD BARDOLPH.   My lord, I'll tell you what;
If my young lord your son have not the day,
Upon mine honor, for a silken point
I'll give my barony: never talk of it.

NORTHUMBERLAND.
Why should that gentleman that rode by Travers
Give then such instances of loss?

LORD BARDOLPH.   Who, he?
He was some hilding* fellow that had stolen   worthless
The horse he rode on, and, upon my life,
Spoke at a venture.*   random
                    Look, here comes more news.
      (MORTON enters.)

NORTHUMBERLAND.
Yea, this man's brow, like to a title-leaf,   60
Foretells the nature of a tragic volume:
So looks the strand whereon the imperious flood
Hath left a witnessed usurpation.*   encroachment
Say, Morton, didst thou come from Shrewsbury?

MORTON.
I ran from Shrewsbury, my noble lord;
Where hateful death put on his ugliest mask
To fright our party.

NORTHUMBERLAND.   How doth my son and brother?
    Thou tremblest; and the whiteness in thy cheek
Is apter than thy tongue to tell thy errand.
Even such a man, so faint, so spiritless,   70

So dull, so dead in look, so woe-begone,
Drew Priam's curtain² in the dead of night,
And would have told him half his Troy was burnt;
But Priam found the fire ere he his tongue—
And I my Percy's death ere thou report'st it.
This thou wouldst say, "Your son did thus and thus;
Your brother thus: so fought the noble Douglas":
Stopping my greedy ear with their bold deeds:
But in the end, to stop my ear indeed,
Thou hast a sigh to blow away this praise,   80
Ending with "Brother, son, and all are dead."

MORTON.

Douglas is living, and your brother, yet;
But, for my lord your son*—   *i.e.*, Hotspur

NORTHUMBERLAND.   Why, he is dead.
See what a ready tongue suspicion hath!
He that but fears the thing he would not know
Hath by instinct knowledge from others' eyes
That what he feared is chanced.*   has happened
                    Yet speak, Morton;
Tell thou an earl his divination lies,
And I will take it as a sweet disgrace
And make thee rich for doing me such wrong.   90

MORTON.

You are too great to be by me gainsaid:*   contradicted
Your spirit is too true, your fears too certain.

NORTHUMBERLAND.

Yet, for all this, say not that Percy's dead.
I see a strange confession in thine eye:
Thou shakest thy head and hold'st it fear or sin
To speak a truth. If he be slain, say so;
The tongue offends not that reports his death:
And he doth sin that doth belie the dead,
Not he which says the dead is not alive.
Yet the first bringer of unwelcome news   100
Hath but a losing office,* and his tongue   duty
Sounds ever after as a sullen bell,
Remembered tolling a departing* friend.³   departed

LORD BARDOLPH.

  I cannot think, my lord, your son is dead.

MORTON.

  I am sorry I should force you to believe
  That which I would to God I had not seen;
  But these mine eyes saw him in bloody state,
  Rendering faint quittance,* wearied and   resistance
    outbreathed,
  To Harry Monmouth; whose swift wrath beat
    down
  The never-daunted Percy to the earth,   110
  From whence with life he never more sprung up.
  In few,* his death, whose spirit lent a fire   in short
  Even to the dullest peasant in his camp,
  Being bruited* once, took fire and heat away   noised
                                        abroad
  From the best-tempered courage in his troops;
  For from his metal* was his party steeled;   mettle
  Which once in him abated, all the rest
  Turned on themselves, like dull and heavy lead:
  And as the thing that's heavy in itself,
  Upon enforcement* flies with greatest speed,   being
                                         forced
  So did our men, heavy in Hotspur's loss,   121
  Lend to this weight such lightness with their fear
  That arrows fled not swifter toward their aim
  Than did our soldiers, aiming at their safety,
  Fly from the field. Then was that noble
    Worcester
  Too soon ta'en prisoner; and that furious Scot,
  The bloody Douglas, whose well-laboring sword
  Had three times slain the appearance of* the king,   what ap-
                                         peared
  'Gan vail* his stomach* and did grace the shame   to lose/
                                         courage
  Of those that turned their backs,[4] and in his flight, 130
  Stumbling in fear, was took.
                     The sum of all
  Is that the king hath won, and hath sent out
  A speedy power to encounter you, my lord,
  Under the conduct of young Lancaster
  And Westmoreland. This is the news at full.

NORTHUMBERLAND.

  For this I shall have time enough to mourn.
  In poison there is physic; and these news,
  Having been well, that would have made me sick,
  Being sick, have in some measure made me well:
  And as the wretch, whose fever-weakened joints,   140
  Like strengthless hinges, buckle under life,
  Impatient of his fit, breaks like a fire
  Out of his keeper's arms, even so my limbs,
  Weakened with grief, being now enraged with
    grief,
  Are thrice themselves.
    (*As he casts his crutch and kerchief away.*)
          Hence, therefore, thou nice crutch!
  A scaly gauntlet now with joints of steel
  Must glove this hand: and hence, thou
    sickly quoif!*   sick man's cap
  Thou art a guard too wanton* for the head   frivolous
  Which princes, fleshed* with conquest, aim to hit. made fierce
  Now bind my brows with iron; and approach   150
  The ragged'st* hour that time and spite dare bring roughest
  To frown upon the enraged Northumberland!
  Let heaven kiss earth! Now let not Nature's hand
  Keep the wild flood confined! Let order die!
  And let this world no longer be a stage
  To feed contention in a lingering act;
  But let one spirit of the first-born Cain
  Reign in all bosoms, that, each heart being set
  On bloody courses, the rude scene may end,
  And darkness be the burier of the dead!   160

TRAVERS.

  This strainèd passion doth you wrong, my lord.

LORD BARDOLPH.

  Sweet earl, divorce not wisdom from your honor.

MORTON.

  The lives of all your loving complices*   allies
  Lean on your health; the which, if you give o'er
  To stormy passion, must perforce decay.
  You cast* the event* of war, my noble lord,   forecast/ outcome

And summed the account of chance, before you
　said
"Let us make head."* It was your presurmise,   raise an
That, in the dole* of blows, your son might drop: army
You knew he walked o'er perils, on an edge,   dealing
                                                         170
More likely to fall in than to get o'er;
You were advised* his flesh was capable   aware
Of* wounds and scars and that his forward spirit   liable to
Would lift him where most trade* of danger   press
　ranged:
Yet did you say "Go forth"; and none of this,
Though strongly apprehended, could restrain
The stiff-borne* action. What hath then befallen,   obstinate
Or what hath this bold enterprise brought forth,
More than that being which was like to be?

LORD BARDOLPH.

We all that are engagèd to* this loss   involved in
Knew that we ventured on such dangerous seas   181
That if we wrought out life 'twas ten to one.[5]
And yet we ventured, for the gain proposed
Choked the respect* of likely peril feared;   consideration
And since we are o'erset,* venture again.   overthrown
Come, we will all put forth,* body and goods.   stake
                                                        everything
MORTON.

'Tis more than time: and, my most noble lord,
I hear for certain, and do speak the truth,
The gentle Archbishop of York is up
With well-appointed powers. He is a man   190
Who with a double surety binds his followers.
My lord your son had only but the corpse,*   living
But shadows and the shows of men, to fight;*   bodies
For that same word, rebellion, did divide   fight with
The action of their bodies from their souls;
And they did fight with queasiness,* constrained   disgust
As men drink potions, that their weapons only
Seemed on our side; but, for their spirits and souls,
This word rebellion, it had froze them up,
As fish are in a pond. But now the bishop   200
Turns insurrection to religion:

Supposed sincere and holy in his thoughts,
He's followed both with body and with mind;
And doth enlarge* his rising with the blood   extend the
Of fair King Richard, scraped from Pomfret   scope of
  stones;[6]
Derives from heaven his quarrel and his cause;
Tells them he doth bestride a bleeding land,
Gasping for life under great Bolingbroke:
And more and less* do flock to follow him.   high and
    low

NORTHUMBERLAND.

I knew of this before; but, to speak truth,   210
This present grief had wiped it from my mind.
  Go in with me; and counsel every man
The aptest way for safety and revenge:
Get posts and letters, and make* friends with   collect
  speed:
Never so few, and never yet more need.
  (*They go in together.*)

SCENE 2. A street in London.

(SIR JOHN FALSTAFF *enters, followed by his* PAGE,
a small boy, who bears his sword and buckler.)

FALSTAFF.

Sirrah, you giant, what says the doctor to my
water?

PAGE.

He said, sir, the water itself was a good healthy
water; but, for the party that owed* it, he might   owned
have more diseases than he knew for.

FALSTAFF.

Men of all sorts take a pride to gird at* me: the   deride
brain of this foolish-compounded clay, man, is not
able to invent any thing that tends to laughter,
more than I invent or is invented on me: I am not
only witty in myself, but the cause that wit is in   10
other men.

  I do here walk before thee like a sow that hath

overwhelmed all her litter but one. If the prince
put thee into my service for any other reason than
to set* me off, why then I have no judgment.   show
Thou whoreson mandrake,⁷ thou art fitter to be
worn in my cap than to wait at my heels. I was
never manned with* an agate till now:⁸ but I will   attended
                                                         by
inset you neither in gold nor silver, but in vile   20
apparel, and send you back again to your master,
for a jewel—the juvenal,* the prince your master,   juvenile
whose chin is not yet fledged.* I will sooner have   feathered
a beard grow in the palm of my hand than he
shall get one on his cheek; and yet he will not
stick to say* his face is a face-royal:⁹ God may   stick at
                                                         saying
finish it when he will, 'tis not a hair amiss yet: he
may keep it still at a face-royal, for a barber shall
never earn sixpence out of it; and yet he'll be   30
crowing as if he had writ man* ever since his   reached
                                                         manhood
father was a bachelor. He may keep his own
grace, but he's almost out of mine, I can assure
him.

What said Master Dombledon about the satin
for my short cloak and my slops?*   breeches

PAGE.

He said, sir, you should procure him better assur-
ance than Bardolph: he would not take his band*   bond
and yours; he liked not the security.

FALSTAFF.

Let him be damned, like the glutton! Pray God   40
his tongue be hotter! A whoreson Achitophel!¹⁰
A rascally yea-forsooth knave! To bear a gentleman in hand,* and then stand upon security! The   delude a
                                                         gentleman
whoreson smooth pates*¹¹ do now wear nothing   heads
but high shoes, and bunches of keys at their
girdles; and if a man is through with them in
honest taking up, then they must stand upon security. I had as lief they would put ratsbane in
my mouth as offer to stop it with security. I
looked a' should have sent me two and twenty   50
yards of satin, as I am a true knight, and he sends

me security. Well, he may sleep in security; for
he hath the horn of abundance, and the lightness
of his wife shines through it:[12] and yet cannot he
see, though he have his own lanthorn* to light   lantern
him.

　　Where's Bardolph?

PAGE.

He's gone into Smithfield to buy your worship a
horse.

FALSTAFF.

I bought him in Paul's,[13] and he'll buy me a horse
in Smithfield: an I could get me but a wife in the
stews,* I were manned, horsed, and wived.   bordellos/
　　(*The* LORD CHIEF-JUSTICE, *accompanied by* SERV-   61
ANT, *enters at a distance.*)

PAGE (*aside to* FALSTAFF).

Sir, here comes the nobleman that committed the
prince for striking him about Bardolph.

FALSTAFF (*aside to* PAGE).

Wait close;* I will not see him.   conceal
　　(*Starts to walk away.*)   yourself

CHIEF-JUSTICE (*to* SERVANT).

What's he that goes there?

SERVANT.

Falstaff, an 't please your lordship.

CHIEF-JUSTICE.

He that was in question for* the robbery?   questioned
                                                  about/69
SERVANT.

He, my lord: but he hath since done good service
at Shrewsbury; and, as I hear, is now going with
some charge* to the Lord John of Lancaster.   troops

CHIEF-JUSTICE.

What, to York? Call him back again.

SERVANT (*calling*).

Sir John Falstaff!

FALSTAFF (*aside to* PAGE).

Boy, tell him I am deaf.

PAGE (*to* SERVANT).

You must speak louder; my master is deaf.   79

CHIEF-JUSTICE.

I am sure he is, to the hearing of anything good.
(*To* SERVANT.)
Go, pluck him by the elbow; I must speak with
him.

SERVANT (*pulling at* FALSTAFF's *sleeve*).

Sir John!

FALSTAFF.

What!   A young knave, and begging!   Is there
not wars?   Is there not employment?   Doth not
the king lack subjects?   Do not the rebels need
soldiers?   Though it be a shame to be on any side
but one, it is worse shame to beg than to be on the
worst side, were it worse than the name of rebel-
lion can tell how to make it.   90

SERVANT.

You mistake me, sir.

FALSTAFF.

Why, sir, did I say you were an honest man?   Setting my knighthood and my soldiership aside, I
had lied in my throat, if I had said so.

SERVANT.

I pray you, sir, then set your knighthood and
your soldiership aside; and give me leave to tell
you, you lie in your throat, if you say I am any
other than an honest man.

FALSTAFF.

I give thee leave to tell me so!   I lay aside that
which grows to* me!   If thou gettest any leave   is part of/
of me, hang me; if thou takest leave, thou wert   100
better be hanged.   You hunt counter:* hence!   the wrong
Avaunt!   way

SERVANT (*pointing out the* LORD CHIEF-JUSTICE).

Sir, my lord would speak with you.

CHIEF-JUSTICE.

Sir John Falstaff, a word with you.

FALSTAFF.

My good lord!   God give your lordship good
time of day.   I am glad to see your lordship

abroad: I heard say your lordship was sick: I
hope your lordship goes abroad by advice. Your
lordship, though not clean past your youth, hath   110
yet some smack* of age in you, some relish of the   savor
saltness of time;[14] and I most humbly beseech your
lordship to have a reverent care of your health.

CHIEF-JUSTICE.

Sir John, I sent for you before your expedition
to Shrewsbury.

FALSTAFF.

An 't please your lordship, I hear his majesty is
returned with some discomfort* from Wales.   dejection

CHIEF-JUSTICE.

I talk not of his majesty. You would not come
when I sent for you.   121

FALSTAFF.

And I hear, moreover, his highness is fallen into
this same whoreson apoplexy.

CHIEF-JUSTICE.

Well, God mend him! I pray you, let me speak
with you.

FALSTAFF.

This apoplexy is, as I take it, a kind of lethargy,
an 't please your lordship; a kind of sleeping in
the blood, a whoreson tingling.

CHIEF-JUSTICE.

What tell you me of it? Be it as it is.   130

FALSTAFF.

It hath it original from much grief, from study
and perturbation of the brain: I have read the
cause of his effects in Galen:[15] it is a kind of deafness.

CHIEF-JUSTICE.

I think you are fallen into the disease; for you
hear not what I say to you.

FALSTAFF.

Very well, my lord, very well: rather, an 't please
you, it is the disease of not listening, the malady
of not marking, that I am troubled withal.   140

CHIEF-JUSTICE.

To punish you by the heels* would amend the *i.e.*, in the stocks
attention of your ears; and I care not if I do
become your physician.

FALSTAFF.

I am as poor as Job, my lord, but not so patient:
your lordship may minister the potion of imprisonment to me in respect of poverty; but how
I should be your patient to follow your prescriptions, the wise may make some dram of a scruple,¹⁶
or indeed a scruple itself.

CHIEF-JUSTICE.

I sent for you, when there were matters against   150
you for your life, to come speak with me.

FALSTAFF.

As I was then advised by my learned counsel in
the laws of this land*-service, I did not come.   army

CHIEF-JUSTICE.

Well, the truth is, Sir John, you live in great
infamy.

FALSTAFF.

He that buckles him* in my belt cannot live in less.   himself

CHIEF-JUSTICE.

Your means are very slender, and your waste is   160
great.

FALSTAFF.

I would it were otherwise; I would my means
were greater, and my waist slenderer.

CHIEF-JUSTICE.

You have misled the youthful prince.

FALSTAFF.

The young prince hath misled me: I am the fellow with the great belly, and he my dog.

CHIEF-JUSTICE.

Well, I am loath to gall a new-healed wound: your
day's service at Shrewsbury hath a little gilded
over your night's exploit on Gadshill: you may
thank the unquiet time for your quiet o'er-posting*   escaping
that action.   171

FALSTAFF.

My lord?

CHIEF-JUSTICE.

But since all is well, keep it so: wake not a sleeping wolf.

FALSTAFF.

To wake a wolf is as bad as to smell a fox.*

be suspicious

CHIEF-JUSTICE.

What! You are as a candle, the better part burnt out.

FALSTAFF.

A wassail* candle my lord, all tallow: if I did say of wax, my growth would approve the truth.

festival

181

CHIEF-JUSTICE.

There is not a white hair on your face but should have his effect of gravity.

FALSTAFF.

His effect of gravy, gravy, gravy.[17]

CHIEF-JUSTICE.

You follow the young prince up and down, like his ill angel.

FALSTAFF.

Not so, my lord; your ill angel is light; but I hope he that looks upon me will take me without weighing: and yet, in some respects, I grant, I cannot go: I cannot tell. Virtue* is of so little regard in these costermonger* times[18] that true valor is turned bear-herd: pregnancy* is made a tapster, and hath his quick wit wasted in giving reckonings: all the other gifts appertinent* to man, as the malice of this age shapes them, are not worth a gooseberry. You that are old consider not the capacities of us that are young; you do measure the heat of our livers with the bitterness of your galls: and we that are in the vaward* of our youth, I must confess, are wags too.

190

courage

peddler

quick wit

appertaining

vanguard
200

CHIEF-JUSTICE.

Do you set down your name in the scroll of youth, that are written down old with all the characters

of age? Have you not a moist eye? A dry hand?
A yellow cheek? A white beard? A decreasing leg?
An increasing belly? Is not your voice broken?
Your wind short? Your chin double? Your wit
single? And every part about you blasted with
antiquity? And will you yet call yourself young?
Fie, fie, fie, Sir John!   209

FALSTAFF.

My lord, I was born about three of the clock in the
afternoon, with a white head and something a
round belly. For my voice, I have lost it with
halloing and singing of anthems. To approve
my youth further, I will not: the truth is, I am
only old in judgment and understanding; and he
that will caper with me for a thousand marks, let
him lend me the money, and have at him! For
the box of the ear that the prince gave you, he
gave it like a rude prince, and you took it like a
sensible lord. I have checked* him for it, and the   reproved/
young lion repents; marry, not in ashes and sack-   220
cloth, but in new silk and old sack.

CHIEF-JUSTICE.

Well, God send the prince a better companion!

FALSTAFF.

God send the companion a better prince! I cannot
rid my hands of him.

CHIEF-JUSTICE.

Well, the king hath severed you and Prince Harry:
I hear you are going with Lord John of Lan-
caster against the Archbishop and the Earl of
Northumberland.   230

FALSTAFF.

Yea; I thank your pretty sweet wit for it. But look
you pray, all you that kiss my lady Peace at home,
that our armies join not in a hot day; for, by the
Lord, I take but two shirts out with me, and I
mean not to sweat extraordinarily: if it be a hot
day, and I brandish anything but a bottle, I would
I might never spit white* again. There is not a   have a dry
                                                                   mouth

dangerous action can peep out his head but I am
thrust upon it: well, I cannot last ever: but it was   240
always yet the trick of our English nation, if they
have a good thing, to make it too common. If ye
will needs say I am an old man, you should give
me rest. I would to God my name were not so
terrible to the enemy as it is: I were better to be
eaten to death with a rust than to be scoured to
nothing with perpetual motion.

CHIEF-JUSTICE.

Well, be honest, be honest; and God bless your
expedition!

FALSTAFF.

Will your lordship lend me a thousand pound to
furnish me forth?   251

CHIEF-JUSTICE.

Not a penny, not a penny; you are too impatient
to bear crosses.

    Fare you well: commend me to my cousin
Westmoreland.

    (*The* CHIEF-JUSTICE *and his* SERVANT *leave.*)

FALSTAFF.

If I do, fillip* me with a three-man beetle.*¹⁹ A   strike/
man can no more separate age and covetousness   rammer
than a'* can part young limbs and lechery: but the   he
gout galls the one, and the pox pinches the other;
and so both the degrees* prevent* my curses.   conditions/
    Boy!   anticipate
          260

PAGE.

Sir?

FALSTAFF.

What money is in my purse?

PAGE.

Seven groats and two pence.

FALSTAFF.

I can get no remedy against this consumption of
the purse: borrowing only lingers and lingers it
out, but the disease is incurable. (*Giving him
letters.*) Go bear this letter to my Lord of Lan-

caster; this to the prince; this to the Earl of Westmoreland; and this to old Mistress Ursula, whom
I have weekly sworn to marry since I perceived   270
the first white hair on my chin. About it: you
know where to find me.

    (*The* PAGE *goes.*)

A pox of this gout! Or, a gout of this pox! For
the one or the other plays the rogue with my great
toe. 'Tis no matter if I do halt;* I have the wars   **limp**
for my color,* and my pension shall seem the more   **excuse**
reasonable. A good wit will make use of anything:
I will turn diseases to commodity.*   **profit**

    (FALSTAFF *goes.*)

SCENE 3. York. A room in the ARCHBISHOP'S palace.

    (*The* ARCHBISHOP *enters, with* LORD HASTINGS,
LORD MOWBRAY, and LORD BARDOLPH.)

ARCHBISHOP.
  Thus have you heard our cause and known our
    means;
  And, my most noble friends, I pray you all,
  Speak plainly your opinions of our hopes.
  And first, lord marshal, what say you to it?
MOWBRAY.
  I well allow* the occasion of our arms;*   **grant/war**
  But gladly would be better satisfied
  How in* our means we should advance ourselves   **within**
  To look with forehead bold and big enough
  Upon the power and puissance of the king.
HASTINGS.
  Our present musters grow upon the file*   **list/10**
  To five and twenty thousand men of choice;
  And our supplies* live largely in the hope   **reinforcements**
  Of great Northumberland, whose bosom burns
  With an incensèd fire of injuries.
LORD BARDOLPH.
  The question then, Lord Hastings, standeth thus;

Whether our present five and twenty thousand
May hold up head* without Northumberland?   its head

HASTINGS.

With him, we may.

LORD BARDOLPH.

             Yea, marry, there's the point:
But if without him we be thought too feeble,
My judgment is, we should not step too far   20
Till we had his assistance by the hand;
For in a theme so bloody-faced as this
Conjecture, expectation, and surmise
Of aids incertain* should not be admitted.   uncertain

ARCHBISHOP.

'Tis very true, Lord Bardolph; for indeed
It was young Hotspur's case at Shrewsbury.

LORD BARDOLPH.

It was, my lord; who lined* himself with hope,   fortified
Eating the air on promise of supply,
Flattering himself in project of a power
Much smaller than the smallest of his thoughts: 30
And so, with great imagination
Proper* to madmen, led his powers to death   peculiar
And winking* leaped into destruction.   shutting
                                      his eyes

HASTINGS.

But, by your leave, it never yet did hurt
To lay down likelihoods and forms* of hope.   estimates

LORD BARDOLPH.

Yes, if this present quality of war,
Indeed the instant* action: a cause on foot   immediate
Lives so in hope as in an early spring
We see the appearing buds; which to prove fruit,
Hope gives not so much warrant as despair   40
That frosts will bite them.[20]
                          When we mean to build,
We first survey the plot, then draw the model;
And when we see the figure of the house,
Then must we rate the cost of the erection;
Which if we find outweighs ability,
What do we then but draw anew the model

In fewer offices,* or at last desist   rooms
To build at all? Much more, in this great work,
Which is almost to pluck a kingdom down
And set another up, should we survey   50
The plot of situation and the model,
Consent* upon a sure foundation,   agree
Question surveyors, know our own estate,*   resources
How able such a work to undergo,
To weigh against his* opposite[21]; or else   its
We fortify in* paper and in figures,   on
Using the names of men instead of men:
Like one that draws the model of a house
Beyond his power to build it; who, half through,   59
Gives o'er and leaves his part-created cost*   *i.e.*, house
A naked subject* to the weeping clouds   object
And waste for churlish winter's tyranny.

HASTINGS.

Grant that our hopes, yet likely of fair birth,
Should be still-born, and that we now possessed
The utmost man* of* expectation,   in men/
      within
I think we are a body strong enough,
Even as we are, to equal* with the king.   be equal

LORD BARDOLPH.

What, is the king but five and twenty thousand?

HASTINGS.

To us no more; nay, not so much, Lord Bardolph.
For his divisions, as the times do brawl,   70
Are in three heads: one power against the French,
And one against Glendower; perforce a third
Must take up us: so is the unfirm king
In three divided; and his coffers sound
With hollow poverty and emptiness.

ARCHBISHOP.

That he should draw his several strengths together
And come against us in full puissance,
Need not be dreaded.

HASTINGS.   If he should do so,
He leaves his back unarmed, the French and Welsh
Baying him at the heels: never fear that.   80

LORD BARDOLPH.

Who is it like should lead his forces hither?

HASTINGS.

The Duke of Lancaster and Westmoreland;
Against the Welsh, himself and Harry Monmouth:
But who is substituted 'gainst the French,
I have no certain notice.

ARCHBISHOP.   Let us on,
And publish the occasion of* our arms.   reason for
The commonwealth is sick of their own choice;
Their over-greedy love hath surfeited:
An habitation giddy and unsure
Hath he that buildeth on the vulgar heart.   90
    O thou fond* many, with what loud applause   foolish
Didst thou beat heaven with blessing Bolingbroke,
Before he was what thou wouldst have him be!
And being now trimmed* in thine own desires,   arrayed
Thou, beastly feeder, art so full of him,
That thou provokest thyself to cast him up.
So, so, thou common dog, didst thou disgorge
Thy glutton bosom of the royal Richard;
And now thou wouldst eat thy dead vomit up,
And howl'st to find it. What trust is in these times?   100
They that, when Richard lived, would have him
    die,
Are now become enamored on* his grave: of
Thou, that threw'st dust upon his goodly head
When through proud London he came sighing on
After the admired heels of Bolingbroke,
Criest now "O earth, yield us that king again,
And take thou this!"
                    O thoughts of men accursed!
Past and to come seems best; things present worst.

MOWBRAY.

Shall we go draw* our numbers and set on?*   assemble/
                                                                                                   march

HASTINGS.

We are time's subjects, and time bids be gone.   110
    (*They go.*)

ACT II

Scene 1. A street in London.

(*The* HOSTESS *of the Boar's Head Tavern enters,
followed by the two sheriff's officers,* FANG *and*
SNARE, *and* FANG'S BOY.)

HOSTESS.

Master Fang, have you entered the action?* — brought suit

FANG.

It is entered.

HOSTESS.

Where's your yeoman?* Is 't a lusty yeoman? — sheriff's assistant
Will a' stand to 't?* — fight well

FANG (*to his* BOY).

Sirrah, where's Snare?

HOSTESS.

O Lord, ay! Good Master Snare.

SNARE (*steps forward*).

Here, here.

FANG.

Snare, we must arrest Sir John Falstaff.

HOSTESS.

Yea, good Master Snare; I have entered him and
all.

11

SNARE.

It may chance cost some of us our lives, for he will
stab.

HOSTESS.

Alas the day! Take heed of him; he stabbed me
in mine own house, and that most beastly. In good
faith, he cares not what mischief he does, if his

weapon be out; he will foin* like any devil; he   thrust
will spare neither man, woman, nor child.

FANG.

If I can close with him, I care not for his thrust.   21

HOSTESS.

No, nor I neither: I'll be at your elbow.

FANG.

An I but fist* him once; an a' come but within my   punch
vice*—   grasp

HOSTESS.

I am undone by his going; I warrant you, he's an
infinitive thing* upon my score.* Good Master   amount/
Fang, hold him sure: good Master Snare, let him   reckoning
not 'scape. A' comes continuantly to Pie-corner—
saving your manhoods—to buy a saddle; and he is
indited to dinner to the Lubber's-head in Lum-   30
bert street, to Master Smooth's the silkman: I pray
yet, since my exion* is entered and my case so   *i.e.,*
openly known to the world, let him be brought   action
in to* his answer. A hundred mark is a long one   to make
for a poor lone woman to bear: and I have borne,
and borne, and borne, and have been fubbed off,*   put off
and fubbed off, and fubbed off, from this day to
that day, that it is a shame be be thought on. There
is no honesty in such dealing; unless a woman
should be made an ass and a beast, to bear every   40
knave's wrong. (*Looking down the street.*) Yon-
der he comes; and that arrant malmsey*-nose   malmsey
knave, Bardolph, with him. Do your offices,* do   wine
your offices: Master Fang and Master Snare, do   duty
me, do me, do me your offices.

    (FALSTAFF, *attended by the* PAGE, *enters with his*
    servant BARDOLPH.)

FALSTAFF.

How now! Whose mare's dead? What's the
matter?

FANG (*stepping forward*).

Sir John, I arrest you at the suit of Mistress Quickly.   49

FALSTAFF.

Away, varlets! Draw, Bardolph: cut me off the
villain's head: throw the quean* in the channel.*   slut/
    (*They all struggle. The* HOSTESS *attacks* FALSTAFF.)   gutter

HOSTESS.

Throw me in the channel! I'll throw thee in the
channel. Wilt thou? Wilt thou? Thou bastardly
rogue! Murder, murder! Ah, thou honey-suckle
villain! Wilt thou kill God's officers and the king's?
Ah, thou honey-seed rogue! Thou are a honey-
seed, a man-queller,* and a woman-queller.   slayer

FALSTAFF.

Keep them off, Bardolph.   60

FANG (*calling for help*).

A rescue! A rescue!

HOSTESS.

Good people, bring a rescue or two. (*To* FAL-
STAFF.) Thou wo't,* wo't thou? Thou wo't, wo't   wilt
ta?* Do, do, thou rogue! Do, thou hemp-seed!*   thou/gal-
                                                          lows-bird

FALSTAFF (*to the* HOSTESS, *as the struggle continues*).

Away, you scullion! You rampallian!* You fus-   wretch
tilarian! I'll tickle your catastrophe.*   backside
    (*The* LORD CHIEF-JUSTICE *enters, with* ATTEND-
    ANTS.)

CHIEF-JUSTICE.

What is the matter? Keep the peace here, ho!
    (*The brawl stops.*)

HOSTESS.

Good my lord, be good to me. I beseech you,
stand to me.   70

CHIEF-JUSTICE.

How now, Sir John! what* are you brawling here?   why
Doth this become your place, your time, and busi-
    ness?
You should have been well on your way to York.
    (*To one of the* OFFICERS.)
Stand from him, fellow: wherefore hang'st upon
    him?

HOSTESS.

O my most worshipful lord, an 't please your grace,
I am a poor widow of Eastcheap, and he is arrested
at my suit.

CHIEF-JUSTICE.

For what sum?

HOSTESS.

It is more than for some, my lord: it is for all, all
I have. He hath eaten me out of house and home:
he hath put all my substance into that fat belly of   80
his. (*Turning to* FALSTAFF.) But I will have some
of it out again, or I will ride thee o' nights like
the mare.*   night-
                                                                  mare

FALSTAFF.

I think I am as like to ride the mare, if I have any
vantage of ground to get up.

CHIEF-JUSTICE.

How comes this, Sir John? Fie! What man of
good temper would endure this tempest of ex-
clamation? Are you not ashamed to enforce a
poor widow to so rough a course to come by her
own?   90

FALSTAFF (*to the* HOSTESS).

What is the gross sum that I owe thee?

HOSTESS.

Marry, if thou wert an honest man, thyself and the   partly
money too. Thou didst swear to me upon a parcel-*
gilt goblet, sitting in my Dolphin-chamber, at the
round table, by a sea-coal fire, upon Wednesday
in Wheeson* week, when the prince broke thy   Whitsun
head for liking* his father to a singing-man of   compar-
Windsor,²² thou didst swear to me then, as I was   ing
washing thy wound, to marry me and make me
my lady thy wife. Canst thou deny it? Did not   100
goodwife Keech, the butcher's wife, come in then
and call me gossip Quickly? Coming in to borrow
a mess* of vinegar; telling us she had a good dish   dishful
of prawns; whereby thou didst desire to eat some;
whereby I told thee they were ill for a green

wound? And didst thou not, when she was gone
downstairs, desire me to be no more so familiarity
with such poor people; saying that ere long they
should call me madam? And didst thou not kiss   110
me and bid me fetch thee thirty shillings? I put
thee now to thy book-oath: deny it, if thou canst.

FALSTAFF.

My lord, this is a poor mad soul; and she says up
and down the town that her eldest son is like you:
she hath been in good case,* and the truth is,   well
poverty hath distracted her. But for these foolish   to do
officers, I beseech you I may have redress against
them.

CHIEF-JUSTICE.

Sir John, Sir John, I am well acquainted with your   120
manner of wrenching the true cause the false way.
It is not a confident brow; nor the throng of words
that come with such more than impudent sauciness
from you, can thrust me from a level* considera-   just
tion: you have, as it appears to me, practiced
upon* the easy-yielding spirit of this woman, and   victim-
made her serve your uses both in purse and in   ized
person.

HOSTESS.

Yea, in truth, my lord.

CHIEF-JUSTICE (*to the* HOSTESS).

Pray thee, peace. (*To* FALSTAFF.) Pay her the
debt you owe her, and unpay the villainy you have   130
done her: the one you may do with sterling money,
and the other with current* repentance.   genuine

FALSTAFF.

My lord, I will not undergo this sneap* without   rebuke
reply. You call honorable boldness impudent
sauciness: if a man will make courtesy and say
nothing, he is virtuous: no, my lord, my humble
duty remembered, I will not be your suitor. I say
to you, I do desire deliverance from these officers,
being upon hasty* employment in the king's   urgent
affairs.   140

CHIEF-JUSTICE.

You speak as having* power to do wrong: but   *if you
answer in the effect of your reputation, and satisfy   had
the poor woman.

FALSTAFF.

Come hither, hostess.

(*As* FALSTAFF *takes the* HOSTESS *aside,* GOWER
enters and hands a paper to the CHIEF-JUSTICE.)

CHIEF-JUSTICE.

Now, Master Gower, what news?

GOWER.

The king, my lord, and Harry Prince of Wales
Are near at hand: the rest the paper tells.

FALSTAFF (*to the* HOSTESS *as the* CHIEF-JUSTICE *turns
aside to read the paper.*)

As I am a gentleman.

HOSTESS.

Faith, you said so before.

FALSTAFF.

As I am a gentleman. Come, no more words of it.   151

HOSTESS.

By this heavenly ground I tread on, I must be
fain* to pawn both my plate and the tapestry of   *content
my dining-chambers.

FALSTAFF.

Glasses, glasses, is the only drinking: and for thy
walls, a pretty slight drollery,* or the story of the   *comic
Prodigal, or the German hunting in water-work,*   picture
is worth a thousand of these bed-hangings and these   water-
fly-bitten tapestries. Let it be ten pound, if thou   color
canst. Come, an 'twere not for thy humors,*   160
there's not a better wench in England. Go, wash   *moods
thy face, and draw* the action. Come, thou must   *withdraw
not be in this humor with me; does not know me?
Come, come, I know thou wast set on to this.

HOSTESS.

Pray thee, Sir John, let it be but twenty nobles:*   *gold
i' faith, I am loath to pawn my plate, so God save   coins
me, la!

169

FALSTAFF.

Let it alone; I'll make other shift:* you'll be a
fool still.*

find other
means
always

HOSTESS.

Well, you shall have it, though I pawn my gown.
I hope you'll come to supper. You'll pay me all
together?

FALSTAFF.

Will I live? (*To* BARDOLPH.) Go with her, with
her; hook on,* hook on.

stick
with her

HOSTESS.

Will you have Doll Tearsheet meet you at supper?

FALSTAFF.

No more words; let's have her.

(*The* HOSTESS *and* BARDOLPH *leave, followed by
the sheriff's* OFFICERS *and the* BOY.)

CHIEF-JUSTICE (*as he finishes reading*).

I have heard better news.

FALSTAFF.

What's the news, my lord?   180

CHIEF-JUSTICE (*to* GOWER).

Where lay the king last night?

GOWER.

At Basingstoke, my lord.

FALSTAFF.

I hope, my lord, all's well: what is the news, my
lord?

CHIEF-JUSTICE.

Come all his forces back?

GOWER.

No; fifteen hundred foot, five hundred horse,
Are marched up to my lord of Lancaster,
Against Northumberland and the Archbishop.

FALSTAFF.

Comes the king back from Wales, my noble lord?

CHIEF-JUSTICE.

You shall have letters of me presently: 190
Come, go along with me, good Master Gower.

FALSTAFF.

My lord!

CHIEF-JUSTICE.

What's the matter?

FALSTAFF (*ignoring the* CHIEF-JUSTICE).

Master Gower, shall I entreat you with me to dinner?

GOWER.

I must wait upon my good lord here. I thank you, good Sir John.

CHIEF-JUSTICE.

Sir John, you loiter here too long, being you are to take soldiers up* in counties as you go.   recruit/200

FALSTAFF.

Will you sup with me, Master Gower?

CHIEF-JUSTICE.

What foolish master taught you these manners, Sir John?

FALSTAFF.

Master Gower, if they become me not, he was a fool that taught them me. (*To the* CHIEF-JUSTICE.) This is the right fencing grace,* my lord; tap for   style
tap, and so part fair.

CHIEF-JUSTICE.

Now the Lord lighten thee! Thou art a great fool.

(*They go their separate ways.*)

SCENE 2. Another street in London.

(PRINCE HENRY *and* POINS *enter.*)

PRINCE.

Before God, I am exceeding weary.

POINS.

Is't come to that? I had thought weariness durst not have attached* one of so high blood.   attacked

PRINCE.

Faith, it does me; though it discolors the com-
plexion of* my greatness to acknowledge it. Doth
it not show vilely in me to desire small* beer?

*i.e.,
causes
to blush
weak

POINS.

Why, a prince should not be so loosely studied*
as to remember so weak a composition.

disposed
10

PRINCE.

Belike* then my appetite was not princely got;
for, by my troth, I do now remember the poor
creature, small beer. But, indeed, these humble
considerations make me out of love with my
greatness. What a disgrace is it to me to remember thy name! Or to know thy face tomorrow!
Or to take note how many pair of silk stockings
thou hast, viz. these, and those that were thy
peach-colored ones! Or to bear* the inventory of
thy shirts, as, one for superfluity and another for
use! But that the tenniscourt-keeper knows better
than I; for it is a low ebb of linen with thee when
thou keepest not racket there; as thou hast not
done a great while, because the rest of thy low
countries have made a shift to eat up thy holland:
and God knows, whether those that bawl out the
ruins of thy linen shall inherit his kingdom: but
the midwives say the children are not in the
fault;[23] whereupon the world increases, and kin-
dreds are mightily strengthened.

most
likely

bear in
mind

20

30

POINS.

How ill it follows, after you have labored so hard,
you should talk so idly! Tell me, how many good
young princes would do so, their fathers being so
sick as yours at this time is?

PRINCE.

Shall I tell thee one thing, Poins?

POINS.

Yes, faith; and let it be an excellent good thing.

PRINCE.

It shall serve among wits of no higher breeding than thine.

POINS.

Go to; I stand the push* of your one thing that you will tell.

*await the thrust
41*

PRINCE.

Marry, I tell thee, it is not meet that I should be sad, now my father is sick: albeit I could tell to thee, as to one it pleases me, for fault of a better, to call my friend, I could be sad, and sad indeed too.

POINS.

Very hardly* upon such a subject.

unlikely

PRINCE.

By this hand, thou thinkest me as far in the devil's book as thou and Falstaff for obduracy and persistency: let the end try* the man. But I tell thee, my heart bleeds inwardly that my father is so sick: and keeping such vile company as thou art hath in reason taken from me all ostentation of sorrow.

*50
test*

POINS.

The reason?

PRINCE.

What wouldst thou think of me, if I should weep?

POINS.

I would think thee a most princely hypocrite.

59

PRINCE.

It would be every man's thought; and thou art a blessed fellow to think as every man thinks: never a man's thought in the world keeps the road-way better than thine: every man would think me an hypocrite indeed. And what accites* your most worshipful thought to think so?

excites

POINS.

Why, because you have been so lewd and so much engraffed* to Falstaff.

attached

PRINCE.

And to thee.

POINS.

By this light, I am well spoke on; I can hear it   70
with mine own ears: the worst that they can say
of me is that I am a second brother and that I
am a proper* fellow of my hands; and those two   clever
things, I confess, I cannot help.

(*Looking down the street.*)

By the mass, here comes Bardolph.

PRINCE.

And the boy that I gave Falstaff:

(BARDOLPH *and the* PAGE *enter.*)

a' had him from me Christian; and look, if the fat
villain have not transformed him ape.*   into an
                                              ape

BARDOLPH.

God save your grace!

PRINCE.

And yours, most noble Bardolph!

BARDOLPH (*to the* PAGE).

Come, you virtuous ass, you bashful fool, must   80
you be blushing? Wherefore blush you now?
What a maidenly man-at-arms are you become!
Is 't such a matter to get a pottlepot's* maidenhead?   tank-
                                                            ard's

PAGE.

A' calls me e'en now, my lord, through a red
lattice,* and I could discern no part of his face   *i.e.*, ale-
from the window. At last I spied his eyes, and   house
methought he had made two holes in the ale-
wife's* new petticoat and so peeped through.   alehouse
                                                   keeper's

PRINCE (*to* POINS).

Has not the boy profited?   90

BARDOLPH.

Away, you whoreson upright rabbit, away!

PAGE.

Away, you rascally Althæa's dream,[24] away!

PRINCE.

Instruct us, boy; what dream, boy?

PAGE.

Marry, my lord, Althæa dreamed she was delivered of a fire-brand; and therefore I tell him
her dream.

PRINCE.

A crown's worth of good interpretation: there
'tis, boy.   100
    (*He gives him a coin.*)

POINS.

O, that this good blossom could be kept from
cankers!* Well, there is sixpence to preserve thee.   canker
    (*He gives the* PAGE *a sixpence.*)   worms

BARDOLPH.

An you do not make him hanged among you, the
gallows shall have wrong.*   been
                                                             wronged
PRINCE.

And how doth thy master, Bardolph?

BARDOLPH.

Well, my lord. He heard of your grace's coming
to town: there's a letter for you.
    (*He gives the letter to the* PRINCE, *who takes it
    and reads.*)

POINS.

Delivered with good respect. And how doth the
martlemas, your master?²⁵   110

BARDOLPH.

In bodily health, sir.

POINS.

Marry, the immortal part needs a physician; but
that moves not him: though that be sick, it dies
not.

PRINCE.

I do allow this wen* to be as familiar with me as   wart
my dog; and he holds his place;
    (*Handing* POINS *the letter.*)
for look you how he writes.

POINS (*reads*).

"John Falstaff, knight—" every man must know
that, as oft as he has occasion to name himself: 120

even like those that are kin to the king; for they never prick their finger but they say, "There's some of the king's blood spilt." "How comes that?" says he, that takes upon him not to conceive.* The answer is as ready as a borrower's cap,* "I am the king's poor cousin, sir."

understand
i.e., is to be doffed

PRINCE.

Nay, they will be kin to us, or they will fetch it from Japhet.[26] But to the letter:

POINS (*reads*).

"Sir John Falstaff, knight, to the son of the king, nearest his father, Harry Prince of Wales, greeting." Why, this is a certificate.

130

PRINCE.

Peace!

POINS (*reads*).

"I will imitate the honorable Romans in brevity—"
He sure means brevity in breath, short-winded.
"I commend me to thee, I commend thee, and I leave thee. Be not too familiar with Poins; for he misuses thy favors so much, that he swears thou art to marry his sister Nell. Repent at idle times as thou mayest; and so, farewell.

141

"Thine, by yea and no, which is as much as to say, as thou usest him, JACK FALSTAFF with my familiars; JOHN with my brothers and sisters; and SIR JOHN with all Europe."

My lord, I'll steep this letter in sack and make him eat it.

PRINCE.

That's to make him eat twenty of his words. But do you use me thus, Ned? Must I marry your sister?

151

POINS.

God send the wench no worse fortune! But I never said so.

PRINCE.

Well, thus we play the fools with the time, and

the spirits of the wise sit in the clouds and mock us.

    (*To* BARDOLPH.)

Is your master here in London?

BARDOLPH.

    Yea, my lord.

PRINCE.

    Where sups he? Doth the old boar feed in the old frank?*   sty/160

BARDOLPH.

    At the old place, my lord, in Eastcheap.

PRINCE.

    What company?

PAGE.

    Ephesians, my lord, of the old church.[27]

PRINCE.

    Sup any women with him?

PAGE.

    None, my lord, but old Mistress Quickly and Mistress Doll Tearsheet.

PRINCE.

    What pagan may that be?

PAGE.

    A proper gentlewoman, sir, and a kinswoman of my master's.   170

PRINCE.

    Even such kin as the parish heifers are to the town bull.

    (*To* POINS.)

Shall we steal upon them, Ned, at supper?

POINS.

    I am your shadow, my lord; I'll follow you.

PRINCE.

    Sirrah, you boy, and Bardolph, no word to your master that I am yet come to town. There's for your silence.

    (*He gives them each some money.*)

BARDOLPH.

    I have no tongue, sir.   179

PAGE.

    And for* mine, sir, I will govern it.   as for

PRINCE.

    Fare you well; go.

      (BARDOLPH *and the* PAGE *leave.*)

    This Doll Tearsheet should be some road.*   a harlot

POINS.

    I warrant you, as common as the way between
    Saint Alban's and London.

PRINCE.

    How might we see Falstaff bestow* himself to-   deport
    night in his true colors, and not ourselves be seen?

POINS.

    Put on two leathern jerkins and aprons, and wait
    upon him at his table as drawers.   191

PRINCE.

    From a God to a bull?[28] A heavy descension!
    It was Jove's case. From a prince to a prentice? A
    low transformation! That shall be mine; for in
    everything the purpose must weigh with* the   equal
    folly. Follow me, Ned.

      (*They go.*)

SCENE 3. Warkworth. Before NORTHUMBERLAND's castle.

      (NORTHUMBERLAND, LADY NORTHUMBERLAND, *and*
      LADY PERCY, HOTSPUR's *widow, come out of the*
      castle.)

NORTHUMBERLAND.

    I pray thee, loving wife, and gentle daughter,
    Give even way* unto my rough affairs: free scope
    Put not you on the visage of the times
    And be like them to Percy troublesome.

LADY NORTHUMBERLAND.

    I have given over.* I will speak no more: up
    Do what you will: your wisdom be your guide.

NORTHUMBERLAND.

Alas, sweet wife, my honor is at pawn;*   pledged
And, but* my going, nothing can redeem it.   except

LADY PERCY.

O yet, for God's sake, go not to these wars!
The time was, father, that you broke your word,   10
When you were more endeared* to it than now;   bound
When your own Percy, when my heart's dear
    Harry,
Threw many a northward look to see his father
Bring up his powers: but he did long in vain.
Who then persuaded you to stay at home?
There were two honors lost, yours and your son's.
For yours, the God of heaven brighten it!
For his, it stuck* upon him as the sun   settled
In the gray vault of heaven, and by his light
Did all the chivalry of England move   20
To do brave acts: he was indeed the glass
Wherein the noble youth did dress themselves:
He had no legs that practiced not his gait;
And speaking thick, which nature made his
    blemish,
Became the accents of the valiant;
For those that could speak low and tardily
Would turn their own perfection to abuse,
To seem like him: so that in speech, in gait,
In diet, in affections* of delight,   choice
In military rules, humors of blood,*   capricious
                                                             emotion
He was the mark* and glass, copy and book,   beacon
That fashioned others. And him—O wondrous
    him!   32
O miracle of men!—him did you leave,
Second to none, unseconded by you,
To look upon the hideous god of war
In disadvantage; to abide a field
Where nothing but the sound of Hotspur's name
Did seem defensible! So you left him!
Never, O never, do his ghost* the wrong   spirit

To hold your honor more precise and nice   40
With others than with him!
               Let them alone:
The marshal and the archbishop are strong.
Had my sweet Harry had but half their numbers,
Today might I, hanging on Hotspur's neck,
Have talked of Monmouth's grave.

NORTHUMBERLAND.   Beshrew your heart,
Fair daughter, you do draw my spirits from me
With new lamenting ancient oversights.
But I must go and meet with danger there,
Or it will seek me in another place
And find me worse provided.

LADY NORTHUMBERLAND.   O, fly to Scotland,   50
Till that the nobles and the armèd commons
Have of their puissance* made a little taste.   power

LADY PERCY.

If they get* ground and vantage of the king,   gain
Then join you with them, like a rib of steel,
To make strength stronger; but, for all our loves,
First let them try themselves. So did your son;
He was so suffered:* so came* I a widow;   permitted/
And never shall have length of life enough   became
To rain upon remembrance with mine eyes,
That it may grow and sprout as high as heaven,   60
For recordation* to my noble husband.   a memorial

NORTHUMBERLAND.

Come, come, go in with me. 'Tis with my mind
As with the tide swelled up unto his height,
That makes a still-stand, running neither way:
Fain* would I go to meet the archbishop,   willingly
But many thousand reasons hold me back.
I will resolve for* Scotland: there am I,   decide on
Till time and vantage* crave my company.   opportunity
    (*They go back into the castle.*)

SCENE 4. London. The Boar's Head Tavern in Eastcheap.

(*Two* DRAWERS *enter, one of them with a dish.*)

FIRST DRAWER.

What the devil hast thou brought there? Apple-
johns?* Thou knowest Sir John cannot endure
an apple-john.

i.e., kind
of apple

SECOND DRAWER.

Mass, thou sayest true. The prince once set a dish
of apple-johns before him, and told him there
were five more Sir Johns, and, putting off his hat,
said "I will now take my leave of these six dry,
round, old, withered knights." It angered him to
the heart. But he hath forgot that.

10

FIRST DRAWER.

Why, then, cover,* and set them down: and see
if thou canst find out Sneak's noise;* Mistress
Tearsheet would fain hear some music. Dispatch:
the room where they supped is too hot; they'll
come in straight.

i.e., set
the table
band

SECOND DRAWER.

Sirrah, here will be the prince and Master Poins
anon;* and they will put on two of our jerkins
and aprons; and Sir John must not know of it:
Bardolph hath brought word.

immedi-
ately

20

FIRST DRAWER.

By the mass, here will be old Utis:*29 it will be
an excellent stratagem.

great
sport

SECOND DRAWER.

I'll see if I can find out Sneak.

(*The* SECOND DRAWER *hurries out, as* HOTSPUR
enters with DOLL TEARSHEET.)

HOSTESS.30

I' faith, sweetheart, methinks now you are in an
excellent good temperality: your pulsidge beats as
extraordinarily as heart would desire; and your

color, I warrant you, is as red as any rose, in
good truth, la! But, i' faith, you have drunk too
much canaries; and that's a marvelous searching
wine, and it perfumes the blood ere one can say   30
"What's this?" How do you now?

DOLL.

Better than I was: hem!

HOSTESS.

Why, that's well said; a good heart's worth gold.
    (*Listening.*)
Lo, here comes Sir John.
    (FALSTAFF *enters, singing.*)

FALSTAFF.

"When Arthur first in court"
    (*To the* FIRST DRAWER.)
—Empty the jordan.*   chamber-
                                                           pot
    (FIRST DRAWER *goes, and* FALSTAFF *sings again.*)
"And was a worthy king."
    How now, Mistress Doll!

HOSTESS.

Sick of a calm;* yea, good faith.   qualm—*i.e.,*
                                                           nausea/40

FALSTAFF.

So is all her sect;* an they be once in a calm,   sex
they are sick.

DOLL.

You muddy rascal, is that all the comfort you give
me?

FALSTAFF.

You make fat rascals,[31] Mistress Doll.

DOLL.

I make them! Gluttony and diseases make them.
I make them not.

FALSTAFF.

If the cook help to make the gluttony, you help
to make the diseases, Doll: we catch of you, Doll,
we catch of you; grant that, my poor virtue, grant
that.   51

DOLL.

Yea, joy, our chains and our jewels.

FALSTAFF.

"Your brooches, pearls, and ouches:"* for to serve   gems
bravely is to come halting* off, you know: to   limping
come off the breach with his pike bent bravely,
and to surgery bravely; to venture upon the
charged chambers bravely—

DOLL.

Hang yourself, you muddy conger,* hang your-   eel
self!   59

HOSTESS.

By my troth, this is the old fashion; you two
never meet but you fall to some discord. You are
both, i' good truth, as rheumatic as two dry toasts;
you cannot one bear with another's confirmities.*   infirmities
What the good-year! One must bear, and that
must be you: you are the weaker vessel, as they
say, the emptier vessel.

DOLL.

Can a weak empty vessel bear such a huge full
hogshead? There's a whole merchant's venture of
Bourdeaux* stuff in him; you have not seen a   *i.e.*, Bor-
...lk* better stuffed in the hold. Come, I'll be   deaux wine
friends with th e, Jack: thou art going to the   large ship
wars; and wheth I shall ever see thee again or   71
no, there is nobody c res.

(FIRST DRAWER *returns.*)

FIRST DRAWER.

Sir, Ancient* Pistol's below, and would speak   Ensign
with you.

DOLL.

Hang him, swaggering rascal! Let him not come
hither: it is the foul-mouthedst rogue in England.

HOSTESS.

If he swagger, let him not come here: no, by my   80
faith; I must live among my neighbors; I'll* no   I'll have
swaggerers: I am in good name and fame with the
very best. Shut the door; there comes no swaggerers here: I have not lived all this while to have
swaggering now. Shut the door, I pray you.

FALSTAFF.

Dost thou hear, hostess?

HOSTESS.

Pray ye, pacify yourself, Sir John: there comes no swaggerers here.

FALSTAFF.

Dost thou hear? It is mine ancient.   89

HOSTESS.

Tilly-fally,* Sir John, ne'er tell me: your ancient swaggerer comes not in my doors. I was before Master Tisick, the debuty, t' other day; and, as he said to me, 'twas no longer ago than Wednesday last, "I' good faith, neighbor Quickly," says he— Master Dumbe, our minister,[32] was by then— "neighbor Quickly," says he, "receive those that are civil; for," said he, "you are in an ill name": now a' said so, I can tell whereupon;* "for," says he, "you are an honest woman, and well thought on; therefore take heed what guests you receive: receive," says he, "no swaggering companions." There comes none here: you would bless you* to hear what he said: no, I'll no swaggerers.

fiddle-sticks

where-fore

100

yourself

FALSTAFF.

He's no swaggerer, hostess; a tame cheater,[33] i' faith; you may stroke him as gently as a puppy greyhound: he'll not swagger with a Barbary* hen, if her feathers turn back in any show of resistance. Call him up, drawer.

guinea

(FIRST DRAWER *goes*.)

HOSTESS.

Cheater, call you him? I will bar no honest man my house, nor no cheater: but I do not love swaggering, by my troth; I am the worse, when one says swagger. Feel, masters, how I shake. Look you, I warrant you.

110

DOLL.

So you do, hostess.

HOSTESS.

Do I? Yea, in very truth, do I, an 'twere* an   as if I
aspen leaf: I cannot abide swaggerers.   were

(PISTOL *enters, followed by* BARDOLPH *and the*
PAGE.[34])

PISTOL.

God save you, Sir John!   119

FALSTAFF.

Welcome, Ancient Pistol. Here, Pistol, I charge*   pledge
you with a cup of sack: do you discharge upon*   charge
mine hostess.   it to

PISTOL.

I will discharge upon her, Sir John, with two
bullets.

FALSTAFF.

She is pistol-proof, sir; you shall hardly offend
her.

HOSTESS.

Come, I'll drink no proofs nor no bullets: I'll
drink no more than will do me good, for no man's
pleasure, I.

PISTOL.

Then to you, Mistress Dorothy; I will charge you.   131

DOLL.

Charge me! I scorn you, scurvy companion.*   fellow
What! You poor, base, rascally, cheating, lack-
linen mate! Away, you moldy rogue, away! I
am meat for your master.

PISTOL.

I know you, Mistress Dorothy.

DOLL.

Away, you cut-purse rascal! You filthy bung,*   pick-
away! By this wine, I'll thrust my knife in your   pocket
moldy chaps,* an you play the saucy cuttle*   jaws/
with me. Away, you bottle-ale rascal! You basket-   cut-purse
hilt* stale juggler, you! Since when, I pray you,   sword
sir? God's light, with two points on your shoulder?   trick
Much!*   140
                                                    not much!

PISTOL.

God let me not live, but I will murder your ruff* | collar
for this.

FALSTAFF.

No more, Pistol; I would not have you go off here.
Discharge yourself of our company, Pistol.

HOSTESS.

No, good Captain Pistol. Not here, sweet captain. | 150

DOLL.

Captain! Thou abominable damned cheater, art
thou not ashamed to be called captain? An cap-
tains were of my mind, they would truncheon* | cudgel
you out, for taking their names upon you before
you have earned them. You a captain! You slave,
for what? For tearing a poor whore's ruff in a
bawdy-house? He a captain! Hang him, rogue!
He lives upon moldy stewed prunes and dried
cakes. A captain! God's light, these villains will
make the word as odious as the word "occupy";* | fornicate
which was an excellent good word before it was | 161
ill sorted:* Therefore captains had need look to 't. | com-panioned

BARDOLPH.

Pray thee, go down, good ancient.

FALSTAFF.

Hark thee hither, Mistress Doll.

PISTOL.

Not I: I tell thee what, Corporal Bardolph, I could
tear her: I'll be revenged of her.

PAGE.

Pray thee, go down.

PISTOL.

I'll see her damned first; to Pluto's damned lake, | 170
by this hand, to the infernal deep, with Erebus and
tortures vile also. Hold hook and line, say I.
Down, down, dogs! down, faitors!* Have we | swindlers
not Hiren here?[35]

HOSTESS.

Good Captain Peesel, be quiet; 'tis very late, i'
faith: I beseek you now, aggravate your choler.

PISTOL.

These be good humors,* indeed! Shall pack-   fancies
horses
And hollow pampered jades of Asia,
Which cannot go but thirty mile a-day,
Compare with Cæsars, and with Cannibals,   180
And Trojan Greeks? Nay, rather damn them with
King Cerberus; and let the welkin* roar.[36]   heavens
Shall we fall foul* for toys?   quarrel

HOSTESS.

By my troth, captain, these are very bitter words.

BARDOLPH.

Be gone, good ancient: this will grow to a brawl
anon.

PISTOL.

Die men like dogs! Give crowns like pins! Have
we not Hiren here?   189

HOSTESS.

O' my word, captain, there's none such here.
What the good-year! Do you think I would deny
her? For God's sake, be quiet.

PISTOL.

Then feed, and be fat, my fair Calipolis.[37] Come
give 's some sack.
"Si fortune me tormente, sperato me contento."[38]
Fear we broadsides? No, let the fiend give fire:
Give me some sack: and, sweetheart, lie thou there.
    (*Placing his sword on the table.*)
Come we to full points* here; and are etceteras   stops
nothing?

FALSTAFF.

Pistol, I would be quiet.

PISTOL.

Sweet knight, I kiss thy neif:* what! We have   fist/201
seen the seven stars.*   *i.e.,*
    Pleiades

DOLL.

For God's sake, thrust him downstairs: I cannot
endure such a fustian* rascal.   preten-
    tious

PISTOL.

Thrust him downstairs!   Know we not Galloway nags?

FALSTAFF.

Quoit* him down, Bardolph, like a shove-groat* shilling:[39] nay, an a' do nothing but speak nothing, a' shall be nothing here.

pitch/ shuffle- board

BARDOLPH.

Come, get you downstairs.

PISTOL.

What! Shall we have incision?* Shall we imbrue? *bloodshed*
   (*Snatching up his sword.*)
Then death rock me asleep, abridge my doleful days![40]

211

Why then let grievous, ghastly, gaping wounds
Untwine the Sisters Three! Come, Atrops, I say![41]

HOSTESS.

Here's goodly stuff toward!*

at hand

FALSTAFF (*to the* PAGE).

Give me my rapier, boy.

DOLL.

I pray thee, Jack, I pray thee, do not draw.

FALSTAFF.

Get you downstairs. (*Draws his sword.*)

HOSTESS.

Here's a goodly tumult! I'll forswear keeping house, afore I'll be in these   tirrits and frights.*
So; murder, I warrant now. Alas, alas! Put up your naked weapons, put up your naked weapons.
   (FALSTAFF *drives* PISTOL *out.* BARDOLPH *goes after him.*)

220

i.e., terrors and fits

DOLL.

I pray thee, Jack, be quiet; the rascal's gone. Ah, you whoreson little valiant villain, you!

HOSTESS.

Are you not hurt i' the groin? Me-thought a' made a shrewd* thrust at your belly.
   (BARDOLPH *returns.*)

sharp

FALSTAFF.

Have you turned him out o' doors?

BARDOLPH.

Yea, sir. The rascal's drunk: you have hurt him,   231
sir, i' the shoulder.

FALSTAFF.

A rascal! To brave* me!   *defy*

DOLL (*to* FALSTAFF).

Ah, you sweet little rogue, you! Alas, poor ape,
how thou sweatest! Come, let me wipe thy face;
come on, you whoreson chops: ah, rogue! I' faith,
I love thee: thou art as valorous as Hector of
Troy, worth five of Agamemnon, and ten times
better than the Nine Worthies:⁴² ah, villain!

FALSTAFF.

A rascally slave! I will toss the rogue in a blanket.   241

DOLL.

Do, an thou darest for thy heart: an thou dost,
I'll canvass* thee between a pair of sheets.   *toss*

   (*The* MUSICIANS *enter.*)

PAGE.

The music is come, sir.

FALSTAFF.

Let them play. Play, sirs. Sit on my knee, Doll.
   (*As the music begins, he sits* DOLL *on his lap.*)
A rascal bragging slave! The rogue fled from me
like quicksilver.

DOLL.

I' faith, and thou followedst him like a church.   250
Thou whoreson little tidy Bartholomew boar-pig,
when wilt thou leave fighting o' days and foining*   *thrusting*
o' nights, and begin to patch up thine old body for
heaven?

   (*The* PRINCE *and* POINS *enter at the back, dis-
guised as drawers.*)

FALSTAFF.

Peace, good Doll! Do not speak like a death's-
head; do not bid me remember mine end.

DOLL.

Sirrah, what humor's* the prince of?

dispo-sition

FALSTAFF.

A good shallow young fellow: a' would have made
a good pantler,* a' would ha' chipped* bread well.

pantryman/trimmed

DOLL.

They say Poins has a good wit.

260

FALSTAFF.

He, a good wit? Hang him, baboon! His wit's
as thick as Tewksbury mustard;[43] there 's no more
conceit* in him than is in a mallet.

imagina-tion

DOLL.

Why does the prince love him so, then?

FALSTAFF.

Because their legs are both of a bigness, and a'
plays at quoits well, and eats conger and fennel,
and drinks off candles' ends for flap-dragons, and
rides the wild-mare* with the boys, and jumps
upon joined-stools, and swears with a good grace,
and wears his boots very smooth, like unto the sign
of the leg, and breeds no bate* with telling of discreet stories;[44] and such other gambol faculties*
a' has, that show a weak mind and an able body,
for the which the prince admits him; for the
prince himself is such another: the weight of a
hair will turn the scales between their avoirdupois.

see-saw/270

discord

horseplay

280

PRINCE (*aside to* POINS).

Would not this nave of a wheel have his ears cut
off?

POINS (*aside to the* PRINCE).

Let's beat him before his whore.

PRINCE (*aside to* POINS).

Look, whether the withered elder hath not his
poll* clawed like a parrot.

head

POINS (*aside to the* PRINCE).

Is it not strange that desire should so many years
outlive performance?

FALSTAFF.

Kiss me, Doll.

PRINCE (*aside to* POINS).

Saturn and Venus this year in conjunction! What
says the almanac to that?[45]

POINS (*aside to the* PRINCE).

And, look, whether the fiery Trigon, his man, be
not lisping* to his master's old tables, his note-   making
book, his counsel-keeper.[46]   love/290

FALSTAFF (*to* DOLL).

Thou dost give me flattering busses.*   kisses

DOLL.

By my troth, I kiss thee with a most constant
heart.

FALSTAFF.

I am old, I am old.

DOLL.

I love thee better than I love e'er a scurvy young
boy of them all.

FALSTAFF.

What stuff wilt have a kirtle* of? I shall receive   skirt
money o' Thursday: shalt have a cap tomorrow.
A merry song, come: it grows late; we'll to bed.
Thou 'lt forget me when I am gone.   300

DOLL.

By my troth, thou 'lt set me a-weeping an thou
sayest so: prove that ever I dress myself handsome
till thy return: well, hearken at the end.*   wait and
see

FALSTAFF.

Some sack, Francis.

PRINCE.
POINS. } Anon, anon, sir. (*Coming forward.*)

FALSTAFF.

Ha! A bastard son of the king's? And art not
thou Poins his brother?

PRINCE.

Why, thou globe of sinful continents, what a life
dost thou lead!   310

FALSTAFF.

A better than thou: I am a gentleman: thou art a
drawer.

PRINCE.

Very true, sir; and I come to draw you out by the ears.

HOSTESS (*to the* PRINCE).

O, the Lord preserve thy good grace! By my troth, welcome to London. Now, the Lord bless that sweet face of thine! O Jesu, are you come from Wales?

FALSTAFF.

Thou whoreson mad compound of majesty, by this light flesh and corrupt blood,⁴⁷ thou art welcome.

321

DOLL.

How, you fat fool! I scorn you.

POINS (*aside to the* PRINCE).

My lord, he will drive you out of your revenge and turn all to a merriment, if you take not the heat.*

strike
while hot

PRINCE.

You whoreson candle-*mine, you, how vilely did you speak of me even now before this honest, virtuous, civil gentlewoman!

tallow

HOSTESS.

God's blessing of your good heart! And so she is, by my troth.

330

FALSTAFF.

Didst thou hear me?

PRINCE.

Yea, and you knew me, as you did when you ran away by Gadshill: you knew I was at your back, and spoke it on purpose to try my patience.

FALSTAFF.

No, no, no; not so. I did not think thou wast within hearing.

PRINCE.

I shall drive you then to confess the wilful abuse; and then I know how to handle you.

FALSTAFF.

No abuse, Hal, o' mine honor; no abuse.

340

PRINCE.

Not to dispraise me, and call me pantler and bread-chipper and I know not what?

FALSTAFF.

No abuse, Hal.

POINS.

No abuse?

FALSTAFF.

No abuse, Ned, i' the world; honest Ned, none. I dispraised him before the wicked, that the wicked might not fall in love with him; in which doing, I have done the part of a careful friend and a true subject, and thy father is to give me thanks for it. No abuse, Hal: none, Ned, none: no, faith, boys, none.   350

PRINCE.

See now, whether pure fear and entire cowardice doth not make thee wrong this virtuous gentle-woman to close with us. Is she of the wicked? Is thine hostess here of the wicked? Or is thy boy of the wicked? Or honest Bardolph, whose zeal burns in his nose, of the wicked?

POINS.

Answer, thou dead elm, answer.

FALSTAFF.

The fiend hath pricked down* Bardolph irre-coverable; and his face is Lucifer's privy*-kitchen, where he doth nothing but roast malt-worms.* For the boy, there is a good angel about him; but the devil outbids him too.

marked/ 360
private
topers

PRINCE.

For* the women?   *how about*

FALSTAFF.

For one of them, she is in hell already, and burns* poor souls. For the other, I owe her money; and whether she be damned for that, I know not.

infects

HOSTESS.

No, I warrant you.   369

FALSTAFF.

No, I think thou art not; I think thou art quit for
that. Marry, there is another indictment upon
thee, for suffering flesh to be eaten in thy house,
contrary to the law;[48] for the which I think thou
wilt howl.

HOSTESS.

All victualers do so: what's a joint of mutton or
two in a whole Lent?

PRINCE.

You, gentlewoman—

DOLL.

What says your grace?

FALSTAFF.

His grace says that which his flesh rebels against.   380
    (*A loud knocking is heard.*)

HOSTESS (*calling*).

Who knocks so loud at door? Look to the door
there, Francis.
    (PETO *enters.*)

PRINCE.

Peto, how now! What news?

PETO.

The king your father is at Westminster;
And there are twenty weak and wearied posts*   messengers
Come from the north. And, as I came along,
I met and overtook a dozen captains,
Bare-headed, sweating, knocking at the taverns,
And asking every one for Sir John Falstaff.

PRINCE.

By heavens, Poins, I feel me much to blame,   390
So idly to profane the precious time,
When tempest of commotion,* like the south*   rebellion/
Borne* with black vapor, doth begin to melt   south wind
And drop upon our bare unarmed heads.   laden
Give me my sword and cloak. Falstaff, good night.
    (PRINCE HENRY *leaves, with* POINS *and* PETO.)

FALSTAFF.

Now comes in the sweetest morsel of the night,

and we must hence and leave it unpicked. (*More knocking is heard, and* BARDOLPH *goes out to answer the door.*) More knocking at the door!

(BARDOLPH *returns.*)

How now! What's the matter?   400

BARDOLPH.

You must away to court, sir, presently;
A dozen captains stay at door for you.

FALSTAFF (*to the* PAGE).

Pay the musicians, sirrah.

Farewell, hostess; farewell, Doll. You see, my good wenches, how men of merit are sought after: the undeserver may sleep, when the man of action is called on. Farewell, good wenches: if I be not sent away post,* I will see you again ere I go.   *at once*

DOLL.

I cannot speak; if my heart be not ready to burst—
well, sweet Jack, have a care of thyself.   410

FALSTAFF.

Farewell, farewell.

(FALSTAFF *and* BARDOLPH *leave.*)

HOSTESS.

Well, fare thee well: I have known thee these twenty nine years, come peascod*-time; but an honester and truer-hearted man—well, fare thee well.   *i.e., peas ripening*

BARDOLPH (*within*).

Mistress Tearsheet!

HOSTESS.

What's the matter?

BARDOLPH (*within*).

Bid Mistress Tearsheet come to my master.   419

HOSTESS.

O, run, Doll, run; run, good Doll: come. (DOLL *blubbers.*) Yea, will you come, Doll?

(*They go.*)

ACT III

SCENE 1. Westminster. A room in the palace. Night.

(The KING enters, in night dress, bearing letters, which he hands to a PAGE.)

KING.

Go call the Earls of Surrey and of Warwick;
But, ere they come, bid them o'er-read these
     letters,
And well consider of them: make good speed.
     (The PAGE goes.)
How many thousand of my poorest subjects
Are at this hour asleep! O sleep, O gentle sleep,
Nature's soft nurse, how have I frighted thee,
That thou no more wilt weigh my eyelids down
And steep my senses in forgetfulness?
Why rather, sleep, liest thou in smoky cribs,*   hovels
Upon uneasy* pallets stretching thee   uncomfortable
And hushed with buzzing night-flies to thy slumber,   11
Than in the perfumed chambers of the great,
Under the canopies of costly state,*   splendor
And lulled with sound of sweetest melody?
O thou dull* god, why liest thou with the vile   drowsy
In loathsome beds, and leavest the kingly couch
A watch-case* or a common 'larum-bell?   sentry box
Wilt thou upon the high and giddy mast
Seal up the ship-boy's eyes, and rock his brains
In cradle of the rude imperious surge   20
And in the visitation of the winds,
Who take the ruffian billows by the top,
Curling their monstrous heads and hanging them

With deafening clamor in the slippery clouds,
That, with the hurly,* death itself awakes? — uproar
Canst thou, O partial* sleep, give thy repose — partisan
To the wet sea-boy in an hour so rude,
And in the calmest and most stillest night,
With all appliances and means to boot,
Deny it to a king? Then happy low,* lie down: — lowly folk
Uneasy lies the head that wears a crown. — 31

    (WARWICK *and* SURREY *enter.*)

WARWICK.

Many good morrows to your majesty!

KING.

Is it good morrow, lords?

WARWICK.

'Tis one o'clock, and past.

KING.

Why, then, good morrow to you all, my lords.
Have you read o'er the letters that I sent you?

WARWICK.

We have, my liege.

KING.

Then you perceive the body of our kingdom
How foul* it is; what rank diseases grow, — corrupted
And with what danger, near the heart of it. — 40

WARWICK.

It is but as a body yet distempered;* — disordered
Which to his former strength may be restored
With good advice and little medicine:
My Lord Northumberland will soon be cooled.

KING.

O God! That one might read the book of fate,
And see the revolution* of the times — revolving
Make mountains level, and the continent,
Weary of solid firmness, melt itself
Into the sea! And, other times, to see
The beachy* girdle of the ocean — beached
Too wide for Neptune's hips; how chances mock, — 51
And changes fill the cup of alteration
With divers liquors!

O, if this were seen,
The happiest youth, viewing his progress through,
What perils past, what crosses to ensue,
Would shut the book, and sit him down and die.
'Tis not ten years gone
Since Richard and Northumberland, great friends,
Did feast together, and in two years after
Were they at wars. It is but eight years since   60
This Percy was the man nearest my soul,
Who like a brother toiled in my affairs
And laid his love and life under my foot,
Yea, for my sake, even to the eyes of Richard
Gave him defiance. But which of you was by—
    (*To* WARWICK.)
You, cousin Nevil,* as I may remember—   *i.e.,* Warwick
When Richard, with his eye brimful of tears,
Then checked and rated* by Northumberland,   berated
Did speak these words, now proved a prophecy?
"Northumberland, thou ladder by the which   70
My cousin Bolingbroke ascends my throne";
Though then, God knows, I had no such intent
But that necessity so bowed* the state   bowed down
That I and greatness were compelled to kiss:
"The time shall come," thus did he follow it,
"The time will come, that foul sin, gathering head,
Shall break into corruption": so went on,
Foretelling this same time's condition
And the division of our amity.

WARWICK.

There is a history in all men's lives,   80
Figuring* the nature of the times deceased;   revealing
The which observed, a man may prophesy,
With a near aim, of the main chance of things
As yet not come to life, which in their seeds
And weak beginnings lie intreasurèd.*   stored up
Such things become the hatch and brood of time;
And by the necessary form* of this   logical
King Richard might create a perfect guess   necessity
That great Northumberland, then false to him,

Would of that seed grow to a greater falseness;⠀⠀⠀⠀⠀90
Which should not find a ground to root upon,
Unless on you.

KING.⠀⠀⠀⠀⠀⠀⠀⠀Are these things then necessities?
Then let us meet them like necessities:
And that same word even now cries out on* us:⠀⠀⠀against
They say the bishop and Northumberland
Are fifty thousand strong.

WARWICK.⠀⠀⠀⠀⠀⠀⠀⠀⠀It cannot be, my lord;
Rumor doth double, like the voice and echo,
The numbers of the feared.

⠀⠀⠀⠀⠀⠀⠀⠀⠀⠀⠀⠀⠀Please it your grace
To go to bed. Upon my soul, my lord,
The powers that you already have sent forth⠀⠀⠀⠀100
Shall bring this prize in very easily.
To comfort you the more, I have received
A certain instance* that Glendower is dead.⠀⠀⠀proof
⠀Your majesty hath been this fortnight ill,
And these unseasoned* hours perforce must add⠀⠀ill-timed
Unto your sickness.

KING.⠀⠀⠀⠀⠀⠀⠀I will take your counsel:
And were these inward* wars once out of hand,*⠀⠀civil/ended
We would, dear lords, unto the Holy Land.
⠀(*They go.*)

SCENE 2. Gloucestershire. Before JUSTICE SHALLOW's house.

(MOULDY, SHADOW, WART, FEEBLE, *and* BULLCALF, *all local inhabitants, wait in the background.* JUSTICE SHALLOW *enters from his house and meets* JUSTICE SILENCE.)

SHALLOW.
⠀Come on, come on, come on, sir; give me your
hand, sir, give me your hand, sir: an early stirrer,
by the rood!* And how doth my good cousin⠀⠀⠀cross
Silence?

SILENCE.

Good morrow, good cousin Shallow.

SHALLOW.

And how doth my cousin, your bedfellow? And
your fairest daughter and mine, my god-daughter
Ellen?

SILENCE.

Alas, a black ousel,* cousin Shallow!   blackbird/9

SHALLOW.

By yea and nay, sir, I dare say my cousin William
is become a good scholar. He is at Oxford still,
is he not?

SILENCE.

Indeed, sir, to my cost.

SHALLOW. A' must, then, to the inns o' court shortly.
I was once of Clement's Inn,* where I think they   *i.e.*, law
will talk of mad Shallow yet.   school

SILENCE.

You were called "lusty Shallow" then, cousin.

SHALLOW.

By the mass, I was called anything; and I would   20
have done anything indeed too, and roundly* too. thoroughly
There was I, and little John Doit of Staffordshire,
and black George Barnes, and Francis Pickbone,
and Will Squele, a Cotswold man;⁴⁹ you had not
four such swingebucklers* in all the inns o' court   swash-
again. And I may say to you, we knew where   bucklers
the bona-robas* were and had the best of them   harlots
all at commandment. Then was Jack Falstaff,
now Sir John, a boy, and page to Thomas Mowbray, Duke of Norfolk.

SILENCE.

This Sir John, cousin, that comes hither anon
about soldiers?   31

SHALLOW.

The same Sir John, the very same. I see him
break Skogan's head at the court-gate, when a'
was a crack* not thus high. And the very same   youngster
day did I fight with one Sampson Stockfish, a

fruiterer, behind Gray's Inn. Jesu, Jesu, the mad
days that I have spent! And to see how many of
my old acquaintance are dead!

SILENCE.

We shall all follow, cousin.   39

SHALLOW.

Certain, 'tis certain; very sure, very sure: death,
as the Psalmist saith, is certain to all; all shall die.
How* a good yoke of bullocks at Stamford fair?   how much

SILENCE.

By my troth, I was not there.

SHALLOW.

Death is certain. Is old Double of your town living yet?

SILENCE.

Dead, sir.

SHALLOW.

Jesu, Jesu, dead! A' drew a good bow; and dead!
A' shot a fine shoot. John a Gaunt loved him
well, and betted much money on his head. Dead!   50
A' would have clapped i' the clout* at twelve   *i.e., hit
                                                   the mark
score; and carried you a forehand shaft* a long-range
                                             arrow
fourteen and fourteen and a half,⁵⁰ that it would
have done a man's heart good to see. How a score
of ewes now?

SILENCE.

Thereafter as they be:* a score of good ewes   according
                                                to grade
may be worth ten pounds.

SHALLOW.

And is old Double dead?

SILENCE (*looks down the street*).

Here come two of Sir John Falstaff's men, as I
think.   60

   (BARDOLPH *enters, accompanied by a soldier.*)

BARDOLPH.

Good morrow, honest gentlemen. I beseech you,
which is Justice Shallow?

SHALLOW.

I am Robert Shallow, sir; a poor esquire of this

county, and one of the king's justices of the peace.
What is your good pleasure with me?

BARDOLPH.

My captain, sir, commends him to you; my captain, Sir John Falstaff, a tall* gentleman, by
heaven, and a most gallant leader.

sturdy

SHALLOW.

He greets me well, sir. I knew him a good
backsword* man. How doth the good knight?
May I ask how my lady his wife doth?

70
single-
stick

BARDOLPH.

Sir, pardon; a soldier is better accommodated than
with a wife.

SHALLOW.

It is well said, in faith, sir; and it is well said
indeed, too. Better accommodated! It is good;
yea, indeed, is it: good phrases are surely, and
ever were, very commendable. Accommodated!
It comes of "accommodo": very good; a good
phrase.

79

BARDOLPH.

Pardon me, sir; I have heard the word. Phrase
call you it? By this good day, I know not the
phrase; but I will maintain the word with my
sword to be a soldier-like word, and a word of
exceeding good command, by heaven. Accommodated; that is, when a man is, as they say,
accommodated; or when a man is, being, whereby
a' may be thought to be accommodated; which is
an excellent thing.

SHALLOW.

It is very just.

89

(FALSTAFF enters.)

Look, here comes good Sir John. Give me your
good hand, give me your worship's good hand:
by my troth, you like* well and bear your years
very well: welcome, good Sir John.

look

FALSTAFF.

I am glad to see you well, good Master Robert Shallow. Master Surecard, as I think?

SHALLOW.

No, Sir John; it is my cousin Silence, in commis-
sion* with me.   office

FALSTAFF.

Good Master Silence, it well befits you should be of the peace.

SILENCE.

Your good worship is welcome.   100

FALSTAFF.

Fie! This is hot weather, gentlemen. Have you provided me here half a dozen sufficient* men?   fit

SHALLOW.

Marry, have we, sir. Will you sit?

FALSTAFF.

Let me see them, I beseech you.

SHALLOW.

Where's the roll? Where's the roll? Where's the roll? Let me see, let me see, let me see. So, so, so, so, so, so, so: yea, marry, sir: Ralph Mouldy! Let them appear as I call; let them do so, let them do so. Let me see: where is Mouldy?   111

MOULDY (steps forward).

Here, an 't please you.

SHALLOW.

What think you, Sir John? A good-limbed fellow; young, strong, and of good friends.

FALSTAFF.

Is thy name Mouldy?

MOULDY.

Yea, an 't please you.

FALSTAFF.

'Tis the more time thou were used.

SHALLOW.

Ha, ha, ha! Most excellent, i' faith! Things that are moldy lack use: very singular good! In faith, well said, Sir John, very well said.

FALSTAFF (*to* SHALLOW, *who checks* MOULDY'*s name
on the list*).

Prick him.*51 _{list him/}

MOULDY.

I was pricked well enough before, an you could
have let me alone: my old dame will be undone
now for one to do her husbandry* and her drudg- farm work
ery. You need not to have pricked me; there are
other men fitter to go out than I.

FALSTAFF.

Go to: peace, Mouldy. You shall go. Mouldy, it
is time you were spent.* expended

MOULDY.

Spent! 129

SHALLOW.

Peace, fellow, peace; stand aside: know you where
you are? (MOULDY *steps aside*.) For the other, Sir
John: let me see: Simon Shadow!

FALSTAFF.

Yea, marry, let me have him to sit under: he's
like to be a cold soldier.

SHALLOW.

Where's Shadow?
(SHADOW *steps forward*.)

SHADOW.

Here, sir.

FALSTAFF.

Shadow, whose son art thou?

SHADOW.

My mother's son, sir.

FALSTAFF.

Thy mother's son! Like enough, and thy father's
shadow:* so the son of the female is the shadow image/
of the male: it is often so, indeed; but much of 140
the father's substance!

SHALLOW.

Do you like him, Sir John?

FALSTAFF.

Shadow will serve for summer; prick him, for we

have a number of shadows* to fill up the muster-book.⁵² *i.e., false entries*

> (SHALLOW *checks* SHADOW's *name, and* SHADOW *moves back.*)

SHALLOW.

Thomas Wart!

FALSTAFF.

Where's he?

WART (*steps forward*).

Here, sir.

FALSTAFF.

Is thy name Wart?   150

WART.

Yea, sir.

FALSTAFF.

Thou art a very ragged wart.

SHALLOW.

Shall I prick him down, Sir John?

FALSTAFF.

It were* superfluous; for his apparel is built upon *would be* his back and the whole frame stands* upon pins:⁵³ *depends* prick him no more.

> (WART *steps aside.*)

SHALLOW.

Ha, ha, ha! you can do it, sir; you can do it: I commend you well. Francis Feeble!

FEEBLE (*steps forward*).

Here, sir.

FALSTAFF.

What trade art thou, Feeble?   160

FEEBLE.

A woman's tailor, sir.

SHALLOW.

Shall I prick him, sir?

FALSTAFF.

You may: but if he had been a man's tailor, he'd ha' pricked you. (*To* FEEBLE.) Wilt thou make as many holes in an enemy's battle* as thou hast *army* done in a woman's petticoat?

FEEBLE.

I will do my good will, sir: you can have no more.

FALSTAFF.

Well said, good woman's tailor! Well said, coura-
geous Feeble! Thou wilt be as valiant as the
wrathful dove or most magnanimous* mouse.
Prick the woman's tailor: well—Master Shallow—
deep, Master Shallow.

170

brave

FEEBLE (*as* SHALLOW *checks off his name*).

I would Wart might have gone, sir.

FALSTAFF.

I would thou wert a man's tailor, that thou
mightst mend him and make him fit to go. I cannot put him to* a private soldier that is the leader
of so many thousands.* Let that suffice, most
forcible Feeble.

enlist
him as
i.e., lice

FEEBLE.

It shall suffice, sir.

180

FALSTAFF.

I am bound to thee, reverend Feeble. Who is next?

SHALLOW.

Peter Bullcalf o' the green!*

i.e., village
green

FALSTAFF.

Yea, marry, let's see Bullcalf.

BULLCALF (*steps forward*).

Here, sir.

FALSTAFF.

'Fore God, a likely fellow! Come, prick me Bullcalf till he roar again.

BULLCALF.

O Lord! Good my lord captain—

FALSTAFF.

What, dost thou roar before thou art pricked?

190

BULLCALF.

O Lord, sir! I am a diseased man.

FALSTAFF.

What disease hast thou?

BULLCALF.

A whoreson cold, sir, a cough, sir, which I caught
with ringing in the king's affairs upon his corona-
tion-day, sir.

FALSTAFF.

Come, thou shalt go to the wars in a gown;* we
will have away* thy cold; and I will take such
order that thy friends shall ring for thee. (BULL-
CALF *steps aside*.) Is here all?

dressing gown
get rid of

199

SHALLOW.

Here is two more called than your number; you
must have but four here, sir. And so, I pray you,
go in with me to dinner.

FALSTAFF.

Come, I will go drink with you, but I cannot
tarry dinner. I am glad to see you, by my troth,
Master Shallow.

SHALLOW.

O, Sir John, do you remember since we lay all
night in the windmill in Saint George's field?[54]

FALSTAFF.

No more of that, good Master Shallow, no more
of that.

SHALLOW.

Ha! 'Twas a merry night. And is Jane Nightwork alive?

211

FALSTAFF.

She lives, Master Shallow.

SHALLOW.

She never could away with* me.

endure

FALSTAFF.

Never, never; she would always say she could not
abide Master Shallow.

SHALLOW.

By the mass, I could anger her to the heart. She
was then a bona-roba. Doth she hold her own
well?

FALSTAFF.

Old, old, Master Shallow.

219

SHALLOW.

Nay, she must be old; she cannot choose but be old; certain she's old; and had Robin Nightwork by old Nightwork before I came to Clement's Inn.

SILENCE.

That's fifty five years ago.

SHALLOW.

Ha, cousin Silence, that thou hadst seen that that this knight and I have seen! Ha, Sir John, said I well?

FALSTAFF.

We have heard the chimes at midnight, Master Shallow.   229

SHALLOW.

That we have, that we have, that we have; in fai*th, Sir John, we have: our watchword was "Hem* boys!" Come, let's to dinner; come, let's to dinner. Jesus, the days that we have seen! Come, come.   *drink up*

(FALSTAFF *and the* JUSTICE *go into the house.*)

BULLCALF (*takes* BARDOLPH *aside and gives him money*).

Good Master Corporate Bardolph, stand* my   *act as* friend; and here's four Harry ten shillings in French crowns for you.[55] In very truth, sir, I had as lief be hanged, sir, as go: and yet, for mine own part, sir, I do not care; but rather, because I am unwilling, and, for mine own part, have a   240 desire to stay with my friends; else, sir, I did not care, for mine own part, so much.

BARDOLPH.

Go to; stand aside.

MOULDY (*moving to* BARDOLPH, *as* BULLCALF *steps aside*).

And, good master corporal captain, for my old dame's sake, stand my friend: she has nobody to do anything about her when I am gone; and she is old, and cannot help herself. You shall have forty, sir.

BARDOLPH.

Go to; stand aside.   249

(BARDOLPH *takes money and* MOULDY *steps aside.*)

FEEBLE.

By my troth, I care not; a man can die but once: we owe God a death: I'll ne'er bear a base mind: an 't be my destiny, so; an 't be not, so: no man is too good to serve 's prince; and let it go which way it will, he that dies this year is quit for the next.

BARDOLPH.

Well said; thou 'rt a good fellow.

FEEBLE.

Faith, I'll bear no base mind.

(FALSTAFF *and the* JUSTICE *return from the house.*)

FALSTAFF.

Come, sir, which men shall I have?

SHALLOW.

Four of which you please.

BARDOLPH (*takes* FALSTAFF *aside*).

Sir, a word with you: I have three pound to free Mouldy and Bullcalf.   261

FALSTAFF.

Go to; well.

SHALLOW.

Come, Sir John, which four will you have?

FALSTAFF.

Do you choose for me.

SHALLOW.

Marry, then, Mouldy, Bullcalf, Feeble and Shadow.

FALSTAFF.

Mouldy and Bullcalf: for you, Mouldy, stay at home till you are past service. And for your part, Bullcalf, grow till you come unto it:* I will none   reach it
of you.   271

SHALLOW.

Sir John, Sir John, do not yourself wrong: they
are your likeliest men, and I would have you
served with the best.

FALSTAFF.

Will you tell me, Master Shallow, how to choose
a man? Care I for the limb, the thewes, the
stature, bulk, and big assemblance* of a man!   assembly
Give me the spirit, Master Shallow. Here's Wart;
you see what a ragged appearance it is: a' shall
charge* you and discharge* you with the motion   load/fire
of a pewterer's hammer, come off and on swifter   280
than he that gibbets* on the brewer's bucket.⁵⁶   hangs
And this same half-faced fellow, Shadow; give me
this man: he presents no mark to the enemy; the
foeman may with as great aim* level at the edge   target
of a penknife. And for a retreat; how swiftly will
this Feeble the woman's tailor run off! O, give
me the spare men, and spare me the great ones.
    Put me a caliver* into Wart's hand, Bardolph.   musket/
                                                           290
BARDOLPH (demonstrates manual of arms with his
    gun).

Hold, Wart, traverse;* thus, thus, thus.   march

FALSTAFF (as BARDOLPH gives caliver to WART).

Come, manage me your caliver. (As WART goes
through manual of arms.) So: very well: go to:
very good, exceeding good. O, give me always a
little, lean, old, chapt, bald shot. Well said,* i'   done
faith, Wart; thou 'rt a good scab. Hold, there's
a tester* for thee. (Gives WART a coin.)   sixpence

SHALLOW.

He is not his craft's master; he doth not do it
right. I remember at Mile-end Green, when I lay
at Clement's Inn—I was then Sir Dagonet in   300
Arthur's show⁵⁷—there was a little quiver* fel-   nimble
low, and a' would manage you his piece thus;
(Taking caliver from WART.) and a' would about
and about, and come you in and come you in:
"rah, tah, tah," would a' say; "bounce"* would   bang

a' say; and away again would a' go, and again
would a' come: I shall ne'er see such a fellow.
(*Gives caliver back to* BARDOLPH.)

FALSTAFF.

These fellows will do well, Master Shallow. God
keep you, Master Silence: I will not use many
words with you. Fare you well, gentlemen both:
I thank you: I must a dozen mile tonight. Bardolph, give the soldiers coats.   311

SHALLOW.

Sir John, the Lord bless you! God prosper your
affairs! God send us peace! At your return visit
our house; let our old acquaintance be renewed:
peradventure I will with ye to the court.

FALSTAFF.

'Fore God, I would you would, Master Shallow.

SHALLOW.

Go to; I have spoke at* a word. God keep you.   in/320

FALSTAFF.

Fare you well, gentle gentlemen. (*The* JUSTICES
go back into the house.) On, Bardolph; lead the
men away. (BARDOLPH *marches the recruits away.*)
As I return, I will fetch off* these justices: I do   get the
see the bottom of Justice Shallow. Lord, Lord,   better of
how subject we old men are to this vice of lying!
This same starved justice hath done nothing but
prate to me of the wildness of his youth, and the
feats he hath done about Turnbull Street;[58] and
every third word a lie, duer* paid to the hearer   more
than the Turk's tribute. I do remember him at   promptly
Clement's Inn like a man made after supper of a   330
cheese-paring. When a' was naked, he was, for all
the world, like a forked radish, with a head fantastically carved upon it with a knife. A' was so
forlorn, that his dimensions to any thick* sight   poor
were invincible.* A' was the very genius of fam-   invisible
ine; yet lecherous as a monkey, and the whores
called him mandrake:[59] a' came ever in the rear-   339

ward of the fashion, and sung those tunes to the overscutched* huswives* that he heard the carmen* whistle, and sware they were his fancies or his goodnights.*

> overused/ hussies
>
> carters
>
> serenades

And now is this Vice's dagger become a squire,[60] and talks as familiarly of John a Gaunt as if he had been sworn brother to him; and I'll be sworn a' ne'er saw him but once in the Tiltyard; and then he burst his head for crowding among the marshal's men. I saw it, and told John a Gaunt he beat his own name; for you might have thrust him and all his apparel into an eel-skin; the case of a treble hautboy* was a mansion for him, a court: and now has he land and beefs.*

> 350
>
> oboe
>
> cattle

Well, I'll be acquainted with him, if I return; and it shall go hard* but I will make him a philosopher's two stones to me:[61] if the young dace* be a bait for the old pike, I see no reason in the law of nature but I may snap at him. Let time shape, and there an end.

> will be strange
>
> *i.e.*, a small fish

(*He goes.*)

ACT IV

Scene 1. Yorkshire. Gaultree Forest.

(*The* ARCHBISHOP OF YORK, *in armor, enters with* LORD MOWBRAY, LORD HASTINGS, *and members of their army, all in battle dress.*)

ARCHBISHOP.
What is this forest called?

HASTINGS.
'Tis Gaultree Forest, an 't shall please your grace.

ARCHBISHOP.
Here stand, my lords; and send discoverers* forth   scouts
To know the numbers of our enemies.

HASTINGS.
We have sent forth already.

ARCHBISHOP.   'Tis well done.
My friends and brethren in these great affairs,
I must acquaint you that I have received
New-dated letters from Northumberland;
Their cold intent, tenor and substance, thus:
Here doth he wish his person, with such powers   10
As might hold sortance* with his quality,   accord
The which he could not levy; whereupon
He is retired, to ripe his growing fortunes,
To Scotland: and concludes in hearty prayers
That your attempts may overlive* the hazard   outlive
And fearful meeting of their opposite.

MOWBRAY.
Thus do the hopes we have in him touch ground
And dash themselves to pieces.

(*A* MESSENGER *enters.*)

HASTINGS.   Now, what news?

MESSENGER.
  West of this forest, scarcely off a mile,
  In goodly form comes on the enemy;   20
  And, by the ground they hide, I judge their
      number
  Upon or near the rate of thirty thousand.

MOWBRAY.
  The just* proportion* that we gave them out.   exact/size
  Let us sway* on and face them in the field.   sweep

ARCHBISHOP (*as he sees* WESTMORELAND *approach*).
  What well-appointed* leader fronts us here?   equipped

MOWBRAY.
  I think it is my Lord of Westmoreland.
      (WESTMORELAND *enters, in armor.*)

WESTMORELAND.
  Health and fair greeting from our general,
  The prince, Lord John, and Duke of Lancaster.

ARCHBISHOP.
  Say on, my Lord of Westmoreland, in peace:
  What does concern* your coming?   is the
                                                      purpose of
WESTMORELAND.   Then, my lord,   30
  Unto your grace do I in chief address
  The substance of my speech. If that rebellion
  Came like itself, in base and abject routs,*   mobs
  Led on by bloody* youth, guarded* with rags,   headstrong/
                                                     decked out
  And countenanced by boys and beggary,
  I say, if damned commotion* so appeared,   sedition
  In his true, native and most proper* shape,   essential
  You, reverend father, and these noble lords
  Had not* been here, to dress the ugly form   would
                                                        not have
  Of base and bloody insurrection   40
  With your fair honors.
                          You, lord archbishop,
  Whose see is by a civil* peace maintained,   orderly
  Whose beard the silver hand of peace hath touched,
  Whose learning and good letters* peace hath   wide
      tutored,   reading
  Whose white investments* figure* innocence,   vestments/
                                                      symbolize
  The dove and very blessed spirit of peace—

Wherefore do you so ill translate* yourself   transform
Out of the speech of peace that bears such grace,
Into the harsh and boisterous tongue of war;
Turning your books to graves, your ink to blood,   50
Your pens to lances and your tongue divine
To a loud trumpet and a point* of war?   signal

ARCHBISHOP.

Wherefore do I this? So the question stands.
Briefly to this end:* we are all diseased,   sum of the
And with our surfeiting and wanton hours   matter
Have brought ourselves into a burning fever,
And we must bleed for it; of which disease
Our late king, Richard, being infected, died.
But, my most noble Lord of Westmoreland,
I take not on me here as a physician,   60
Nor do I as* an enemy to peace   in the
Troop* in the throngs of military men;   role of
                                          march
But rather show* awhile like fearful war,   appear
To diet rank* minds sick of happiness   sated
And purge the obstructions which begin to stop
Our very veins of life.
                            Hear me more plainly.
I have in equal balance justly weighed
What wrongs our arms may do, what wrongs we
    suffer,
And find our griefs* heavier than our offenses.   grievances
We see which way the stream of time doth run,   70
And are enforced from our most quiet there
By the rough torrent of occasion;*   crisis
And have the summary of all our griefs,
When time shall serve,* to show in articles,   prove
                                          favorable
Which long ere this we offered to the king,
And might by no suit* gain our audience.   plea
When we are wronged and would unfold our griefs,
We are denied access unto his person
Even by those men that most have done us wrong.
The dangers of the days but newly gone,   80
Whose memory is written on the earth
With yet appearing blood, and the examples

Of every minute's instance,* present now,   happening
Hath put us in these ill-beseeming arms—
Not to break peace or any branch of it,
But to establish here a peace indeed,
Concurring both in name and quality.

WESTMORELAND.

When ever yet was your appeal denied?
Wherein have you been gallèd* by the king?   irritated/89
What peer hath been suborned* to grate on you,   incited
That you should seal this lawless bloody book
Of forged rebellion with a seal divine
And consecrate commotion's bitter edge?

ARCHBISHOP.

My brother general, the commonwealth,
To brother born an household cruelty,
I make my quarrel in particular.[62]

WESTMORELAND.

There is no need of any such redress;
Or if there were, it not belongs to you.

MOWBRAY.

Why not to him in part, and to us all
That feel the bruises of the days before,   100
And suffer the condition of these times
To lay a heavy and unequal hand
Upon our honors?

WESTMORELAND.   O, my good Lord Mowbray,
Construe the times to* their necessities,   according to
And you shall say indeed, it is the time,
And not the king, that doth you injuries.
Yet for your part, it not appears to me
Either from the king or in the present time
That you should have an inch of any ground
To build a grief on: were you not restored   110
To all the Duke of Norfolk's signories,*   estates
Your noble and right well remembered father's?

MOWBRAY.

What thing, in honor, had my father lost,
That need to be revived and breathed in me?
The king that loved him, as the state stood then,

Was force perforce compelled to banish him:
And then that Henry Bolingbroke and he,
Being mounted and both rousèd in their seats,
Their neighing coursers daring of the spur,
Their armèd staves* in charge, their beavers* down,   lances/ visors/120
Their eyes of fire sparkling through sights of steel*   *i.e.*, helmets
And the loud trumpet blowing them together,
Then, then, when there was nothing could have
   stayed
My father from the breast of Bolingbroke,
O, when the king did throw his warder* down,63   staff
His own life hung upon the staff he threw:
Then threw he down himself and all their lives
That by indictment and by dint* of sword   force
Have since miscarried under Bolingbroke.

WESTMORELAND.

You speak, Lord Mowbray, now you know not
   what.   130
The Earl of Hereford* was reputed then   *i.e.*, later Henry IV
In England the most valiant gentleman:
Who knows on whom fortune would then have
   smiled?
But if your father had been victor there,
He ne'er had borne it out of* Coventry: escaped from
For all the country in a general* voice   according
Cried hate upon him; and all their prayers and love
Were set on Hereford, whom they doted on
And blessed and graced indeed, more than the
   king.
But this is mere digression from my purpose.   140
Here come I from our princely general
To know your griefs; to tell you from his grace
That he will give you audience; and wherein
It shall appear that your demands are just,
You shall enjoy them, everything set off*   disregarded
That might so much as think you enemies.

MOWBRAY.

But he hath forced us to compel this offer;
And it proceeds from policy, not love.

WESTMORELAND.

Mowbray, you overween* to take it so—   presume
This offer comes from mercy, not from fear: 150
For, lo! Within a ken* our army lies,   sight
Upon mine honor, all too confident
To give admittance to a thought of fear.
Our battle* is more full of names than yours,   army
Our men more perfect in the use of arms,
Our armor all as strong, our cause the best;
Then reason will* our hearts should be as good.   *i.e.*, will have it
Say you not then our offer is compelled.

MOWBRAY.

Well, by my will we shall admit no parley.

WESTMORELAND.

That argues but the shame of your offense: 160
A rotten case abides no handling.

HASTINGS.

Hath the Prince John a full commission,
In very ample virtue* of his father,   power
To hear and absolutely to determine
Of what conditions we shall stand upon?

WESTMORELAND.

That is intended* in the general's name: implied
I muse* you make so slight a question.   wonder

ARCHBISHOP (*giving him a document*).

Then take, my Lord of Westmoreland, this schedule,
For this contains our general grievances:
Each several article herein redressed,*   to be redressed 171
All members of our cause, both here and hence,
That are insinewed* to this action,   bound together
Acquitted by a true substantial form
And present* execution of our wills*   instant/ wishes
To us and to our purposes confined,
We come within our awful banks* again   respected bounds
And knit our powers to the arm of peace.

WESTMORELAND.

This will I show the general.
                              Please you, lords,
In sight of both our battles we may meet;

And either end in peace—which God so frame!—   180
Or to the place of difference call the swords
Which must decide it.

ARCHBISHOP.   My lord, we will do so.
   (WESTMORELAND *leaves*.)

MOWBRAY.

There is a thing within my bosom tells me
That no conditions of our peace can stand.

HASTINGS.

Fear you not that: if we can make our peace
Upon such large terms and so absolute
As our conditions shall consist* upon,   insist
Our peace shall stand as firm as rocky mountains.

MOWBRAY.

Yea, but our valuation shall be* such   be judged
That every slight and false-derivèd cause,   190
Yea, every idle, nice and wanton reason
Shall to the king taste of this action;
That, were our royal faiths* martyrs in love,   loyalty
We shall be winnowed with so rough a wind
That even our corn shall seem as light as chaff
And good from bad find no partition.*   distinc-
                                                          tion

ARCHBISHOP.

No, no, my lord. Note this; the king is weary
Of dainty and such picking* grievances: trifling
For he hath found to end one doubt by death
Revives two greater in the heirs of life,*   living
                                                          heirs
And therefore will he wipe his tables clean   201
And keep no tell-tale to his memory
That may repeat and history* his loss   record
To new remembrance; for full well he knows
He cannot so precisely weed this land
As his misdoubts* present occasion: 64   suspicions
His foes are so enrooted with his friends
That, plucking to unfix an enemy,
He doth unfasten so and shake a friend:
So that this land, like an offensive wife   210
That hath enraged him on to offer strokes,
As he is striking, holds his infant up

And hangs resolved* correction in the arm   resolved
                                                       upon
That was upreared to execution.

HASTINGS.

Besides, the king hath wasted* all his rods   used up
On late offenders, that he now doth lack
The very instruments of chastisement:
So that his power, like to a fangless lion,
May offer, but not hold.

ARCHBISHOP.   'Tis very true:

And therefore be assured, my good lord marshal,   220
If we do now make our atonement well,
Our peace will, like a broken limb united,
Grow stronger for the breaking.

MOWBRAY.   Be it so.

(WESTMORELAND *returns*.)

Here is returned my Lord of Westmoreland.

WESTMORELAND.

The prince is here at hand: pleaseth your lordship
To meet his grace just* distance 'tween our armies.   equal

MOWBRAY.

Your grace of York, in God's name, then, set forward.

ARCHBISHOP.

Before,* and greet his grace. My lord, we come.   go before
(*They all go*.)

SCENE 2. Another part of Gaultree Forest. An open place.

(*From one side* PRINCE JOHN OF LANCASTER *enters,
with* WESTMORELAND, *officers, and attendants.
From the other side, the* ARCHBISHOP *enters with*
LORD MOWBRAY, LORD HASTINGS, *officers, and attendants*.)

LANCASTER.

You are well encountered here, my cousin
Mowbray.
Good day to you, gentle lord archbishop;

And so to you, Lord Hastings; and to all.
My Lord* of York, it better showed with you   *i.e., Archbishop
When that your flock, assembled by the bell,
Encircled you to hear with reverence
Your exposition on the holy text
Than now to see you here an iron man,
Cheering a rout of rebels with your drum,
Turning the word to sword, and life to death.   10
That man that sits within a monarch's heart,
And ripens in the sunshine of his favor,
Would he abuse the countenance of the king,
Alack, what mischiefs might he set abroach*   *on foot
In shadow of such greatness!

                    With you, lord bishop,
It is even so. Who hath not heard it spoken
How deep you were within the books of God?
To us the speaker in his parliament;
To us the imagined voice of God himself:
The very opener* and intelligencer*   *interpreter/ mediator/20
Between the grace, the sanctities of heaven
And our dull workings.* O, who shall believe   *thinking
But* you misuse the reverence of your place,   *but that
Employ the countenance and grace of heaven,
As a false favorite doth his prince's name,
In deeds dishonorable? You have ta'en up,*   *enlisted
Under the counterfeited zeal of God,
The subjects of his substitute,* my father,   *deputy
And both against the peace of heaven and him
Have here up-swarmed them.*   *brought them in swarms

ARCHBISHOP.   Good my Lord of
   Lancaster,   30
I am not here against your father's peace;
But, as I told my Lord of Westmoreland,
The time misordered* doth, in common sense,   *disordered
Crowd us and crush us to this monstrous* form,   *distorted
To hold our safety up.* I sent your grace   *keep us safe
The parcels* and particulars of our grief,   *details
The which hath been with scorn shoved from the
   court,

Whereon this Hydra* son of war is born;　　*i.e., many-headed
Whose dangerous eyes may well be charmed asleep
With grant of our most just and right desires,　　40
And true obedience, of this madness cured,
Stoop tamely* to the foot of majesty.　　*submissively

MOWBRAY.
If not, we ready are to try our fortunes
To the last man.

HASTINGS.　　　　And though we here fall down,
We have supplies* to second our attempt.　　*reserves
If they miscarry, theirs shall second them:
And so success* of mischief shall be born　　*succession
And heir from heir shall hold this quarrel up
Whiles England shall have generation.*　　*propagation

LANCASTER.
You are too shallow, Hastings, much too shallow,　　50
To sound the bottom of the after-times.

WESTMORELAND.
Pleaseth your grace to answer them directly
How far forth you do like their articles.

LANCASTER.
I like them all, and do allow* them well,　　*approve
And swear he﹐﹐, by the honor of my blood,
My father's purposes have been mistook,
And some about him have too lavishly
Wrested* his meaning and authority.　　*wrenched
My lord, these griefs shall be with speed redressed;
Upon my soul, they shall.

　　　　　　If this may please you,　　60
Discharge your powers unto their several counties,
As we will ours: and here between the armies
Let's drink together friendly and embrace,
That all their eyes may bear those tokens* home　　*i.e., of our pledges
Of our restorèd love and amity.

ARCHBISHOP.
I take your princely word for these redresses.

LANCASTER.
I give it you, and will maintain my word:
And thereupon I drink unto your grace.

HASTINGS (*to an* OFFICER, *as* ATTENDANTS *pour wine*).

Go, captain, and deliver to the army

This news of peace: let them have pay, and part:*   depart/70

I know it will well please them. Hie thee, captain.

  (OFFICER *goes*.)

ARCHBISHOP.

To you, my noble Lord of Westmoreland.

WESTMORELAND (*drinks*).

I pledge your grace; and, if you knew what pains

I have bestowed to breed this present peace,

You would drink freely: but my love to ye

Shall show itself more openly hereafter.

ARCHBISHOP.

I do not doubt you.

WESTMORELAND.   I am glad of it.

Health to my lord and gentle cousin, Mowbray.

MOWBRAY.

You wish me health in very happy season,   79

For I am, on the sudden, something* ill.   somewhat

ARCHBISHOP.

Against* ill chances men are ever merry;   confronted
      by
But heaviness foreruns the good event.

WESTMORELAND.

Therefore be merry, coz; since sudden sorrow

Serves to say thus, "some good thing comes to-

  morrow."

ARCHBISHOP.

Believe me, I am passing* light in spirit.   exceed-
      ingly

MOWBRAY.

So much the worse, if your own rule be true.

  (*Shouts are heard*.)

LANCASTER.

The word of peace is rendered:* hark, how they   pro-
      claimed
  shout!

MOWBRAY.

This had been* cheerful after victory.   would
      have been

ARCHBISHOP.

A peace is of the nature of a conquest,

For then both parties nobly are subdued,   90
And neither party loser.
LANCASTER (*to* WESTMORELAND).
                              Go my lord,
And let our army be dischargèd too.
    (*To* ARCHBISHOP *as* WESTMORELAND *goes.*)
And, good my lord, so please you, let our trains
March by us, that we may peruse the men
We should have coped withal.*   with
ARCHBISHOP.   Go, good Lord
    Hastings,
And, ere they be dismissed, let them march by.
    (HASTINGS *goes.*)
LANCASTER.
I trust, lords, we shall lie* tonight together.   lodge
    (*To* WESTMORELAND *as he returns.*)
Now cousin, wherefore stands our army still?
WESTMORELAND.
The leaders, having charge from you to stand,
Will not go off until they hear you speak.   100
LANCASTER.
They know their duties.
    (HASTINGS *returns.*)
HASTINGS.
My lord, our army is dispersed already:
Like youthful steers unyoked, they take their
    courses
East, west, north, south; or, like a school broke
    up,
Each hurries toward his home and sporting place.*   play-
                                                           ground
WESTMORELAND.
Good tidings, my Lord Hastings—
                              for the which
I do arrest thee, traitor, of high treason.
And you, lord archbishop, and you lord Mow-
    bray—
Of capital treason I attach you both.
    (GUARDS *step forward and arrest* HASTINGS, MOW-
    BRAY, *and the* ARCHBISHOP.)

MOWBRAY.

Is this proceeding just and honorable?   110

WESTMORELAND.

Is your assembly so?

ARCHBISHOP.

Will you thus break your faith?

LANCASTER.   I pawned* thee   pledged
    none:
I promised you redress of these same grievances
Whereof you did complain; which, by mine honor,
I will perform with a most Christian care.
But for you, rebels, look to taste the due
Meet for rebellion and such acts as yours.
Most shallowly* did you these arms commence,   lightly
Fondly* brought here and foolishly sent hence.   foolishly
    Strike up our drums, pursue the scattered stray:*   stragglers
God, and not we, hath safely fought today.   121
Some guard these traitors to the block of death,
Treason' true bed and yielder up of breath.

    (*Drums sound.* PRINCE JOHN *and* WESTMORELAND
    go, followed by the rebels, under guard, and all
    OFFICERS *and* SOLDIERS.)

SCENE 3. Another part of the forest.

    (*Trumpets and drums. Groups of* PRINCE JOHN'S
    men pursuing fleeing rebels are seen. Then FAL-
    STAFF *enters, in armor, and meets* COLEVILE, *also
    in armor.*)

FALSTAFF.

What's your name, sir? Of what condition* are   rank
you, and of what place, I pray?

COLEVILE.

I am a knight, sir; and my name is Colevile of the
dale.

FALSTAFF.

Well, then, Colevile is your name, a knight is your

degree, and your place the dale. Colevile shall be
still your name, a traitor your decree, and the
dungeon your place, a place deep enough; so shall
you be still Colevile of the dale.   10

COLEVILE.

Are not you Sir John Falstaff?

FALSTAFF.

As good a man as he, sir, whoe'er I am. Do ye
yield, sir? Or shall I sweat for you? (*Threatens*
COLEVILE *with drawn sword.*) If I do sweat, they   tears/
are the drops* of thy lovers,* and they weep for   friends
thy death: therefore rouse up fear and trembling,
and do observance* to my mercy.   homage

COLEVILE.

I think you are Sir John Falstaff, and in that
thought yield me.* (*Surrenders his sword.*)   myself/19

FALSTAFF.

I have a whole school of tongues in this belly of
mine, and not a tongue of them all speaks any
other word but my name.⁶⁵ An I had but a belly
of any indifferency,* I were simply the most active   *i.e.,* indif-
fellow in Europe: my womb, my womb, my   ferent size
womb, undoes me. (*Hearing the approaching
troops.*) Here comes our general.

    (PRINCE JOHN OF LANCASTER *enters, with* WEST-
    MORELAND, BLUNT, OFFICERS, *and* SOLDIERS.)

LANCASTER.

The heat is past; follow no further now:⁶⁶
Call in the powers, good cousin Westmoreland.

    (WESTMORELAND *goes.*)

Now, Falstaff, where have you been all this while?
When everything is ended, then you come.   30
These tardy tricks of yours will, on my life
One time or other break some gallows' back.

FALSTAFF.

I would be sorry, my lord, but it should be thus:
I never knew yet but rebuke and check was the
reward of valor. Do you think me a swallow, an
arrow, or a bullet? Have I, in my poor and old

motion, the expedition of thought? I have speeded
hither with the very extremest inch of possibility;
I have foundered* nine score and odd posts:* and _{lamed/post}
here, travel-tainted as I am, have, in my pure and   horses/40
immaculate valor, taken Sir John Colevile of the
dale, a most furious knight and valorous enemy.
But what of that? He saw me, and yielded; that
I may justly say, with the hook-nosed fellow of
Rome,*67 "I came, saw, and overcame."   *i.e., Julius
                                                          Caesar

LANCASTER.

It was more of his courtesy than your deserving.

FALSTAFF.

I know not: here he is, and here I yield him: and   50
I beseech your grace, let it be booked with the rest
of this day's deeds; or, by the Lord, I will have
it in a particular* ballad else,68 with mine own   my own
picture on the top on 't, Colevile kissing my foot:
to the which course if I be enforced, if you do not
all show like gilt two-pences to me, and I in the
clear sky of fame o'ershine you as much as the full
moon doth the cinders of the element,* which   i.e., stars
show like pins' heads to her, believe not the word
of the noble. Therefore let me have right, and
let desert mount.   61

LANCASTER.

Thine's too heavy to mount.

FALSTAFF.

Let it shine, then.

LANCASTER.

Thine's too thick to shine.

FALSTAFF.

Let it do something, my good lord, that may do
me good, and call it what you will.

LANCASTER.

Is thy name Colevile?

COLEVILE.

It is, my lord.

LANCASTER.

A famous rebel art thou, Colevile.   69

FALSTAFF.
  And a famous true subject took him.
COLEVILE.
  I am, my lord, but as my betters are
  That led me hither: had they been ruled by me,
  You should have won them dearer than you have.
FALSTAFF.
  I know not how they sold themselves: but thou,
  like a kind fellow, gavest thyself away gratis; and
  I thank thee for thee.
    (WESTMORELAND *returns.*)
LANCASTER.
  Now, have you left pursuit?
WESTMORELAND.
  Retreat is made and execution stayed.
LANCASTER.
  Send Colevile with his confederates
  To York, to present execution.   80
  Blunt, lead him hence; and see you guard him sure.
    (BLUNT *takes* COLEVILE *out, under guard.*)
  And now dispatch we toward the court, my lords:
  I hear the king my father is sore sick.
  Our news shall go before us to his majesty,
  Which, cousin, you shall bear to comfort him,
  And we with sober* speed will follow you.   deliberate
FALSTAFF.
  My lord, I beseech you, give me leave to go
  Through Gloucestershire: and, when you come to
      court,
  Stand* my good lord, pray, in your good report.   act as
LANCASTER.
  Fare you well, Falstaff: I, in my condition,*   rank/90
  Shall better speak of you than you deserve.
    (*All leave except* FALSTAFF.)
FALSTAFF.
  I would you had but the wit: 'twere better than
  your dukedom. Good faith, this same young sober-
  blooded boy doth not love me; nor a man cannot
  make him laugh; but that's no marvel, he drinks

no wine. There's never none of these demure
boys come to any proof;* for thin drink doth so
over-cool their blood, and making many fish-
meals, that they fall into a kind of male green-
sickness;69 and then, when they marry, they get
wenches. They are generally fools and cowards;
which some of us should be too, but for inflammation.* A good sherris-sack* hath a two-fold operation in it. It ascends me into the brain; dries me
there all the foolish and dull and crudy* vapors
which environ it; makes it apprehensive, quick,
forgetive,* full of nimble fiery and delectable
shapes; which, delivered o'er to the voice, the
tongue, which is the birth, becomes excellent wit.
The second property of your excellent sherris is,
the warming of the blood; which, before cold and
settled, left the liver white and pale, which is the
badge of pusillanimity and cowardice; but the
sherris warms it and makes it course from the in-
wards to the parts extreme: it illumineth the face,
which as a beacon gives warning to all the rest of
this little kingdom, man, to arm; and then the
vital commoners and inland petty spirits muster
me all to their captain, the heart, who, great and
puffed up with this retinue, doth any deed of
courage; and this valor comes of sherris. So that
skill in the weapon is nothing without sack, for
that sets it a-work; and learning a mere hoard of
gold kept by a devil, till sack commences it* and
sets it in act and use.

Hereof comes it that Prince Harry is valiant; for
the cold blood he did naturally inherit of his
father, he hath, like lean, sterile and bare land,
manured, husbanded and tilled with excellent en-
deavor of drinking good and good store of fertile
sherris, that he is become very hot and valiant. If
I had a thousand sons, the first humane principle I
would teach them should be, to forswear thin
potations and to addict themselves to sack.

turn out
well

99

stimu-
lation/
sherry

thick

inventive

110

120

starts
it off

130

(BARDOLPH *enters.*)
How now, Bardolph?

BARDOLPH.
The army is discharged all and gone.

FALSTAFF.
Let them go. I'll through Gloucestershire and
there will I visit Master Robert Shallow, esquire.
I have him already tempering* between my finger   condition-
and my thumb, and shortly will I seal with him.   ing/140
Come away.
(*They go.*)

SCENE 4.⁷⁰ The Palace at Westminster. The Jerusalem
Chamber.⁷¹

(*The* KING *enters with the* EARL OF WARWICK *and
others, including the* PRINCES THOMAS OF CLARENCE
and HUMPHREY OF GLOUCESTER, *and* ATTENDANTS.)

KING.
Now, lords, if God doth give successful end
To this debate* that bleedeth at our doors,   quarrel
We will our youth lead on to higher fields
And draw no swords but what are sanctified.
Our navy is addressed,* our power collected,   prepared
Our substitutes* in absence well invested,*   deputies/
And everything lies level* to our wish: established
Only, we want a little personal strength;   conforms
And pause us, till these rebels, now afoot,
Come underneath the yoke of government.   10

WARWICK.
Both which we doubt not but your majesty
Shall soon enjoy.

KING.   Humphrey, my son of Gloucester,
Where is the prince your brother?

GLOUCESTER.
I think he's gone to hunt, my lord, at Windsor.

KING.

  And how accompanied?

GLOUCESTER.   I do not know, my lord.

KING.

  Is not his brother, Thomas of Clarence, with him?

GLOUCESTER.

  No, my good lord; he is in presence here.

CLARENCE (*stepping forward*).

  What would my lord and father?

KING.

  Nothing but well to thee, Thomas of Clarence.

  How chance thou art not with the prince thy
    brother?   20

  He loves thee, and thou dost neglect him, Thomas;

  Thou hast a better place in his affection

  Than all thy brothers: cherish it, my boy,

  And noble offices thou mayst effect

  Of mediation, after I am dead,

  Between his greatness and thy other brethren.

  Therefore omit* him not; blunt not his love,   *neglect*

  Nor lose the good advantage of his grace

  By seeming cold or careless of his will;

  For he is gracious, if he be observed.*   *shown respect 31*

  He hath a tear for pity and a hand

  Open as day for melting* charity—   *compassionate*

  Yet notwithstanding, being incensed, he's flint,

  As humorous* as winter and as sudden   *changeable*

  As flaws congealèd* in the spring of day.   *icy gusts*

  His temper, therefore, must be well observed:

  Chide him for faults, and do it reverently,

  When you perceive his blood inclined to mirth;

  But, being* moody, give him line and scope,   *when he is*

  Till that his passions, like a whale on ground,   40

  Confound* themselves with working.   *exhaust*

                            Learn

  this, Thomas,

  And thou shalt prove a shelter to thy friend,

  A hoop of gold to bind thy brothers in,

  That the united vessel of their blood,*   *i.e., the royal family*

Mingled with venom of suggestion*—   insinuation
As, force perforce, the age will pour it in—
Shall never leak, though it do work as strong
As aconitum[72] or rash* gunpowder.   fast

CLARENCE.
I shall observe him with all care and love.

KING.
Why art thou not at Windsor with him, Thomas?   50

CLARENCE.
He is not there today; he dines in London.

KING.
And how accompanied? Canst thou tell that?

CLARENCE.
With Poins, and other his continual followers.

KING.
Most subject is the fattest* soil to weeds;   richest
And he, the noble image of my youth,
Is overspread with them: therefore my grief
Stretches itself beyond the hour of death.
The blood weeps from my heart when I do shape
In forms imaginary the unguided days
And rotten times that you shall look upon   60
When I am sleeping with my ancestors.
For when his headstrong riot hath no curb,
When rage and hot blood are his counselors,
When means and lavish* manners meet together,   unrestrained
O, with what wings shall his affections* fly   passions
Towards fronting peril and opposed decay!*   ruin

WARWICK.
My gracious lord, you look beyond* him quite: misjudge
The prince but studies his companions
Like a strange tongue, wherein, to gain the
    language,
'Tis needful that the most immodest word   70
Be looked upon and learned; which one attained,
Your highness knows, comes to no further use
But to be known and hated. So, like gross terms,
The prince will in the perfectness* of time   ripeness
Cast off his followers; and their memory

Shall as a pattern or a measure live,
By which his grace must mete* the lives of others,   appraise
Turning past evils to advantages.

KING.

'Tis seldom when* the bee doth leave her comb   that
In the dead carrion.

    (WESTMORELAND, *in riding dress, enters.*)

                  Who's here? Westmoreland?   80

WESTMORELAND.

Health to my sovereign, and new happiness
Added to that that I am to deliver!
Prince John your son doth kiss your grace's hand:
Mowbray, the Bishop Scroop, Hastings and all
Are brought to the correction of your law;
There is not now a rebel's sword unsheathed,
But Peace puts forth her olive everywhere.
The manner how this action hath been borne
Here at more leisure may your highness read,
    (*Handing over a dispatch.*)
With every course in his particular.   90

KING.

O Westmoreland, thou art a summer bird,
Which ever in the haunch of winter sings
The lifting up* of day.   lengthening
    (HARCOURT, *also in riding dress, enters.*)
                  Look, here's more news.

HARCOURT.

From enemies heaven keep your majesty;
And, when they stand against you, may they fall
As those that I am come to tell you of!
The Earl Northumberland and the Lord Bardolph,
With a great power of English and of Scots,
Are by the sheriff of Yorkshire overthrown:
The manner and true order of the fight   100
This packet, please it you, contains at large.*   in full
    (*Handing over a dispatch.*)

KING.

And wherefore should these good news make me
    sick?

Will Fortune never come with both hands full,
But write her fair words still in foulest letters?
She either gives a stomach and no food;
Such are the poor, in health; or else a feast
And takes away the stomach; such are the rich,
That have abundance and enjoy it not.
I should rejoice now at this happy news;
And now my sight fails, and my brain is giddy: 110
O me! Come near me; now I am much ill.
    (*The* KING *faints. All gather round him.*)

GLOUCESTER.
Comfort, your majesty!

CLARENCE.   O my royal father!

WESTMORELAND.
My sovereign lord, cheer up yourself, look up.

WARWICK.
Be patient, princes; you do know, these fits
Are with his highness very ordinary.
Stand from him, give him air; he'll straight be well.

CLARENCE (*moving aside, with his brother* GLOUCESTER).
No, no, he cannot long hold out these pangs:
The incessant care and labor of his mind
Hath wrought the mure* that should confine it in   wall
So thin that life looks through and will break out.   120

GLOUCESTER.
The people fear* me; for they do observe   frighten
Unfathered* heirs and loathly births of nature.   unnaturally
                                                                              generated
The seasons change their manners, as* the year   as if
Had found some months asleep and leaped them
    over.

CLARENCE.
The river hath thrice flowed,* no ebb between;   been at
                                                                              floodtide
And the old folk, time's doting chronicles,
Say it did so a little time before
That our great-grandsire, Edward, sicked* and died.   sickened
    (*The* KING *stirs.*)

WARWICK.
Speak lower, princes, for the king recovers.

GLOUCESTER.

This apoplexy will certain be his end.   130

KING.

I pray you, take me up, and bear me hence
Into some other chamber: softly, pray.

(ATTENDANTS *carry the* KING *out. The others
follow*.)

SCENE 5. Another chamber in the Palace.

(*The* KING *is lying in bed.* CLARENCE, GLOU-
CESTER, WARWICK, *and others are in attendance*.)

KING.

Let there be no noise made, my gentle friends;
Unless some dull* and favorable hand   soothing
Will whisper music to my weary spirit.

WARWICK (*to a* SERVANT, *who goes out*).

Call for the music in the other room.

KING.

Set me the crown upon my pillow here.

CLARENCE.

His eye is hollow, and he changes* much.   changes
                                                         color
WARWICK.

Less noise, less noise!

(*Music begins to play from another room. The
crown is placed on the* KING'S *pillow.* PRINCE
HENRY *enters*.)

PRINCE.   Who saw the Duke of Clarence?

CLARENCE (*weeping*).

I am here, brother, full of heaviness.

PRINCE.

How now! Rain within doors, and none abroad!
How doth the king?   10

GLOUCESTER.

Exceeding ill.

PRINCE.

Heard he the good news yet? Tell it him.

GLOUCESTER.

He altered much upon the hearing it.

PRINCE.

If he be sick with joy, he'll recover without physic.

WARWICK (*moving to the* PRINCES).

Not so much noise, my lords: sweet prince, speak low;

The king your father is disposed to sleep.

CLARENCE.

Let us withdraw into the other room.

WARWICK (*to* PRINCE HENRY).

Will 't please your grace to go along with us?

PRINCE.

No; I will sit and watch here by the king.   20

(*The others go, leaving* PRINCE HENRY *sitting beside the sleeping* KING.)

Why doth the crown lie there upon his pillow,
Being so troublesome a bedfellow?
O polished perturbation! Golden care!
That keep'st the ports of slumber open wide
To many a watchful* night! Sleep with it now!   wakeful
Yet not so sound and half so deeply sweet
As he whose brow with homely biggen* bound   nightcap
Snores out the watch* of night. O majesty!   period
When thou dost pinch thy bearer, thou dost sit
Like a rich armor worn in heat of day,   30
That scalds with* safety.   while
                                                             giving
                              By his gates of breath
There lies a downy feather which stirs not:
Did he suspire,* that light and weightless down   breathe
Perforce must move.
                              My gracious lord! My father!
This sleep is sound indeed; this is a sleep
That from this golden rigol* hath divorced   circle
So many English kings. Thy due from me
Is tears and heavy sorrows of the blood,
Which nature, love, and filial tenderness,
Shall, O dear father, pay thee plenteously.   40

My due from thee is this imperial crown,
Which, as immediate from thy place and blood,*   in direct
                                 descent
Derives itself to me.
> (*Takes the crown and puts it on.*)
>   Lo, here it sits,
Which God shall guard: and put the world's
   whole strength
Into one giant arm, it shall not force
This lineal honor from me: this from thee
Will I to mine leave, as 'tis left to me.
> (*He goes into an adjoining room.*)

KING (*waking*).
Warwick! Gloucester! Clarence!
> (WARWICK, GLOUCESTER, CLARENCE *and the others
> return.*)

CLARENCE.
Doth the king call?

WARWICK.
What would your majesty? How fares your grace?   50

KING.
Why did you leave me here alone, my lords?

CLARENCE.
We left the prince my brother here, my liege,
Who undertook to sit and watch by you.

KING.
The Prince of Wales! Where is he? Let me see
   him:
He is not here.

WARWICK (*noting the other door*).
This door is open; he is gone this way.

GLOUCESTER.
He came not through the chamber where we
   stayed.

KING.
Where is the crown? Who took it from my
   pillow?

WARWICK.
When we withdrew, my liege, we left it here.

KING.

The prince hath ta'en it hence: go, seek him out.   60
Is he so hasty* that he doth suppose   eager
My sleep my death?
Find him, my Lord of Warwick; chide him hither.
This part* of his conjoins with my disease,   conduct
And helps to end me.
    (WARWICK *goes.*)
                See, sons, what things you are!
How quickly nature falls into revolt
When gold becomes her object!
For this the foolish over-careful fathers
Have broke their sleep with thoughts, their brains
    with care,
Their bones with industry;   70
For this they have engrossed* and pilèd up   amassed
The cankered* heaps of strange-achievèd gold;   tarnished
For this they have been thoughtful to invest*   equip
Their sons with arts and martial exercises,
When, like the bee, culling from every flower
The virtuous sweets,
Our thighs packed with wax, our mouths with
    honey,
We bring it to the hive, and, like the bees,
Are murdered for our pains.[73] This bitter taste
Yield his engrossments* to the ending* father.   accumula-
    (*To* WARWICK *as he re-enters.*)   tions/dying
Now, where is he that will not stay so long   81
Till his friend sickness hath determined* me?   terminated

WARWICK.

My lord, I found the prince in the next room,
Washing with kindly* tears his gentle cheeks,   natural
With such a deep demeanor in great sorrow
That tyranny, which never quaffed but blood,
Would, by beholding him, have washed his knife
With gentle eye-drops.
             He is coming hither.

KING.

But wherefore did he take away the crown?

(PRINCE HENRY *returns, carrying the crown.*)

Lo, where he comes. Come hither to me, Harry.   90
Depart the chamber, leave us here alone.
(*The others leave.*)

PRINCE.

I never thought to hear you speak again.

KING.

Thy wish was father, Harry, to that thought:
I stay too long by thee, I weary thee.
Dost thou so hunger for mine empty chair
That thou wilt needs invest thee with my honors
Before thy hour be ripe? O foolish youth!
Thou seek'st the greatness that will overwhelm
    thee.
Stay but a little; for my cloud of dignity
Is held from falling with so weak a wind   100
That it will quickly drop: my day is dim.
Thou hast stolen that which after some few hours
Were thine without offense; and at my death
Thou hast sealed up* my expectation.   confirmed
Thy life did manifest thou lovedst me not,
And thou wilt have me die assured of it.
Thou hidest a thousand dag˜ ≥rs in thy thoughts,
Which thou hast whetted on t˷ y stony heart,
To stab at half an hour of my life.
    What! Canst thou not forbear* me half an hour?   endure
Then get thee gone and dig my grave thyself,   111
And bid the merry bells ring to thine ear
That thou art crownèd, not that I am dead.
Let all the tears that should bedew my hearse
Be drops of balm to sanctify thy head:[74]
Only compound* me with forgotten dust;   mix
Give that which gave thee life unto the worms.
Pluck down my officers, break my decrees;
For now a time is come to mock at form:*   protocol
Harry the Fifth is crowned: up, vanity!*   folly
Down, royal state!* All you sage counselors,   dignity
    hence!
And to the English court assemble now,   122

From every region, apes of idleness!
Now, neighbor confines,* purge you of your scum: regions
Have you a ruffian that will swear, drink, dance,
Revel the night, rob, murder, and commit
The oldest sins the newest kinds of ways?
Be happy, he will trouble you no more;
England shall double gild his treble guilt,
England shall give him office, honor, might;   130
For the fifth Harry from curbed license plucks
The muzzle of restraint, and the wild dog
Shall flesh his tooth on* every innocent.   into

    O my poor kingdom, sick with civil blows!
When that my care could not withhold thy riots,
What wilt thou do when riot is thy care?
O, thou wilt be a wilderness again,
Peopled with wolves, thy old inhabitants!

PRINCE.

O, pardon me, my liege!⁷⁵ But for my tears,
The moist impediments unto my speech,   140
I had forestalled this dead and deep rebuke
Ere you with grief had spoke and I had heard
The course of it so far.
                There is your crown;
And He that wears the crown immortally
Long guard it yours!
    (*Kneels.*)   If I affect* it more   aspire to
Than as your honor and as your renown,
Let me no more from this obedience* rise,   obeisance
Which my most inward true and duteous spirit
Teacheth, this prostrate and exterior bending.
God witness with me, when I here came in,   150
And found no course of breath within your majesty,
How cold it struck my heart! If I do feign,
O, let me in my present wildness die
And never live to show the incredulous world
The noble change that I have purposèd!
Coming to look on you, thinking you dead,
And dead almost, my liege, to think you were,
I spake unto this crown as having sense,

And thus upbraided it: "The care on thee depending
Hath fed upon the body of my father;   160
Therefore, thou best of gold art worst of gold:
Other, less fine in carat, is more precious,
Preserving life in medicine potable;[76]
But thou, most fine, most honored, most renowned,
Hast eat thy bearer up."
               Thus, my most royal liege,
Accusing it, I put it on my head,
To try with it, as with an enemy
That had before my face murdered my father,
The quarrel of a true inheritor.
But if it did infect my blood with joy,   170
Or swell my thoughts to any strain of pride;
If any rebel or vain spirit of mine
Did with the least affection of a welcome
Give entertainment to the might of it,
Let God forever keep it from my head
And make me as the poorest vassal is
That doth with awe and terror kneel to it!

KING.

O my son,
God put it in thy mind to take it hence,
That thou mightst win the more thy father's love,   180
Pleading so wisely in excuse of it!
  Come hither, Harry, sit thou by my bed;
And hear, I think, the very latest counsel
That ever I shall breathe.
    (*The* PRINCE *moves to sit beside the* KING.)
               God knows, my son,
By what by-paths and indirect crooked ways
I met this crown; and I myself know well
How troublesome it sat upon my head.
To thee it shall descend with better quiet,
Better opinion,* better confirmation;   *i.e.*, public opinion attaining
For all the soil of the achievement* goes
With me into the earth. It seemed in me   191
But as an honor snatched with boisterous hand,
And I had many living to upbraid

My gain of it by their assistances,
Which daily grew to quarrel and to bloodshed,
Wounding supposèd peace: all these bold fears*   dangers
Thou see'st with peril I have answerèd;*   repelled
For all my reign hath been but as a scene
Acting that argument.* And now my death   plot
Changes the mode; for what in me was
    purchased,*   deviously
    obtained/200
Falls upon thee in a more fairer sort;
So thou the garland wear'st successively.*   by right of
    succession
Yet, though thou stand'st more sure than I could do,
Thou art not firm enough, since griefs are green;
And all my friends, which thou must make thy
    friends,
Have but their stings and teeth newly ta'en out;
By whose fell working* I was first advanced,   evil
    plotting
And by whose power I well might lodge a fear
To be again displaced: which to avoid,
I cut them off; and had a purpose now,   210
To lead out many to the Holy Land,
Lest rest and lying* still might make them look   inactivity
Too near unto my state. Therefore, my Harry,
Be it thy course to busy giddy minds
With foreign quarrels; that action, hence borne
    out,
May waste* the memory of the former days.   efface
    More would I, but my lungs are wasted so
That strength of speech is utterly denied me.
How I came by the crown, O God forgive;
And grant it may with thee in true peace live!   220

PRINCE.
My gracious liege,
You won it, wore it, kept it, gave it me;
Then plain and right must my possession be:
Which I with more than with a common pain*   effort
'Gainst all the world will rightfully maintain.
    (PRINCE JOHN OF LANCASTER *enters*.)
KING.
Look, look, here comes my John of Lancaster.

LANCASTER.

Health, peace, and happiness to my royal father!

KING.

Thou bring'st me happiness and peace, son John;
But health, alack, with youthful wings is flown
From this bare withered trunk: upon thy sight*   seeing you
My worldly business makes a period.*   ends
    Where is my Lord of Warwick?

PRINCE (*goes to the door and calls*).

                My Lord of Warwick!   232
    (WARWICK *and the others return.*)

KING.

Doth any name particular belong
Unto the lodging* where I first did swoon?   chamber

WARWICK.

'Tis called Jerusalem, my noble lord.

KING.

Laud be to God! Even there my life must end.
It hath been prophesied to me many years,
I should not die but in Jerusalem,
Which vainly I supposed the Holy Land.   239
But bear me to that chamber; there I'll lie:
In that Jerusalem shall Harry die.
    (ATTENDANTS *take up the* KING *and carry him
    out. The others follow.*)

ACT V

SCENE 1. Gloucestershire. Before SHALLOW's house.

(SHALLOW *and* FALSTAFF *enter, followed by*
BARDOLPH *and the* PAGE.)

SHALLOW.
By cock and pie, sir,[77] you shall not away tonight.
(*Calls.*) What, Davy, I say!

FALSTAFF.
You must excuse me, Master Robert Shallow.

SHALLOW.
I will not excuse you; you shall not be excused;
excuses shall not be admitted; there is no excuse
shall serve; you shall not be excused.   (*Calls.*)
Why, Davy!
(DAVY *enters.*)

DAVY.
Here, sir.   9

SHALLOW.
Davy, Davy, Davy, Davy, let me see, Davy; let
me see, Davy; let me see: yea, marry, William
cook,* bid him come hither. Sir John, you shall
not be excused.

i.e.,
William
the cook

DAVY.
Marry, sir, thus; those precepts* cannot be served.
And, again, sir, shall we sow the headland with
wheat?[78]

writs

SHALLOW.
With red wheat, Davy. But for William cook:
are there no young pigeons?

123

DAVY.

Yes, sir. (*Showing him a paper*.) Here is now
the smith's note* for shoeing and plough-irons.   bill/20

SHALLOW.

Let it be cast* and paid. Sir John, you shall not   added
be excused.

DAVY.

Now, sir, a new link to the bucket must needs be
had. And, sir, do you mean to stop any of William's wages, about the sack he lost the other day
at Hinckley fair?

SHALLOW.

A' shall answer it. Some pigeons, Davy, a couple
of short-legged hens, a joint of mutton, and any
pretty little tiny kickshaws,* tell William cook.   tidbits/30

DAVY.

Doth the man of war stay all night, sir?

SHALLOW.

Yea, Davy. I will use him well: a friend i' the
court is better than a penny in purse. Use his men
well, Davy; for they are arrant knaves, and will
backbite.

DAVY.

No worse than they are backbitten, sir; for they
have marvelous foul linen.

SHALLOW.

Well conceited,* Davy. About thy business, Davy.   put/40

DAVY.

I beseech you, sir, to countenance* William Visor   favor
of Woncot against Clement Perkes of the hill.

SHALLOW.

There is many complaints, Davy, against that Visor:
that Visor is an arrant knave, on my knowledge.

DAVY.

I grant your worship that he is a knave, sir; but
yet, God forbid, sir, but a knave should have some
countenance at his friend's request. An honest
man, sir, is able to speak for himself, when a knave   50
is not. I have served your worship truly, sir, this

eight years; and if I cannot once or twice in a
quarter bear out* a knave against an honest man,   support
I have but a very little credit with your worship.
The knave is mine honest friend, sir; therefore, I
beseech your worship, let him be countenanced.

SHALLOW.

Go to; I say he shall have no wrong. Look about,
Davy. (DAVY *goes*.) Where are you, Sir John?   60
Come, come, come, off with your boots. (*Shaking
hands with* BARDOLPH.) Give me your hand, Master Bardolph.

BARDOLPH.

I am glad to see your worship.

SHALLOW.

I thank thee with all my heart, kind Master Bardolph. (*To the* PAGE.) And welcome, my tall
fellow. Come, Sir John.

FALSTAFF.

I'll follow you, good Master Robert Shallow.
(SHALLOW *goes into the house*.) Bardolph, look to
our horses. (BARDOLPH *and the* PAGE *go*.) If I were   70
sawed into quantities,* I should make four dozen   little
of such bearded hermits' staves as Master Shallow.   pieces
It is a wonderful thing to see the semblable co-
herence* of his men's spirits and his: they, by   obvious
observing of him, do bear themselves like foolish   agreement
justices; he, by conversing with them, is turned
into a justice-like servingman: their spirits are so
married in conjunction with the participation of
society that they flock together in consent, like
so many wild-geese.

If I had a suit to Master Shallow, I would humor   80
his men with the imputation of being near their
master: if to his men, I would curry* with Master   curry
Shallow that no man could better command his   favor
servants. It is certain that either wise bearing or
ignorant carriage* is caught, as men take diseases,   behavior
one of another: therefore let men take heed of
their company. I will devise matter enough out of

this Shallow to keep Prince Harry in continual
laughter the wearing out of six fashions, which   90
is four terms,* or two actions,79 and a' shall laugh   *i.e., twelve
without intervallums.*   months,
                                                        intervals

O, it is much that a lie with a slight oath and a
jest with a sad brow will do with a fellow that
never had the ache in his shoulders! O, you shall
see him laugh till his face be like a wet cloak ill   *i.e., all
laid up!*   wrinkled

SHALLOW (calling from inside).
  Sir John!
FALSTAFF.
  I come, Master Shallow; I come, Master Shallow.
  (He goes in.)

SCENE 2. Westminster. A hall in the Palace.

(WARWICK and the LORD CHIEF-JUSTICE entering
from opposite sides, meet.)

WARWICK.
  How now, my lord chief-justice! Whither away?
CHIEF-JUSTICE.
  How doth the king?
WARWICK.
  Exceeding well; his cares are now all ended.
CHIEF-JUSTICE.
  I hope, not dead.
WARWICK.   He's walked the way of nature;
  And to our purposes he lives no more.
CHIEF-JUSTICE.
  I would his majesty had called me with him:
  The service that I truly did his life
  Hath left me open to all injuries.
WARWICK.
  Indeed I think the young king loves you not.
CHIEF-JUSTICE.
  I know he doth not, and do arm myself   10

To welcome the condition of the time,
Which cannot look more hideously upon me
Than I have drawn it in my fantasy.*   imagination
 (LANCASTER, CLARENCE, GLOUCESTER, WESTMORE-
 LAND, *and* ATTENDANTS *enter at the far end of the*
 hall.)

WARWICK.
Here come the heavy* issue of dead Harry: sad
O that the living Harry had the temper
Of him, the worst of these three gentlemen!
How many nobles then should hold their places,
That must strike sail to spirits of vile sort!⁸⁰

CHIEF-JUSTICE.
O God, I fear all will be overturned!

LANCASTER.
Good morrow, cousin Warwick, good morrow.   20

GLOUCESTER. } Good morrow, cousin.
CLARENCE.

LANCASTER.
We meet like men that had forgot to* speak.   how to

WARWICK.
We do remember; but our argument*   subject
Is all too heavy to admit much talk.

LANCASTER.
Well, peace be with him that hath made us heavy!

CHIEF-JUSTICE.
Peace be with us, lest we be heavier!

GLOUCESTER.
O, good my lord, you have lost a friend indeed;
And I dare swear you borrow not that face
Of seeming sorrow: it is sure your own.

LANCASTER.
Though no man be assured what grace to find,   30
You stand in coldest expectation:
I am the sorrier; would 'twere otherwise.

CLARENCE.
Well, you must now speak* Sir John Falstaff   speak to
 fair*—   amicably
Which swims against your stream of quality.*⁸¹   character

CHIEF-JUSTICE.

Sweet princes, what I did, I did in honor,
Led by the impartial conduct of my soul;
And never shall you see that I will beg
A raggèd and forestalled* remission.⁸²   predetermined
If truth and upright innocency fail me,
I'll to the king my master that is dead,   40
And tell him who hath sent me after him.

    (*The* PRINCE, *now King Henry the Fifth, enters,*
    with ATTENDANTS.)

WARWICK.

Here comes the prince.

CHIEF-JUSTICE.

Good morrow; and God save your majesty!

KING.

This new and gorgeous garment, majesty,
Sits not so easy on me as you think.
Brothers, you mix your sadness with some fear:
This is the English, not the Turkish court;
Not Amurath an Amurath succeeds,⁸³
But Harry Harry. Yet be sad, good brothers,
For, by my faith, it very well becomes you: 50
Sorrow so royally in you appears
That I will deeply put the fashion on
And wear it in my heart: why then, be sad;
But entertain no more of it, good brothers,
Than a joint burden laid upon us all.
    For me, by heaven, I bid you be assured,
I'll be your father and your brother too;
Let me but bear your love, I'll bear your cares.
Yet weep that Harry's dead; and so will I;
But Harry lives that shall convert those tears   60
By number into hours of happiness.

PRINCES.

We hope no other from your majesty.

KING.

You all look strangely* on me.   coldly
    (*To the* LORD CHIEF-JUSTICE.) And you most;
You are, I think, assured I love you not.

CHIEF-JUSTICE.

I am assured, if I be measured rightly,
Your majesty hath no just cause to hate me.

KING.

No!
How might a prince of my great hopes forget
So great indignities you laid upon me?
What! Rate,* rebuke, and roughly send to prison   berate
The immediate heir of England! Was this easy?   71
May this be washed in Lethe and forgotten? 84

CHIEF-JUSTICE.

I then did use the person of* your father;   represent
The image of his power lay then in me:
And, in the administration of his law,
Whiles I was busy for the commonwealth,
Your highness pleasèd to forget my place,
The majesty and power of law and justice,
The image of the king whom I presented,
And struck me in my very seat of judgment;   80
Whereon, as* an offender to your father,   i.e., your being
I gave bold way to my authority
And did commit you. If the deed were ill,
Be you* contented, wearing now the garland,   would you be
To have a son set your decress at nought,
To pluck down justice from your awful* bench,   awesome
To trip the course of law and blunt the sword
That guards the peace and safety of your person—
Nay, more, to spurn at your most royal image   89
And mock your workings* in a second body?*   decrees/ i.e., deputy
Question your royal thoughts, make the case yours:
Be now the father and propose* a son;   suppose
Hear your own dignity so much profaned,
See your most dreadful* laws so loosely slighted,   dreaded
Behold yourself so by a son disdained—
And then imagine me taking your part
And in your power soft silencing your son.
After this cold considerance, sentence me;
And, as you are a king, speak in your state*   capacity

What I have done that misbecame my place,   100
My person, or my liege's sovereignty.

KING.

You are right, justice, and you weigh this well.
Therefore, still bear the balance and the sword:
And I do wish your honors may increase,
Till you do live to see a son of mine
Offend you and obey you, as I did.
So shall I live to speak my father's words:
"Happy am I, that have a man so bold,
That dares do justice on my proper* son;   own
And not less happy, having such a son,   110
That would deliver up his greatness so
Into the hands of justice."
                          You did commit me:
For which, I do commit into your hand
The unstained sword that you have used to bear;
With this remembrance,* that you use the same   reminder
With the like bold, just and impartial spirit
As you have done 'gainst me.
                          There is my hand.
You shall be as a father to my youth:
My voice shall sound as you do prompt mine ear,
And I will stoop* and humble my intents   subdue/120
To your well-practiced wise directions.
    And, princes all, believe me, I beseech you:
My father is gone wild* into his grave,   i.e., carrying
                                                    my wildness
For in his tomb lie my affections;
And with his spirit sadly* I survive,   soberly
To mock the expectation of the world,
To frustrate prophecies and to raze out
Rotten opinion, who hath writ me down
After my seeming.
                  The tide of blood in me
Hath proudly flowed in vanity till now: 130
Now doth it turn and ebb back to the sea,
Where it shall mingle with the state of floods*   ocean
And flow henceforth in formal majesty.
Now call we our high court of parliament:

And let us choose such limbs* of noble counsel,   members
That the great body of our state may go*   walk
In equal rank* with the best governed nation;   keeping
                                                  step
That war, or peace, or both at once, may be
As things acquainted and familiar to us;
In which you, father, shall have foremost hand.   140
  Our coronation done, we will accite,*   summon
As I before remembered,* all our state;*   stated/
                                             parliament
And, God consigning* to my good intents,   consenting
No prince nor peer shall have just cause to say,
God shorten Harry's happy life one day!
  (*The* KING *goes, followed by the others.*)

SCENE 3. Gloucestershire. SHALLOW's garden, with arbor
and fruit trees.

(SHALLOW *enters in conversation with* FALSTAFF
and SILENCE, *followed by* DAVY, BARDOLPH, *and
the* PAGE.)

SHALLOW.
  Nay, you shall see my orchard,* where, in an   garden
  arbor, we will eat a last year's pippin of my own
  graffing,* with a dish of caraways,85 and so forth.   grafting
  Come, cousin Silence. And then to bed.
FALSTAFF.
  'Fore God, you have here a goodly dwelling and a
  rich.
SHALLOW.
  Barren, barren, barren; beggars all, beggars all,
  Sir John. Marry, good air. (*To* DAVY, *who is set-*   *i.e.,* the
  ting a table.) Spread,* Davy; spread, Davy. Well,   table
  said,* Davy.   done/10
FALSTAFF.
  This Davy serves you for good uses; he is your
  serving-man and your husband.*   steward
SHALLOW.
  A good varlet, a good varlet, a very good varlet,

Sir John. By the mass, I have drunk too much sack at supper. A good varlet. Now sit down, now sit down. Come, cousin.
(DAVY *pours the wine.*)

SILENCE.

Ah, sirrah! Quoth-a, we shall
(*Singing.*)
Do nothing but eat, and make good cheer,
And praise God for the merry year;[86]
When flesh* is cheap and females dear,   meat/20
And lusty lads roam here and there
              So merrily,
And ever among so merrily.

FALSTAFF.

There's a merry heart! Good Master Silence, I'll give you a health for that anon.

SHALLOW.

Give Master Bardolph some wine, Davy.

DAVY (*to* BARDOLPH).

Sweet sir, sit; I'll be with you anon; most sweet   29
sir, sit. Master page, good master page, sit. Pro-
face!* What you want* in meat, we'll have in   prosit/
drink; but you must bear;* the heart's all.   lack
(DAVY *goes to refill his wine pitcher.*)   bear with
                                                                        me

SHALLOW.

Be merry, Master Bardolph. And my little soldier there, be merry.

SILENCE (*singing*).

Be merry, be merry, my wife has all;
For women are shrews, both short and tall:
'Tis merry in hall when beards wag all,
      And welcome merry Shrove-tide.[87]
Be merry, be merry.

FALSTAFF.

I did not think Master Silence had been a man of this mettle.   41

SILENCE.

Who, I? I have been merry twice and once ere now.

(DAVY *returns with wine and a dish of apples.*)

DAVY (*to* BARDOLPH).

There's a dish of leather-coats* for you.   russet
                                                   apples

SHALLOW.

Davy!

DAVY (*to* SHALLOW).

Your worship! (*To* BARDOLPH). I'll be with you
straight. (*To* SHALLOW *again*). A cup of wine,
sir?

SILENCE (*singing*).

A cup of wine that's brisk and fine,
And drink unto the leman* mine;   sweetheart
    And a merry heart lives long-a.   50

FALSTAFF.

Well said, Master Silence.

SILENCE.

An we shall be merry, now comes in the sweet o'
the night.

    (DAVY *fills their cups.*)

FALSTAFF.

Health and long life to you, Master Silence.

SILENCE (*singing*).

Fill the cup, and let it come;
I'll pledge you a mile* to the bottom.   if it were
                                                    a mile

SHALLOW.

Honest Bardolph, welcome: if thou wantest any
thing, and wilt not call, beshrew thy heart. (*To*   60
the PAGE). Welcome, my little tiny thief, and welcome indeed too. I'll drink to Master Bardolph,
and to all the cavaleros* about London.   gallants

DAVY (*joins* BARDOLPH *and the* PAGE).

I hope to see London once ere I die.

BARDOLPH.

An I might see you there, Davy—

SHALLOW.

By the mass, you'll crack a quart together, ha!
Will you not, Master Bardolph?

BARDOLPH.

Yea, sir, in a pottle-pot.*   tankard

SHALLOW.

By God's liggens, I thank thee: the knave will
stick by thee, I can assure thee that. A' will not   71
out;* he is true bred.   fail you

BARDOLPH.

And I'll stick by him, sir.

SHALLOW.

Why, there spoke a king. Lack nothing: be merry.
(*Knocking is heard.*) Look who's at door there,
ho! Who knocks?
   (DAVY *goes.*)

FALSTAFF (*to* SILENCE, *who has just drained his cup*).

Why, now you have done me right.

SILENCE (*singing*).

> Do me right,
> And dub me knight:
> Samingo.[88]

Is 't not so?   80

FALSTAFF.

'Tis so.

SILENCE.

Is 't so? Why then, say an old man can do some-
what.* (DAVY *returns.*)   something

DAVY.

An 't please your worship, there's one Pistol come
from the court with news.

FALSTAFF.

From the court! Let him come in.
   (PISTOL *enters.*)
How now, Pistol!

PISTOL.

Sir John, God save you!

FALSTAFF.

What wind blew you hither, Pistol?

PISTOL.

Not the ill wind which blows no man to good.   90
Sweet knight, thou are now one of the greatest
men in this realm.

SILENCE.

By 'r lady, I think a' be, but goodman Puff of
Barson.[89]

PISTOL.

Puff!
Puff in thy teeth, most recreant coward base!
  Sir John, I am thy Pistol and thy friend,
And helter-skelter have I rode to thee,
And tidings do I bring and lucky joys
And golden times and happy news of price.   100

FALSTAFF.

I pray thee now, deliver them like a man of this
world.

PISTOL.

A foutre* for the world and worldlings base!   fig
I speak of Africa and golden joys.

FALSTAFF.

O base Assyrian* knight, what is thy news?   i.e.,
Let King Cophetua know the truth thereof.[90]   heathen

SILENCE (*singing*).

And Robin Hood, Scarlet, and John.

PISTOL.

Shall dunghill curs confront the Helicons?*[91]   i.e.,
And shall good news be baffled?   the muses
Then, Pistol, lay thy head in Furies' lap.   110

SHALLOW.

Honest gentleman, I know not your breeding.

PISTOL.

Why then, lament therefore.

SHALLOW.

Give me pardon, sir: if, sir, you come with news
from the court, I take it there's but two ways,
either to utter them, or to conceal them. I am, sir,
under the king, in some authority.

PISTOL.

Under which king, Besonian?* Speak, or die.   knave

SHALLOW.

Under King Harry.

PISTOL.   Harry the Fourth? Or Fifth?   120
SHALLOW.

Harry the Fourth.

PISTOL.   A foutre for thine office!

Sir John, thy tender lambkin now is king;
Harry the Fifth's the man. I speak the truth:
When Pistol lies, do this.

(*Making a gesture.*)   And fig me, like
The bragging Spaniard.

FALSTAFF.

What, is the old king dead?

PISTOL.

As nail in door: the things I speak are just.

FALSTAFF (*rising*).

Away, Bardolph! Saddle my horse. Master Robert
Shallow, choose what office thou wilt in the land,
'tis thine. Pistol, I will double-charge thee with
dignities.   131

BARDOLPH.

O joyful day!
I would not take a knighthood for my fortune.

PISTOL.

What! I do bring good news.

FALSTAFF (*to* SERVANTS.)

Carry Master Silence to bed. (*To* SHALLOW.)
Master Shallow, my Lord Shallow—be what thou
wilt; I am fortune's steward—get on thy boots:
we'll ride all night. O sweet Pistol! Away, Bardolph! (BARDOLPH *and the* PAGE *go.*) Come, Pistol,
utter more to me; and withal devise something to
do thyself good.

Boot, boot, Master Shallow: I know the young   140
king is sick for me. Let us take any man's horses;
the laws of England are at my commandment.
Blessed are they that have been my friends; and
woe to my lord chief-justice!

PISTOL.

Let vultures vile seize on his lungs also!

"Where is the life that late I led?" say they:
Why, here it is: welcome these pleasant days!
(*They all go.*)

Scene 4. A street in London.

(*Two* BEADLES *enter, dragging* HOSTESS QUICKLY *and* DOLL TEARSHEET.)

HOSTESS.

No, thou arrant knave; I would to God that I
might die, that I might have thee hanged: thou
hast drawn my shoulder out of joint.

FIRST BEADLE.

The constables have delivered her over to me; and
she shall have whipping-cheer enough,[92] I warrant
her: there hath been a man or two lately killed
about her.

DOLL (*indicating her distended waistline*).

Nut-hook, nut-hook,[93] you lie. Come on; I'll tell
thee what, thou damned tripe-visaged rascal, an   10
the child I now go with do miscarry, thou wert
better thou hadst struck thy mother, thou paper-
faced villain.

HOSTESS.

O the Lord, that Sir John were come! He would
make this a bloody day to somebody. But I pray
God the fruit of her womb miscarry!

FIRST BEADLE.

If it do, you shall have a dozen of cushions again;
you have but eleven now. Come, I charge you
both go with me; for the man is dead that you and
Pistol beat amongst you.   19

DOLL.

I'll tell you what, you thin man in a censer, I will
have you as soundly swinged* for this—you blue-   thrashed
bottle rogue, you filthy famished correctioner, if
you be not swinged, I'll forswear half-kirtles.

FIRST BEADLE.

Come, come, you she knight-errant, come.

HOSTESS.

O God, that right should thus overcome might!
Well, of sufferance* comes ease.   suffering

DOLL.

Come, you rogue, come; bring me to a justice.   30

HOSTESS.

Ay, come, you starved blood-hound.

DOLL.

Goodman death, goodman bones!

HOSTESS.

Thou atomy,* thou!   anatomy

DOLL.

Come, you thin thing; come, you rascal.

FIRST BEADLE.

Very well.
   (They all go.)

SCENE 5. A public place near Westminster Abbey.

   (Trumpets sound. Two GROOMS *enter, strewing
   the street with rushes.)*

FIRST GROOM.

More rushes, more rushes.

SECOND GROOM.

The trumpets have sounded twice.

FIRST GROOM.

'Twill be two o'clock ere they come from the
coronation: dispatch, dispatch.
   (They hurry off. FALSTAFF, SHALLOW, PISTOL,
   BARDOLPH, *and the* PAGE *enter, taking their places
   to watch for the procession.)*

FALSTAFF.

Stand here by me, Master Robert Shallow; I will
make the king do you grace.* I will leer* upon favor you/
him as a' comes by; and do but mark the counte-   smile
nance that he will give me.

PISTOL.

God bless thy lungs, good knight.   9

FALSTAFF.

Come here, Pistol; stand behind me. O, if I had
had time to have made new liveries, I would have
bestowed* the thousand pound I borrowed of you.   spent
But 'tis no matter; this poor show doth better: this
doth infer the zeal I had to see him.

SHALLOW.

It doth so.

FALSTAFF.

It shows my earnestness of affection—

SHALLOW.

It doth so.

FALSTAFF.

My devotion—

SHALLOW.

It doth, it doth, it doth.   20

FALSTAFF.

As it were, to ride day and night; and not to deliberate, not to remember, not to have patience to
shift me*—   change my
clothes

SHALLOW.

It is best, certain.

FALSTAFF.

But to stand stained with travel, and sweating with
desire to see him; thinking of nothing else, putting
all affairs else in oblivion, as if there were nothing
else to be done but to see him.   29

PISTOL.

'Tis "semper idem," for "obsque hoc nihil est":
'tis all in every part.[94]

SHALLOW.

'Tis so, indeed.

PISTOL.

My knight, I will inflame thy noble liver,
And make thee rage.
Thy Doll, and Helen of thy noble thoughts,
Is in base durance and contagious prison;
Haled thither
By most mechanical and dirty hand:

Rouse up revenge from ebon den with fell Alecto's
   snake,[95]

For Doll is in.*   Pistol speaks nought but truth.   *i.e., in
                                                          prison
FALSTAFF.

I will deliver her.   41

   (*Shouts are heard from nearby and the trumpets
   sound.*)

PISTOL.

There roared the sea, and trumpet-clangor sounds.
   (*Trumpets continue. The* KING, *in coronation
   robes and crown, enters, followed by a train of*
   PRINCES, LORDS, GENTLEMEN ATTENDANTS, *and*
   GUARDS. *In the train is the* LORD CHIEF-JUSTICE.)

FALSTAFF (*stepping forward*).

God save thy grace, King Hal! My royal Hal!

PISTOL.

The heavens thee guard and keep, most royal imp
   of fame!

FALSTAFF.

God save thee, my sweet boy!

KING.

My lord chief-justice, speak to that vain man.

CHIEF-JUSTICE (*to* FALSTAFF).

Have you your wits? Know you what 'tis you
   speak?

FALSTAFF.

My king! My Jove! I speak to thee, my heart!   50

KING.

I know thee not, old man. Fall to thy prayers.
How ill white hairs become a fool and jester!
I have long dreamed of such a kind of man,
So surfeit-swelled, so old and so profane;
But, being awaked, I do despise my dream.
Make less thy body hence, and more thy grace;
Leave gormandizing; know the grave doth gape
For thee thrice wider than for other men.
Reply not to me with a fool-born jest:
Presume not that I am the thing I was;   60
For God doth know, so shall the world perceive,

That I have turned away my former self;
So will I those that kept me company.
When thou dost hear I am as I have been,
Approach me, and thou shalt be as thou wast,
The tutor and the feeder of my riots.*   excesses
Till then, I banish thee, on pain of death,
As I have done the rest of my misleaders,
Not to come near our person by ten mile.
For competence* of life I will allow you,   maintenance
That* lack of means enforce you not to evil;   so that
And, as we hear you do reform yourselves,   72
We will, according to your strengths and qualities,
Give you advancement.

    (*To the* LORD CHIEF-JUSTICE.)

                Be it your charge, my lord,
To see performed the tenor of our word.
    Set on.

    (*The* KING *and the procession leave.*)

FALSTAFF.

Master Shallow, I owe you a thousand pound.

SHALLOW.

Yea, marry, Sir John; which I beseech you to let
me have* home with me.   take it/80

FALSTAFF.

That can hardly be, Mister Shallow. Do not you
grieve at this: I shall be sent for in private to him.
Look you, he must seem thus to the world. Fear
not your advancements: I will be the man yet that
shall make you great.

SHALLOW.

I cannot well perceive how, unless you should
give me your doublet and stuff me out with straw.
I beseech you, good Sir John, let me have five
hundred of my thousand.

FALSTAFF.

Sir, I will be as good as my word. This that you
heard was but a color.*96   pretense/
                                                               91
SHALLOW.

A color that I fear you will die in, Sir John.

FALSTAFF.

Fear no colors: go with me to dinner. Come,
Lieutenant Pistol; come, Bardolph. I shall be sent
for soon at night.
(*The* LORD CHIEF-JUSTICE *returns, with* PRINCE
JOHN *and* OFFICERS.)

CHIEF-JUSTICE (*to the* OFFICERS).

Go, carry Sir John Falstaff to the Fleet:*   *i.e., a Lon-*
Take all his company along with him.   *don prison*

FALSTAFF.

My lord, my lord—

CHIEF-JUSTICE.

I cannot now speak. I will hear you soon.   100
(*To the* OFFICERS.)
Take them away.

PISTOL.

Si fortuna me tormenta, spero contenta.
(*The* OFFICERS *lead* FALSTAFF *and his companions
away.*)

LANCASTER.

I like this fair proceeding of the king's.
He hath intent his wonted followers
Shall all be very well provided for;
But all are banished till their conversations*   *behavior*
Appear more wise and modest to the world.

CHIEF-JUSTICE.

And so they are.

LANCASTER.

The king hath called his parliament, my lord.

CHIEF-JUSTICE.

He hath.   110

LANCASTER.

I will lay odds that, ere this year expire,
We bear our civil swords and native fire
As far as France: I heard a bird so sing,
Whose music, to my thinking, pleased the king.
Come, will you hence?
(*They go.*)

EPILOGUE

Spoken by a Dancer

First my fear; then my courtesy;* last my speech. curtsy
My fear is, your displeasure; my courtesy, my
duty; and my speech, to beg your pardons. If you
look for a good speech now, you undo me: for
what I have to say is of mine own making; and
what indeed I should say will, I doubt,* prove fear
mine own marring. But to the purpose, and so to
the venture. Be it known to you, as it is very
well, I was lately here in the end of a displeasing
play, to pray your patience for it and to promise 10
you a better. I meant indeed to pay you with this;
which, if like an ill venture it come unluckily
home, I break,* and you, my gentle creditors, become bankrupt
lose. Here I promised you I would be, and here I
commit my body to your mercies: bate* me allow
some* and I will pay you some, and, as most debt- something
ors do, promise you infinitely.

If my tongue cannot entreat you to acquit me,
will you command me to use my legs? And yet
that were but light payment, to dance out of your 20
debt. But a good conscience will make any possible satisfaction, and so would I. All the gentlewomen here have forgiven me: if the gentlemen
will not, then the gentlemen do not agree with
the gentlewomen, which was never seen before in
such an assembly.

One word more, I beseech you. If you be not
too much cloyed* with fat meat, our humble gorged
author will continue the story, with Sir John in it,

and make you merry with fair Katharine of
France: where, for anything I know, Falstaff shall
die of a sweat, unless already a' be killed with
your hard opinions; for Oldcastle died a martyr,
and this is not the man. My tongue is weary;
when my legs are too, I will bid you good night:
and so kneel down before you: but, indeed, to
pray for the queen.

30

Selected Commentaries

Most of the commentators on *Henry IV, Part II*, devote their attention exclusively to the rejection of Falstaff; they explain, condemn or lament Hal's summary dismissal of his boon companion. One school of critics, of which Hudson is a prime representative, shows that the worst traits of Falstaff develop as the play proceeds, until every thoughtful observer of his conduct must realize that he has become no fit intimate for Hal. Bradley thinks that, if we have read the Prince's character aright, we should not be surprised at his rejection of Falstaff, for his growing hardness and his adoption of crafty political devices make the banishment thoroughly in character. Wilson believes that the Falstaff of *Part II* is a different creature from the joyous rogue of *Part I;* he has blossomed out into a self-satisfied pink of gentility, who is more humorous to us than to himself. By the end of the play our sympathy has ebbed away from this ridiculous figure. Still, there remain those who insist that Falstaff is the same character throughout the two plays; he triumphs so successfully over the traditional roles of braggart and clown that we resent the Prince's heartless public humiliation of the old rascal.

Tillyard emancipates criticism of *Henry IV, Part II*, from its concentration on the two principal characters in the drama by reminding his readers that *Part II* is in essence a chronicle history play. He finds that drama an epic of Shakespeare's England. Falstaff has become a representative of the ubiquitous London sharp who deceives and fleeces his innocent victims. Justice Shallow, in spite of his folly, along with Silence and Davy, introduces us to country life in Elizabethan England. Even the minor characters fill in the details of the broad canvas. Mistress Quickly, for example, is the type of all stupid good-natured lower-class women.

After attending to all these learned analyses and explanations of the unusual delight taken in the *Henry IV* plays, we turn with joyful assent to Dr. Johnson's tribute to the "unimitated, unimitable Falstaff." We share his belief that it is the perpetual gaiety of this reprobate, his unfailing power of exciting laughter, that gives to these *Henry IV* plays their timeless popularity.

SAMUEL JOHNSON (1709–1784)

Dr. Johnson, more than other critics of his age, responded to the appeal of Shakespeare's genius. In judicious but sympathetic fashion he paid tribute to the poet's power to penetrate to the essence of the characters and of the situation he presents.

THE UNIVERSAL POPULARITY OF THE HENRY IV DRAMAS
(from: *Johnson on Shakespeare*, edited by
Sir Walter Raleigh, 1908)

ACT V. SCENE viii.

KING. *I banish thee, on pain of death.*

Mr. *Rowe* [Nicholas Rowe, 1674–1718, the first editor of Shakespeare] observes, that many readers lament to see *Falstaff* so hardly used by his old friend. But if it be considered that the fat knight has never uttered one sentiment of generosity, and with all his power of exciting mirth, has nothing in him that can be esteemed, no great pain will be suffered from the reflection that he is compelled to live honestly, and maintained by the king, with a promise of advancement when he shall deserve it.

I think the poet more blameable for *Poins*, who is always represented as joining some virtues with his vices, and is therefore treated by the prince with apparent distinction, yet he does nothing in the time of action, and though after the bustle is over he is again a favourite, at last vanishes without notice. *Shakespeare* certainly lost him by heedlessness, in the multiplicity of his characters, the variety of his action, and his eagerness to end the play.

Act V. Scene ix.

chief justice. *Go, carry Sir* John Falstaff *to the* Fleet.

I do not see why *Falstaff* is carried to the Fleet. We have never lost sight of him since his dismission from the king; he has committed no new fault, and therefore incurred no punishment; but the different agitations of fear, anger, and surprise in him and his company, made a good scene to the eye; and our authour, who wanted them no longer on the stage, was glad to find this method of sweeping them away.

I fancy every reader, when he ends this play, cries out with *Desdemona, O most lame and impotent conclusion!* As this play was not, to our knowledge, divided into acts by the authour, I could be content to conclude it with the death of *Henry* the fourth.

In that Jerusalem shall Harry *dye.* These scenes which now make the fifth act of *Henry* the fourth, might then be the first of *Henry* the fifth; but the truth is, that they do unite very commodiously to either play. When these plays were represented, I believe they ended as they are now ended in the books; but *Shakespeare* seems to have designed that the whole series of action from the beginning of *Richard* the second, to the end of *Henry* the fifth, should be considered by the reader as one work, upon one plan, only broken into parts by the necessity of exhibition.

None of *Shakespeare's* plays are more read than the first and second parts of *Henry* the fourth. Perhaps no authour has ever in two plays afforded so much delight. The great events are interesting, for the fate of kingdoms depends upon them; the slighter occurrences are diverting, and, except one or two, sufficiently probable; the incidents are multiplied with wonderful fertility of invention, and the characters diversified with the utmost nicety of discernment, and the profoundest skill in the nature of man.

The prince, who is the hero both of the comick and tragick part, is a young man of great abilities and violent passions, whose sentiments are right, though his actions are wrong; whose virtues are obscured by negligence, and whose understanding is dissipated by levity. In his idle hours he is rather loose than wicked, and when the occasion forces out his latent qualities, he is great without effort, and brave without tumult. The trifler is roused into a hero, and the hero again reposes in the trifler. This character is great, original, and just.

Piercy is a rugged soldier, cholerick, and quarrelsome, and has only the soldier's virtues, generosity and courage.

But *Falstaff* unimitated, unimitable *Falstaff*, how shall I describe thee? Thou compound of sense and vice; of sense which may be admired but not esteemed, of vice which may be despised, but hardly detested. *Falstaff* is a character loaded with faults, and with those faults which naturally produce contempt. He is a thief, and a glutton, a coward, and a boaster, always ready to cheat the weak, and prey upon the poor; to terrify the timorous and insult the defenceless. At once obsequious and malignant, he satirises in their absence those whom he lives by flattering. He is familiar with the prince only as an agent of vice, but of this familiarity he is so proud as not only to be supercilious and haughty with common men, but to think his interest of importance to the duke of *Lancaster*. Yet the man thus corrupt, thus despicable, makes himself necessary to the prince that despises him, by the most pleasing of all qualities, perpetual gaiety, by an unfailing power of exciting laughter, which is the more freely indulged, as his wit is not of the splendid or ambitious kind, but consists in easy escapes and sallies of levity, which make sport but raise no envy. It must be observed that he is stained with no enormous or sanguinary crimes, so that his licentiousness is not so offensive but that it may be borne for his mirth.

The moral to be drawn from this representation is, that no man is more dangerous than he that with a will to corrupt, hath the power to please; and that neither wit nor honesty ought to think themselves safe with such a companion when they see *Henry* seduced by *Falstaff*.

* * *

H. N. HUDSON (1814–1886)

Henry N. Hudson, an American clergyman, was a representative of the best nineteenth-century Shakespearian criticism, both British and American. Until recently his penchant for passing moral judgments on the characters in the plays and his persistent method of treating dramatic figures like living persons has led to neglect and even scorn of his work.

Now many commentators find his appraisals of characters and situations just, and often searching. Dover Wilson believes Hudson to be the only nineteenth-century critic who completely understands Shakespeare's conception of Prince Hal.

THE CONDUCT AND COMPANIONS OF FALSTAFF'S LATER CAREER
(from: *Shakespeare, His Life, Art, and Characters,* 1881)

In all that happens to Falstaff, the being cast off at last by the Prince is the only thing that really hurts his feelings. And as this is the only thing that hurts him, so it is the only one that does him any good: for he is strangely inaccessible to inward suffering; and yet nothing but this can make him better. His character keeps on developing, and growing rather worse, to the end of the play; and there are some positive indications of a hard bad heart in him. His abuse of Shallow's hospitality is exceedingly detestable, and argues that hardening of all within which tells far more against a man than almost any amount of mere sensuality. For it is a great mistake to suppose that our sensual vices, though they may and often do work the most harm to ourselves, are morally the worst. The malignant vices, those that cause us to take pleasure in the pain or damage of others,—it is in these that Hell is most especially concentrated. Satan is neither a glutton nor a wine-bibber; he himself stoops not to the lusts of the flesh, though he delights to see his poor dupes eaten up by them: but to gloat over or to feast on the agonies that one inflicts, this is truly Satanic. In the matter about Justice Shallow we are let into those worse traits of Falstaff, such as his unscrupulous and unrelenting selfishness, which had else escaped our dull perceptions, but which, through all the disguises of art, have betrayed themselves to the apprehensive discernment of Prince Henry. Thus we here come upon the delicate thread which connects that sapient Justice with what I have stated to be the main purpose of the drama. The bad usage which Falstaff puts upon Shallow has the effect of justifying to us the usage which he at last receives from the Prince. And something of the kind was needful in order to bring the Prince's character off from such an act altogether bright and sweet in our regard. For, after sharing so long in the man's prodigality of mental exhilaration, to shut down upon him so, was pretty hard.

I must not leave Sir John without remarking how he is a sort of public brain from which shoot forth nerves of communication through all the limbs and members of the commonwealth. The most broadly-representative, perhaps, of all ideal characters, his conversations are as diversified as his capabilities; so that through him the vision is let forth into a long-drawn yet clear perspective of old English life and manners. What a circle of vices and obscurities and nobilities are sucked into his train! how various in size and quality the orbs that revolve around him and shine by his light! from the immediate heir of England and the righteous Lord Chief Justice to poor Robin Ostler who died of one idea, having "never joy'd since the price of oats rose." He is indeed a multitudinous man; and can spin fun enough out of his marvellous brain to make all the world "laugh and grow fat."

We have had several glimpses of Mrs. Quickly, the Hostess of Eastcheap. She is well worth a steady looking at. One of the most characteristic passages in the play is her account of Falstaff's engagement to her; which has been aptly commented on by Coleridge as showing how her mind runs altogether in the rut of actual events. She can think of things only in the precise order of their occurrence, having no power to select such as touch her purpose, and to detach them from the circumstantial irrelevancies with which they are consorted in her memory.

In keeping with this mental peculiarity, her character savours strongly of her whereabout in life; she is plentifully trimmed with vices and vulgarities, and these all taste rankly of her place and calling, thus showing that she has as much of moral as of mental passiveness. Notwithstanding, she always has an odour of womanhood about her, even her worst features being such as none but a woman could have. Nor is her character, with all its ludicrous and censurable qualities, unrelieved, as we have seen, by traits of generosity that relish equally of her sex. It is even doubtful whether she would have entertained Sir John's proposals of marriage so favourably, but that at the time of making them he was in a condition to need her kindness. Her woman's heart could not stint itself from the plump old sinner when he had wounds to be dressed and pains to be soothed. And who but a woman could speak such words of fluttering eagerness as she speaks in urging on his arrest: "Do your offices, do your offices, Master Fang and Master Snare; do me, do me, do me your offices"; where her heart seems palpitating with an anxious hope that her present action may make another occasion for her kind ministrations? Sometimes, indeed, she gets wrought up to a pretty high pitch of temper, but she cannot hold herself there; and between her turns of anger and her returns to sweetness there is room for more of womanly feeling than I shall venture to describe. And there is still more of the woman in the cunning simplicity—or is it simpleness? —with which she manages to keep her good opinion of Sir John; as when, on being told that at his death "he cried out of women, and said they were devils incarnate," she replies, "'A never could abide carnation; 't was a colour he never liked"; as if she could find no sense in his words but what would stand smooth with her interest and her affection.

It is curious to observe how Mrs. Quickly dwells on the confines of virtue and shame, and sometimes plays over the borders, ever clinging to the reputation, and perhaps to the consciousness, of the one, without foreclosing the invitations of the other. For it is very evident that even in her worst doings she hides from herself their ill-favour under a fair name; as people often paint the cheeks of their vices, and then look them sweetly in the face, though they cannot but know the paint is all that keeps them from being unsightly and loathsome. In her case, however, this may spring, in part, from a simplicity not unlike that which sometimes causes little children to shut their eyes at what affrights them, and then think themselves safe. And yet she shows considerable knowledge of the world; is not without shrewdness in her way; but, in truth, the world her soul lives in, and grows intelligent of, is itself a discipline of moral obtuseness; and this is one reason why she loves it. On the whole, therefore, Mrs. Quickly must be set down as a naughty woman; the Poet clearly meant her so; and, in mixing so much of good with the general preponderance of bad in her composition, he has shown a rare spirit of wisdom, such as may well remind us that "both good men and bad men are apt to be less so than they seem."

Such is one formation of life to which the Poet conducts us by a pathway leading from Sir John. But we have an avenue opening out from him into a much richer formation.

Aside from the humour of the characters themselves, there is great humour of art in the bringing-together of Falstaff and Shallow. Whose risibilities are not quietly shaken up to the centre, as he studies the contrast between them, and the sources of their interest in each other? Shallow is vastly proud of his acquaintance with Sir John, and runs over with consequentiality as he reflects upon it. Sir John understands this perfectly, and is drawn to him quite as much for the pleasure of making a butt of him as in the hope of currying a road to his purse.

One of the most potent spots in Justice Shallow is the exulting self-complacency with which he remembers his youthful essays in profligacy; wherein, though without suspecting it, he was the sport and byword of his companions; he having shown in them the same boobyish alacrity as he now shows in prating about them. His reminiscences in this line are superlatively diverting, partly, perhaps, as reminding us of a perpetual sort of people, not unfrequently met with in the intercourse of life.

Another choice spot in Shallow is a huge love or habit of talking on when he has nothing to say; as though his tongue were hugging and kissing his words. Thus, when Sir John asks to be excused from staying with him over night: "I will not excuse you; you shall not be excused; excuses shall not be admitted; there is no excuse shall serve; you shall not be excused." And he lingers upon his words and keeps rolling them over in his mouth with a still keener relish in the garden after supper. This fond caressing of his phrases springs not merely from sterility of thought, but partly also from that vivid self-appreciation which causes him to dwell with such rapture on the spirited sallies of his youth.

One more point about fetches the compass of his genius, he being considerable mainly for his loquacious thinness. It is well instanced in his appreciation of Sir John's witticism on Mouldy, one of the recruits he is taking up:

FALSTAFF. Is thy name Mouldy?
MOULDY. 'Yea, an 't please you.
FALSTAFF. 'Tis the more time thou wert used.
SHALLOW. Ha, ha, ha! most excellent, i' faith! things that are mouldy lack use: very singular good! In faith, well said, Sir John; very well said.

The mixture of conceit and sycophancy here is charming. Of course it is not so much the wit as his own perception of the wit, that the critic admires.

One would suppose the force of feebleness had done its best in Shallow, yet it is made to do several degrees better in his cousin, Justice Silence. The tautology of the one has its counterpart in the taciturnity of the other. And Shallow's habit in this may have grown, in part, from talking to his cousin, and getting no replies; for Silence has scarce life enough to answer, unless it be to echo the question. The only faculty he seems to have is memory, and he has not force enough of his own to set even this in motion; nothing but excess of wine can make it stir. So that his taciturnity is but the proper outside of his essential vacuity, and springs from sheer dearth of soul. He is indeed a stupendous platitude of a man! The character is poetical by a sort of inversion; as extreme ugliness sometimes has the effect of beauty, and fascinates the eye.

Shakespeare evinces a peculiar delight sometimes in weaving poetical conceptions round the leanest subjects; and we have no finer instance of this than where Silence, his native sterility of brain being overcome by the working of sack on his memory, keeps pouring forth snatches from old ballads. How delicately comical the volubility with which he trundles off the fag-ends of popular ditties, when in "the sweet of the night" his heart has grown rich with the exhilaration of wine! Who can ever forget the exquisite humour of the contrast between Silence dry and Silence drunk?

In this vocal flow of Silence we catch the right spirit and style of old English mirth. For he must have passed his life in an atmosphere of song, since it was only by dint of long custom and endless repetition that so passive a memory as his could have got stored with such matter. And the snatches he sings are fragments of old minstrelsy "that had long been heard in the squire's hall and the yeoman's chimney-corner," where friends and neighbours were wont to "sing aloud old songs, the precious music of the heart."

These two sapient Justices are admirably fitted to each other, for indeed they have worn together. Shallow highly appreciates his kinsman, who in turn looks up to him as his great man, and as a kind of superior nature. It were hardly fair to quit them without referring to their piece of dialogue about old Double; where in all the ludicrous oddity of the thing we have touches that "feelingly persuade us what we are." And I suppose there is none so poor shell of humanity but that, if we apply our ear, and listen intently, "from within are heard murmurings whereby the monitor expresses mysterious union with its native sea." It is considerable that this bit of dialogue occurs at our first meeting with the speakers; as if on purpose to set and gauge our feelings aright towards them; to forestall and prevent an overmuch rising of contempt for them; which is probably about the worst feeling we can cherish.

The drama of *King Henry the Fourth*, taking the two Parts as artistically one, is deservedly ranked among the very highest of Shakespeare's achievements. The characterization, whether for quantity or quality or variety, or again whether regarded in the individual development or the dramatic combination, is above all praise. And yet, large and free as is the scope here given to invention, the parts are all strictly subordinated to the idea of the whole as an historical drama; insomuch that even Falstaff, richly ideal as is the character, everywhere helps on the history; a whole century of old English wit and sense and humour being crowded together and compacted in him. And one is surprised withal, upon reflection, to see how many scraps and odd minutes of intelligence are here to be met with. The Poet seems indeed to have been almost everywhere, and brought away some tincture and relish of the place; as though his body were set full of eyes, and every eye took in matter of thought and memory: here we have the smell of eggs and butter; there we turn up a fragment of old John of Gaunt; elsewhere we chance upon a pot of Tewksbury mustard; again we hit a bit of popular superstition, how Earl Douglas "runs o' horseback up a hill perpendicular": on the march with Falstaff, we contemplate "the cankers of a calm world and a long peace"; at Clement's Inn we hear "the chimes at midnight"; at Master Shallow's we "eat a last year's pippin of my own grafting, with a dish of caraways and so forth": now we are amidst the poetries of chivalry and the felicities of victory; now amidst the obscure sufferings of war, where its inexorable iron hand enters the widow's cottage, and snatches away the land's humblest comforts. And so I might go on indefinitely, the particulars in this kind being so numerous as might well distract the mind, yet so skilfully composed that the number seems not large, till by a special effort of thought one goes to viewing them severally. And these particulars, though so unnoticed or so little noticed in the detail, are nevertheless so ordered that they all tell in the result. How strong is the principle of organic unity and life pervading the whole, may be specially instanced in Falstaff; whose sayings everywhere so fit and cleave to the circumstances, to all the oddities of connection and situation out of which they grow; have such a mixed smacking, such a various and composite relish, made up from all the peculiarities of the person by whom, the occasion wherein, and the purpose for which they are spoken, that they cannot be detached and set out by themselves without thwarting or greatly marring their force and flavour. Thus in the farthest extremities of the work we feel the beatings of one common heart. On the whole, we may safely affirm with Dr. Johnson, that "perhaps no author has ever, in two plays, afforded so much delight."

* * *

A. C. BRADLEY (1851–1935)

Bradley's Shakespeare criticism was the culmination of the movement that had originated in the work of Morgann and was developed by great romantic critics like Coleridge and Hazlitt. His detractors accuse him of substituting interest in the psychology of the characters for essentially dramatic considerations. Yet his interpretations of the principal figures in the four great tragedies has been generally accepted. Although it is the fashion of some contemporary critics to express a low opinion of the tendency of his work, it still holds the high place in the minds of many intelligent readers that it held for an entire generation of nineteenth-century students of Shakespeare.

THE REJECTION OF FALSTAFF
(from: *Oxford Lectures on Poetry*, 1909)

Of the two persons principally concerned in the rejection of Falstaff, Henry, both as Prince and as King, has received, on the whole, full justice from readers and critics. Falstaff, on the other hand, has been in one respect the most unfortunate of Shakespeare's famous characters. All of them, in passing from the mind of their creator into other minds, suffer change; they tend to lose their harmony through the disproportionate attention bestowed on some one feature, or to lose their uniqueness by being conventionalised into types already familiar. But Falstaff was degraded by Shakespeare himself. The original character is to be found alive in the two parts of *Henry IV.*, dead in *Henry V.*, and nowhere else. But not very long after these plays were composed, Shakespeare wrote, and he afterwards revised, the very entertaining piece called *The Merry Wives of Windsor*. Perhaps his company wanted a new play on a sudden; or perhaps, as one would rather believe, the tradition may be true that Queen Elizabeth, delighted with the Falstaff scenes of *Henry IV.*, expressed a wish to see the hero of them again, and to see him in love. Now it was no more possible for Shakespeare to show his own Falstaff in love than to turn twice two into five. But he could write in haste—the tradition says, in a fortnight—a comedy or farce differing from all his other plays in this, that its scene is laid in English middle-class life, and that it is prosaic almost to the end. And among the characters he could introduce a disreputable fat old knight with attendants, and could call them Falstaff, Bardolph, Pistol, and Nym. And he could represent this knight assailing, for financial purposes, the virtue of two matrons, and in the event baffled, duped, treated like dirty linen, beaten, burnt, pricked, mocked, insulted, and, worst of all, repentant and didactic. It is horrible. It is almost enough to convince one that Shakespeare himself could sanction the parody of Ophelia in the *Two Noble Kinsmen*. But it no more touches the real Falstaff than Ophelia is degraded by that parody. To picture the real Falstaff befooled like the Falstaff of the *Merry Wives* is like imagining Iago the gull of Roderigo, or Becky Sharp the dupe of Amelia Osborne. Before he had been served the least of these tricks he would have had his brains taken out and buttered, and have given them to a dog for a New Year's gift. I quote the words of the impostor, for after all Shakespeare made him and gave to him a few sentences worthy of Falstaff himself. But they are only a few—one side of a sheet of notepaper would contain them. And yet critics have solemnly debated at what period in his life Sir John endured the gibes of Master Ford, and whether we should put this comedy between the two parts of *Henry IV.*, or between the second of them and *Henry V*. And the Falstaff of the general reader, it is to be feared, is an impossible conglomerate of two distinct characters, while the Falstaff of the mere playgoer is certainly much more like the impostor than the true man.

The separation of these two has long ago been effected by criticism, and is insisted on in almost all competent estimates of the character of Falstaff. I do not propose to attempt a full account either of this character or of that of Prince Henry, but shall connect the remarks I have to make on them with a question which does not appear to have been satisfactorily discussed—the question of the rejection of Falstaff by the Prince on his accession to the throne. What do we feel, and what are we meant to feel, as we witness this rejection? And what does our feeling imply as to the characters of Falstaff and the new King?

1.

Sir John, you remember, is in Gloucestershire, engaged in borrowing a thousand pounds from Justice Shallow; and here Pistol, riding helter-skelter from London, brings him the great news that the old King is as dead as nail in door, and that Harry the Fifth is the man. Sir John, in wild excitement, taking any man's horses, rushes to London; and he carries Shallow with him, for he longs to reward all his friends. We find him standing with his companions just outside Westminster Abbey, in the crowd that is waiting for the King to come out after his coronation. He himself is stained with travel, and has had no time to spend any of the thousand pounds in buying new liveries for his men. But what of that? This poor show only proves his earnestness of affection, his devotion, how he could not deliberate or remember or have patience to shift himself, but rode day and night, thought of nothing else but to see Henry, and put all affairs else in oblivion, as if there were nothing else to be done but to see him. And now he stands sweating with desire to see him, and repeating and repeating this one desire of his heart—"to see him." The moment comes. There is a shout within the Abbey like the roaring of the sea, and a clangour of trumpets, and the doors open and the procession streams out.

FALSTAFF. God save thy grace, King Hal! my royal Hal!
PISTOL. The heavens thee guard and keep, most royal imp of fame!

FALSTAFF. God save thee, my sweet boy!
KING. My Lord Chief Justice, speak to that vain man.
CHIEF JUSTICE. Have you your wits? Know you what 'tis
you speak?
FALSTAFF. My King! my Jove! I speak to thee, my heart!
KING. I know thee not, old man: fall to thy prayers;
How ill white hairs become a fool and jester!
I have long dream'd of such a kind of man,
So surfeit-swell'd, so old and so profane;
But being awaked I do despise my dream.
Make less thy body hence, and more thy grace;
Leave gormandizing; know the grave doth gape
For thee thrice wider than for other men.
Reply not to me with a fool-born jest:
Presume not that I am the thing I was;
For God doth know, so shall the world perceive,
That I have turn'd away my former self;
So will I those that kept me company.
When thou dost hear I am as I have been,
Approach me, and thou shalt be as thou wast,
The tutor and the feeder of my riots:
Till then, I banish thee, on pain of death,
As I have done the rest of my misleaders,
Not to come near our person by ten mile.
For competence of life I will allow you,
That lack of means enforce you not to evil:
And, as we hear you do reform yourselves,
We will, according to your strengths and qualities,
Give you advancement. Be it your charge, my lord,
To see perform'd the tenour of our word.
Set on.

The procession passes out of sight, but Falstaff and his
friends remain. He shows no resentment. He comforts himself, or tries to comfort himself—first, with the thought that
he has Shallow's thousand pounds, and then, more seriously,
I believe, with another thought. The King, he sees, must look
thus to the world; but he will be sent for in private when
night comes, and will yet make the fortunes of his friends.
But even as he speaks, the Chief Justice, accompanied by
Prince John, returns, and gives the order to his officers:

> Go, carry Sir John Falstaff to the Fleet;
> Take all his company along with him.

Falstaff breaks out, "My lord, my lord," but he is cut short
and hurried away; and after a few words between the Prince

and the Chief Justice the scene closes, and with it the drama.

What are our feelings during this scene? They will depend on our feelings about Falstaff. If we have not keenly enjoyed the Falstaff scenes of the two plays, if we regard Sir John chiefly as an old reprobate, not only a sensualist, a liar, and a coward, but a cruel and dangerous ruffian, I suppose we enjoy his discomfiture and consider that the King has behaved magnificently. But if we *have* keenly enjoyed the Falstaff scenes, if we have enjoyed them as Shakespeare surely meant them to be enjoyed, and if, accordingly, Falstaff is not to us solely or even chiefly a reprobate and ruffian, we feel, I think, during the King's speech, a good deal of pain and some resentment; and when, without any further offence on Sir John's part, the Chief Justice returns and sends him to prison, we stare in astonishment. These, I believe, are, in greater or less degree, the feelings of most of those who really enjoy the Falstaff scenes (as many readers do not). Nor are these feelings diminished when we remember the end of the whole story, as we find it in *Henry V.*, where we learn that Falstaff quickly died, and, according to the testimony of persons not very sentimental, died of a broken heart. Suppose this merely to mean that he sank under the shame of his public disgrace, and it is pitiful enough: but the words of Mrs. Quickly, "The king has killed his heart"; of Nym, "The king hath run bad humours on the knight; that's the even of it"; of Pistol,

> Nym, thou hast spoke the right,
> His heart is fracted and corroborate,

assuredly point to something more than wounded pride; they point to wounded affection, and remind us of Falstaff's own answer to Prince Hal's question, "Sirrah, do I owe you a thousand pound?" "A thousand pound, Hal? a million: thy love is worth a million: thou owest me thy love."

Now why did Shakespeare end his drama with a scene which, though undoubtedly striking, leaves an impression so unpleasant? I will venture to put aside without discussion the idea that he meant us throughout the two plays to regard Falstaff with disgust or indignation, so that we naturally feel nothing but pleasure at his fall; for this idea implies that kind of inability to understand Shakespeare with which it is idle to argue. And there is another and a much more ingenious suggestion which must equally be rejected as impossible. According to it, Falstaff, having listened to the King's speech, did not seriously hope to be sent for by him in private; he fully realised the situation at once, and was only making game of Shallow; and in his immediate turn upon Shallow when the King goes out, "Master Shallow, I owe you a thousand pound," we are meant to see his humorous superiority to any rebuff, so that we end the play with the delightful feeling that, while Henry has done the right thing, Falstaff, in his outward over-throw, has still proved himself inwardly invincible. This sug-gestion comes from a critic who understands Falstaff, and in the suggestion itself shows that he understands him. But it provides no solution, because it wholly ignores, and could not account for, that which follows the short conversation with Shallow. Falstaff's dismissal to the Fleet, and his subsequent death, prove beyond doubt that his rejection was meant by Shakespeare to be taken as a catastrophe which not even his humour could enable him to surmount.

Moreover, these interpretations, even if otherwise admis-sible, would still leave our problem only partly solved. For what troubles us is not only the disappointment of Falstaff, it is the conduct of Henry. It was inevitable that on his acces-sion he should separate himself from Sir John, and we wish nothing else. It is satisfactory that Sir John should have a competence, with the hope of promotion in the highly im-probable case of his reforming himself. And if Henry could not trust himself within ten miles of so fascinating a com-panion, by all means let him be banished that distance: we do not complain. These arrangements would not have prevented a satisfactory ending: the King could have communicated his decision, and Falstaff could have accepted it, in a private interview rich in humour and merely touched with pathos. But Shakespeare has so contrived matters that Henry could not send a private warning to Falstaff even if he wished to, and in their public meeting Falstaff is made to behave in so infatuated and outrageous a manner that great sternness on the King's part was unavoidable. And the curious thing is that Shakespeare did not stop here. If this had been all we should have felt pain for Falstaff, but not, perhaps, resent-ment against Henry. But two things we do resent. Why, when this painful incident seems to be over, should the Chief Justice return and send Falstaff to prison? Can this possibly be meant for an act of private vengeance on the part of the Chief Justice, unknown to the King? No; for in that case Shakespeare would have shown at once that the

King disapproved and cancelled it. It must have been the King's own act. This is one thing we resent; the other is the King's sermon. He had a right to turn away his former self, and his old companions with it, but he had no right to talk all of a sudden like a clergyman; and surely it was both ungenerous and insincere to speak of them as his "misleaders," as though in the days of Eastcheap and Gadshill he had been a weak and silly lad. We have seen his former self, and we know that it was nothing of the kind. He had shown himself, for all his follies, a very strong and independent young man, deliberately amusing himself among men over whom he had just as much ascendency as he chose to exert. Nay, he amused himself not only among them, but at their expense. In his first soliloquy—and first soliloquies are usually significant—he declares that he associates with them in order that, when at some future time he shows his true character, he may be the more wondered at for his previous aberrations. You may think he deceives himself here; you may believe that he frequented Sir John's company out of delight in it and not merely with this cold-blooded design; but at any rate he *thought* the design was his one motive. And, that being so, two results follow. He ought in honour long ago to have given Sir John clearly to understand that they must say good-bye on the day of his accession. And, having neglected to do this, he ought not to have lectured him as his misleader. It was not only ungenerous, it was dishonest. It looks disagreeably like an attempt to buy the praise of the respectable at the cost of honour and truth. And it succeeded. Henry *always* succeeded.

You will see what I am suggesting, for the moment, as a solution of our problem. I am suggesting that our fault lies not in our resentment at Henry's conduct, but in our surprise at it; that if we had read his character truly in the light that Shakespeare gave us, we should have been prepared for a display both of hardness and of policy at this point in his career. And although this suggestion does not suffice to solve the problem before us, I am convinced that in itself it is true. Nor is it rendered at all improbable by the fact that Shakespeare has made Henry, on the whole, a fine and very attractive character, and that here he makes no one express any disapprobation of the treatment of Falstaff. For in similar cases Shakespeare is constantly misunderstood. His readers expect him to mark in some distinct way his approval or disapproval of that which he represents; and hence where *they* disapprove and *he* says nothing, they fancy that he does *not* disapprove, and they blame his indifference, like Dr. Johnson, or at the least are puzzled. But the truth is that he shows the fact and leaves the judgment to them. And again, when he makes us like a character we expect the character to have no faults that are not expressly pointed out, and when other faults appear we either ignore them or try to explain them away. This is one of our methods of conventionalising Shakespeare. We want the world's population to be neatly divided into sheep and goats, and we want an angel by us to say, "Look, that is a goat and this is a sheep," and we try to turn Shakespeare into this angel. His impartiality makes us uncomfortable: we cannot bear to see him, like the sun, lighting up everything and judging nothing. And this is perhaps especially the case in his historical plays, where we are always trying to turn him into a partisan. He shows us that Richard II. was unworthy to be king, and we at once conclude that he thought Bolingbroke's usurpation justified; whereas he shows merely, what under the conditions was bound to exist, an inextricable tangle of right and unright. Or, Bolingbroke being evidently wronged, we suppose Bolingbroke's statements to be true, and are quite surprised when, after attaining his end through them, he mentions casually on his deathbed that they were lies. Shakespeare makes us admire Hotspur heartily; and accordingly, when we see Hotspur discussing with others how large his particular slice of his mother-country is to be, we either fail to recognise the monstrosity of the proceeding, or recognising it, we complain that Shakespeare is inconsistent. Prince John breaks a tottering rebellion by practising a detestable fraud on the rebels. We are against the rebels, and have heard high praise of Prince John, but we cannot help seeing that his fraud is detestable; so we say indignantly to Shakespeare, "Why, you told us he was a sheep"; whereas, in fact, if we had used our eyes we should have known beforehand that he was the brave, determined, loyal, cold-blooded, pitiless, unscrupulous son of a usurper whose throne was in danger.

To come, then, to Henry. Both as prince and as king he is deservedly a favourite, and particularly so with English readers, being, as he is, perhaps the most distinctively English of all Shakespeare's men. In *Henry V.* he is treated as a national hero. In this play he has lost much of the wit which in him seems to have depended on contact with Falstaff, but he has also laid aside the most serious faults of his youth. He inspires in a high degree fear, enthusiasm, and affection; thanks to his beautiful modesty he has the charm which is lacking to another mighty warrior, Coriolanus; his youthful escapades have given him an understanding of simple folk, and sympathy with them; he is the author of the saying, "There is some soul of goodness in things evil"; and he is much more obviously religious than most of Shakespeare's heroes. Having these and other fine qualities, and being without certain dangerous tendencies which mark the tragic heroes, he is, perhaps, the most *efficient* character drawn by Shakespeare, unless Ulysses, in *Troilus and Cressida,* is his equal. And so he has been described as Shakespeare's ideal man of action; nay, it has even been declared that here for once Shakespeare plainly disclosed his own ethical creed, and showed us his ideal, not simply of a man of action, but of a man.

But Henry is neither of these. The poet who drew Hamlet and Othello can never have thought that even the ideal man of action would lack that light upon the brow which at once transfigures them and marks their doom. It is as easy to believe that, because the lunatic, the lover, and the poet are not far apart, Shakespeare would have chosen never to have loved and sung. Even poor Timon, the most inefficient of the tragic heroes, has something in him that Henry never shows. Nor is it merely that his nature is limited: if we follow Shakespeare and look closely at Henry, we shall discover with the many fine traits a few less pleasing. Henry IV. describes him as the noble image of his own youth; and, for all his superiority to his father, he is still his father's son, the son of the man whom Hotspur called a "vile politician." Henry's religion, for example, is genuine, it is rooted in his modesty; but it is also superstitious—an attempt to buy off supernatural vengeance for Richard's blood; and it is also in part political, like his father's projected crusade. Just as he went to war chiefly because, as his father told him, it was the way to keep factious nobles quiet and unite the nation, so when he adjures the Archbishop to satisfy him as to his right to the French throne, he knows very well that the Archbishop *wants* the war, because it will defer and perhaps prevent what he considers the spoliation of the Church. This same strain of policy is what Shakespeare marks in the first soliloquy in *Henry IV.*, where the prince describes his riotous life as a mere scheme to win him glory later. It implies that readiness to use other people as means to his own ends which is a conspicuous feature in his father; and it reminds us of his father's plan of keeping himself out of the people's sight while Richard was making himself cheap by his incessant public appearances. And if I am not mistaken there is a further likeness. Henry is kindly and pleasant to every one as Prince, to every one deserving as King; and he is so not merely out of policy: but there is no sign in him of a strong affection for any one, such an affection as we recognise at a glance in Hamlet and Horatio, Brutus and Cassius, and many more. We do not find this in *Henry V.*, not even in the noble address to Lord Scroop, and in *Henry IV.* we find, I think, a liking for Falstaff and Poins, but no more: there is no more than a liking, for instance, in his soliloquy over the supposed corpse of his fat friend, and he never speaks of Falstaff to Poins with any affection. The truth is, that the members of the family of Henry IV. have love for one another, but they cannot spare love for any one outside their family, which stands firmly united, defending its royal position against attack and instinctively isolating itself from outside influence.

Thus I would suggest that Henry's conduct in his rejection of Falstaff is in perfect keeping with his character on its unpleasant side as well as on its finer; and that, so far as Henry is concerned, we ought not to feel surprise at it. And on this view we may even explain the strange incident of the Chief Justice being sent back to order Falstaff to prison (for there is no sign of any such uncertainty in the text as might suggest an interpolation by the players). Remembering his father's words about Henry, "Being incensed, he's flint," and remembering in *Henry V.* his ruthlessness about killing the prisoners when he is incensed, we may imagine that, after he had left Falstaff and was no longer influenced by the face of his old companion, he gave way to anger at the indecent familiarity which had provoked a compromising scene on the most ceremonial of occasions and in the presence alike of court and crowd, and that he sent the Chief Justice back to take vengeance. And this is consistent with the fact that in the next play we find Falstaff shortly afterwards not only freed from prison, but unmolested in his old haunt in Eastcheap, well within ten miles of Henry's person. His anger had soon passed, and he knew that the requisite effect had been produced both on Falstaff and on the world.

But all this, however true, will not solve our problem. It seems, on the contrary, to increase its difficulty. For the natural conclusion is that Shakespeare *intended* us to feel resentment against Henry. And yet that cannot be, for it implies that he meant the play to end disagreeably; and no one who understands Shakespeare at all will consider that supposition for a moment credible. No; he must have meant the play to end pleasantly, although he made Henry's action consistent. And hence it follows that he must have intended our sympathy with Falstaff to be so far weakened when the rejection-scene arrives that his discomfiture should be satisfactory to us; that we should enjoy this sudden reverse of enormous hopes (a thing always ludicrous if sympathy is absent); that we should approve the moral judgment that falls on him; and so should pass lightly over that disclosure of unpleasant traits in the King's character which Shakespeare was too true an artist to suppress. Thus our pain and resentment, if we feel them, are wrong, in the sense that they do not answer to the dramatist's intention. But it does not follow that they are wrong in a further sense. They may be right, because the dramatist has missed what he aimed at. And this, though the dramatist was Shakespeare, is what I would suggest. In the Falstaff scenes he overshot his mark. He created so extraordinary a being, and fixed him so firmly on his intellectual throne, that when he sought to dethrone him he could not. The moment comes when we are to look at Falstaff in a serious light, and the comic hero is to figure as a baffled schemer; but we cannot make the required change, either in our attitude or in our sympathies. We wish Henry a glorious reign and much joy of his crew of hypocritical politicians, lay and clerical; but our hearts go with Falstaff to the Fleet, or, if necessary, to Arthur's bosom or wheresomever he is.

In the remainder of the lecture I will try to make this view clear. And to that end we must go back to the Falstaff of the body of the two plays, the immortal Falstaff, a character almost purely humorous, and therefore no subject for moral judgments. I can but draw an outline, and in describing one aspect of his character must be content to hold another in reserve.

2.

Up to a certain point Falstaff is ludicrous in the same way as many other figures, his distinction lying, so far, chiefly in the mere abundance of ludicrous traits. *Why* we should laugh at a man with a huge belly and corresponding appetites; at the inconveniences he suffers on a hot day, or in playing the footpad, or when he falls down and there are no levers at hand to lift him up again; at the incongruity of his un-wieldy bulk and the nimbleness of his spirit, the infirmities of his age and his youthful lightness of heart; at the enormity of his lies and wiles, and the suddenness of their exposure and frustration; at the contrast between his reputation and his real character, seen most absurdly when, at the mere mention of his name, a redoubted rebel surrenders to him—*why*, I say, we should laugh at these and many such things, this is no place to inquire; but unquestionably we do. Here we have them poured out in endless profusion and with that air of careless ease which is so fascinating in Shakespeare; and with the enjoyment of them I believe many readers stop. But while they are quite essential to the character, there is in it much more. For these things by themselves do not explain why, beside laughing at Falstaff, we are made happy by him and laugh *with* him. He is not, like Parolles, a mere *object* of mirth.

The main reason why he makes us so happy and puts us so entirely at our ease is that he himself is happy and entirely at his ease. "Happy" is too weak a word; he is in bliss, and we share his glory. Enjoyment—no fitful pleasure crossing a dull life, nor any vacant convulsive mirth—but a rich deep-toned chuckling enjoyment circulates continually through all his being. If you ask *what* he enjoys, no doubt the answer is, in the first place, eating and drinking, taking his ease at his inn, and the company of other merry souls. Compared with these things, what we count the graver interests of life are nothing to him. But then, while we are under his spell, it is impossible to consider these graver interests; gravity is to us, as to him, inferior to gravy; and what he does enjoy he enjoys with such a luscious and good-humoured zest that we sympathise and he makes us happy. And if any one objected, we should answer with Sir Toby Belch, "Dost thou think, because thou art virtuous, there shall be no more cakes and ale?"

But this, again, is far from all. Falstaff's ease and enjoyment are not simply those of the happy man of appetite; they are those of the humorist, and the humorist of genius. Instead of being comic to you and serious to himself, he is more ludicrous to himself than to you; and he makes himself out more ludicrous than he is, in order that he and others may laugh. Prince Hal never made such sport of Falstaff's person as he himself did. It is *he* who says that his skin hangs about him like an old lady's loose gown, and that he walks before his page like a sow that hath o'erwhelmed all her litter but one. And he jests at himself when he is alone just as much as when others are by. It is the same with his appetites. The direct enjoyment they bring him is scarcely so great as the enjoyment of laughing at this enjoyment; and for all his addiction to sack you never see him for an instant with a brain dulled by it, or a temper turned solemn, silly, quarrelsome, or pious. The virtue it instils into him, of filling his brain with nimble, fiery, and delectable shapes—this, and his humorous attitude towards it, free him, in a manner, from slavery to it; and it is this freedom, and no secret longing for better things (those who attribute such a longing to him are far astray), that makes his enjoyment contagious and prevents our sympathy with it from being disturbed.

The bliss of freedom gained in humour is the essence of Falstaff. His humour is not directed only or chiefly against obvious absurdities; he is the enemy of everything that would interfere with his ease, and therefore of anything serious, and especially of everything respectable and moral. For these things impose limits and obligations, and make us the subjects of old father antic the law, and the categorical imperative, and our station and its duties, and conscience, and reputation, and other people's opinions, and all sorts of nuisances. I say he is therefore their enemy; but I do him wrong; to say that he is their enemy implies that he regards them as serious and recognises their power, when in truth he refuses to recognise them at all. They are to him absurd; and to reduce a thing *ad absurdum* is to reduce it to nothing and to walk about free and rejoicing. This is what Falstaff does with all the would-be serious things of life, sometimes only by his words, sometimes by his actions too. He will make truth appear absurd by solemn statements, which he utters with perfect gravity and which he expects nobody to believe; and honour, by demonstrating that it cannot set a leg, and that neither the living nor the dead can possess it; and law, by evading all the attacks of its highest representative and almost forcing him to laugh at his own defeat; and patriotism, by filling his pockets with the bribes offered by competent soldiers who want to escape service, while he takes in their stead the halt and maimed and the gaol-birds; and duty, by showing how he labours in his vocation—of thieving; and courage, alike by mocking at his own capture of Colvile and gravely claiming to have killed Hotspur; and war, by offering the Prince his bottle of sack when he is asked for a sword; and religion, by amusing himself with remorse at odd times when he has nothing else to do; and the fear of death, by maintaining perfectly untouched, in the face of imminent peril and even while he *feels* the fear of death, the very same power of dissolving it in persiflage that he shows when he sits at ease in his inn. These are the wonderful achievements which he performs, not with the sourness of a cynic, but with the gaiety of a boy. And, therefore, we praise him, we laud him, for he offends none but the virtuous, and denies that life is real or life is earnest, and delivers us from the oppression of such nightmares, and lifts us into the atmosphere of perfect freedom.

No one in the play understands Falstaff fully, any more than Hamlet was understood by the persons round him. They are both men of genius. Mrs. Quickly and Bardolph are his slaves, but they know not why. "Well, fare thee well," says the hostess whom he has pillaged and forgiven; "I have known thee these twenty-nine years, come peas-cod time, but an honester and truer-hearted man—well, fare thee well." Poins and the Prince delight in him; they get him into corners for the pleasure of seeing him escape in ways they cannot imagine; but they often take him much too seriously. Poins, for instance, rarely sees, the Prince does not always see, and moralising critics never see, that when Falstaff speaks ill of a companion behind his back, or writes to the Prince that Poins spreads it abroad that the Prince is to marry his sister, he knows quite well that what he says will be repeated, or rather, perhaps, is absolutely indifferent whether it be repeated or not, being certain that it can only give him an opportunity for humour. It is the same with his lying, and almost the same with his cowardice, the two main vices laid to his charge even by sympathisers. Falstaff is neither a liar nor a coward in the usual sense, like the typical cowardly boaster of comedy. He tells his lies either for their own humour, or on purpose to get himself into a difficulty. He rarely expects to be believed, perhaps never. He abandons a statement or contradicts it the moment it is made. There is scarcely more intent in his lying than in the humorous exaggerations which he pours out in soliloquy just as much as when others are by. Poins and the Prince understand this in part. You see them waiting eagerly to convict him, not that they may really put him to shame, but in order to enjoy the greater lie that will swallow up the less. But their sense of humour lags behind his. Even the Prince seems to accept as half-serious that remorse of his which passes so suddenly into glee at the idea of taking a purse, and his request to his friend to bestride him if he should see him down in the battle. Bestride Falstaff! "Hence! Wilt thou lift up Olympus?"

Again, the attack of the Prince and Poins on Falstaff and the other thieves on Gadshill is contrived, we know, with a view to the incomprehensible lies it will induce him to tell. But when, more than rising to the occasion, he turns two men in buckram into four, and then seven, and then nine, and then eleven, almost in a breath, I believe they partly misunderstand his intention, and too many of his critics misunderstand it altogether. Shakespeare was not writing a mere farce. It is preposterous to suppose that a man of Falstaff's intelligence would utter these gross, palpable, open lies with the serious intention to deceive, or forget that, if it was too dark for him to see his own hand, he could hardly see that the three misbegotten knaves were wearing Kendal green. No doubt, if he *had* been believed, he would have been hugely tickled at it, but he no more expected to be believed than when he claimed to have killed Hotspur. Yet he is supposed to be serious even then. Such interpretations would destroy the poet's whole conception; and of those who adopt them one might ask this out of some twenty similar questions: —When Falstaff, in the men in buckram scene, begins by calling twice at short intervals for sack, and then a little later calls for more and says, "I am a rogue if I drunk to-day," and the Prince answers, "O villain, thy lips are scarce wiped since thou drunk'st last," do they think that *that* lie was meant to deceive? And if not, why do they take it for granted that the others were? I suppose they consider that Falstaff was in earnest when, wanting to get twenty-two yards of satin on trust from Master Dombledon the silk-mercer, he offered Bardolph as security; or when he said to the Chief Justice about Mrs. Quickly, who accused him of breaking his promise to marry her, "My lord, this is a poor mad soul, and she says up and down the town that her eldest son is like you"; or when he explained his enormous bulk by exclaiming, "A plague of sighing and grief! It blows a man up like a bladder"; or when he accounted for his voice being cracked by declaring that he had "lost it with singing of anthems"; or even when he sold his soul on Good-Friday to the devil for a cup of Madeira and a cold capon's leg. Falstaff's lies about Hotspur and the men in buckram do not essentially differ from these statements. There is nothing serious in any of them except the refusal to take anything seriously.

This is also the explanation of Falstaff's cowardice, a subject on which I should say nothing if Maurice Morgann's essay [See Bantam edition, *Henry IV, Part I*, pp. 139-148], now more than a century old, were better known. That Falstaff sometimes behaves in what we should generally call a cowardly way is certain; but that does not show that he was a coward; and if the word means a person who feels painful fear in the presence of danger, and yields to that fear in spite of his better feelings and convictions, then assuredly Falstaff was no coward. The stock bully and boaster of comedy is one, but not Falstaff. It is perfectly clear in the first place that, though he had unfortunately a reputation for stabbing and caring not what mischief he did if his weapon were out, he had not a reputation for cowardice. Shallow remembered him five-and-fifty years ago breaking Scogan's head at the court-gate when he was a crack not thus high; and Shallow knew him later a good back-swordsman. Then we lose sight of him till about twenty years after, when his association with Bardolph began; and that association implies that by the time he was thirty-five or forty he had sunk into the mode of life we witness in the plays. Yet, even as we see him there, he remains a person of consideration in the army. Twelve captains hurry about London searching for him. He is present at the Council of War in the King's tent at Shrewsbury, where the only other persons are the King, the two princes, a nobleman and Sir Walter Blunt. The messenger who brings the false report of the battle to Northumberland mentions, as one of the important incidents, the death of Sir John Falstaff. Colvile, expressly described as a famous rebel, surrenders to him as soon as he hears his name. And if his own wish that his name were not so terrible to the enemy, and his own boast of his European reputation, are not evidence of the first rank, they must not be entirely ignored in presence of these other facts. What do these facts mean? Does Shakespeare put them all in with no purpose at all, or in defiance of his own intentions? It is not credible.

And when, in the second place, he look at Falstaff's actions, what do we find? He boldly confronted Colvile, he was quite ready to fight with him, however pleased that Colvile, like a kind fellow, gave himself away. When he saw Henry and Hotspur fighting, Falstaff, instead of making off in a panic, stayed to take his chance if Hotspur should be the victor. He *led* his hundred and fifty ragamuffins where they were peppered, he did not *send* them. To draw upon Pistol and force him downstairs and wound him in the shoulder was no great feat, perhaps, but the stock coward would have shrunk from it. When the Sheriff came to the inn to arrest him for an offence whose penalty was death, Falstaff, who was hidden behind the arras, did not stand there quaking for fear, he immediately fell asleep and snored. When he stood in the battle reflecting on what would happen if the weight of his paunch should be increased by that of a bullet, he cannot have been in a tremor of craven fear. He *never* shows such fear; and surely the man who, in danger of his life, and with no one by to hear him, meditates thus: "I like not such grinning honour as Sir Walter hath. Give me life: which if I can save, so; if not, honour comes unlooked-for, and there's an end," is not what we commonly call a coward.

"Well," it will be answered, "but he ran away on Gadshill; and when Douglas attacked him he fell down and shammed dead." Yes, I am thankful to say, he did. For of course he did not want to be dead. He wanted to live and be merry. And as he had reduced the idea of honour *ad absurdum*, had scarcely any self-respect, and only a respect for reputation as a means of life, naturally he avoided death when he could do so without a ruinous loss of reputation, and (observe) with the satisfaction of playing a colossal practical joke. For *that* after all was his first object. If his one thought had been to avoid death he would have have faced Douglas at all, but would have run away as fast as his legs could carry him; and unless Douglas had been one of those exceptional Scotchmen who have no sense of humour, he would never have thought of pursuing so ridiculous an object as Falstaff running. So that, as Mr. Swinburne remarks, Poins is right when he thus distinguishes Falstaff from his companions in robbery: "For two of them, I know them to be as true-bred cowards as ever turned back; and for the third, if he fight longer than he sees reason, I'll forswear arms." And the event justifies this distinction. For it is exactly thus that, according to the original stage-direction, Falstaff behaves when Henry and Poins attack him and the others. The rest run away at once; Falstaff, here as afterwards with Douglas, fights for a blow or two, but finding himself deserted and outmatched, runs away also. Of course. He saw no reason to stay. *Any* man who had risen superior to all serious motives would have run away. But it does not follow that he would run from mere fear, or be, in the ordinary sense, a coward.

3.

The main source, then, of our sympathetic delight in Falstaff is his humorous superiority to everything serious, and the freedom of soul enjoyed in it. But, of course, this is not the whole of his character. Shakespeare knew well enough that perfect freedom is not to be gained in this manner; we are ourselves aware of it even while we are sympathising with Falstaff; and as soon as we regard him seriously it becomes obvious. His freedom is limited in two main ways. For one thing he cannot rid himself entirely of respect for all that he professes to ridicule. He shows a certain pride in his rank: unlike the Prince, he is haughty to the drawers, who call him a proud Jack. He is not really quite indifferent to reputation. When the Chief Justice bids him pay his debt to Mrs. Quickly for his reputation's sake, I think he feels a twinge, though to be sure he proceeds to pay her by borrowing from her. He is also stung by any thoroughly serious imputation on his courage, and winces at the recollection of his running away on Gadshill; he knows that his behaviour there certainly looked cowardly, and perhaps he remembers that he would not have behaved so once. It is, further, very significant that, for all his dissolute talk, he has never yet allowed the Prince and Poins to *see* him as they saw him afterwards with Doll Tearsheet; not, of course, that he has any moral shame in the matter, but he knows that in such a situation he, in his old age, must appear contemptible—not a humorist but a mere object of mirth. And, finally, he has affection in him—affection, I think, for Poins and Bardolph, and certainly for the Prince; and that is a thing which he cannot jest out of existence. Hence, as the effect of his rejection shows, he is not really invulnerable. And then, in the second place, since he is in the flesh, his godlike freedom has consequences and conditions; consequences, for there is something painfully wrong with his great toe; conditions, for he cannot eat and drink for ever without money, and his purse suffers from consumption, a disease for which he can find no remedy. As the Chief Justice tells him, his means are very slender and his waste great; and his answer, "I would it were otherwise; I would my means were greater and my waist slenderer," though worth much money, brings none in. And so he is driven to evil deeds; not only to cheating his tailor like a gentleman, but to fleecing Justice Shallow, and to highway robbery, and to cruel depredations on the poor woman whose affection he has secured. All this is perfectly consistent with the other side of his character, but by itself it makes an ugly picture.

Yes, it makes an ugly picture when you look at it seriously. But then, surely, so long as the humorous atmosphere is preserved and the humorous attitude maintained, you do not look at it so. You no more regard Falstaff's misdeeds morally than you do the much more atrocious misdeeds of Punch or Reynard the Fox. You do not exactly ignore them, but you attend only to their comic aspect. This is the very spirit of comedy, and certainly of Shakespeare's comic world, which is one of make-believe, not merely as his tragic world is, but in a further sense—a world in which gross improbabilities are accepted with a smile, and many things are welcomed as merely laughable which, regarded gravely, would excite anger and disgust. The intervention of a serious spirit breaks up such a world, and would destroy our pleasure in Falstaff's company. Accordingly through the greater part of these dramas Shakespeare carefully confines this spirit to the scenes of war and policy, and dismisses it entirely in the humorous parts. Hence, if *Henry IV.* had been a comedy like *Twelfth Night*, I am sure that he would no more have ended it with the painful disgrace of Falstaff than he ended *Twelfth Night* by disgracing Sir Toby Belch.

But *Henry IV.* was to be in the main a historical play, and its chief hero Prince Henry. In the course of it his greater and finer qualities were to be gradually revealed, and it was to end with beautiful scenes of reconciliation and affection between his father and him, and a final emergence of the wild Prince as a just, wise, stern, and glorious King. Hence, no doubt, it seemed to Shakespeare that Falstaff at last must be disgraced, and must therefore appear no longer as the invincible humorist, but as an object of ridicule and even of aversion. And probably also his poet's insight showed him that Henry, as he conceived him, *would* behave harshly to Falstaff in order to impress the world, especially when his mind had been wrought to a high pitch by the scene with his dying father and the impression of his own solemn consecration to great duties.

This conception was a natural and a fine one; and if the execution was not an entire success, it is yet full of interest. Shakespeare's purpose being to work a gradual change in our feelings towards Falstaff, and to tinge the humorous atmosphere more and more deeply with seriousness, we see him carrying out this purpose in the Second Part of *Henry IV.* Here he separates the Prince from Falstaff as much as he can, thus withdrawing him from Falstaff's influence, and weakening in our minds the connection between the two. In the First Part we constantly see them together; in the Second (it is a remarkable fact) only once before the rejection. Further, in the scenes where Henry appears apart from Falstaff, we watch him growing more and more grave, and awakening more and more poetic interest; while Falstaff, though his humour scarcely flags to the end, exhibits more and more of his seamy side. This is nowhere turned to the full light in Part I.; but in Part II. we see him as the heartless destroyer of Mrs. Quickly, as a ruffian seriously defying the Chief Justice because his position as an officer on service gives him power to do wrong, as the pike preparing to snap up the poor old dace Shallow, and (this is the one scene where Henry and he meet) as the worn-out lecher, not laughing at his servitude to the flesh but sunk in it. Finally, immediately before the rejection, the world where he is king is exposed in all its sordid criminality when we find Mrs. Quickly and Doll arrested for being concerned in the death of one man, if not more, beaten to death by

their bullies; and the dangerousness of Falstaff is empha-
sised in his last words as he hurries from Shallow's house to
London, words at first touched with humour but at bottom
only too seriously meant: "Let us take any man's horses; the
laws of England are at my commandment. Happy are they
which have been my friends, and woe unto my Lord Chief
Justice." His dismissal to the Fleet by the Chief Justice is the
dramatic vengeance for that threat.

Yet all these excellent devices fail. They cause us momen-
tary embarrassment at times when repellent traits in Falstaff's character are disclosed; but they fail to change our
attitude of humour into one of seriousness, and our sympathy into repulsion. And they were bound to fail, because
Shakespeare shrank from adding to them the one device
which would have ensured success. If, as the Second Part of
Henry IV. advanced, he had clouded over Falstaff's humour
so heavily that the man of genius turned into the Falstaff of
the *Merry Wives,* we should have witnessed his rejection
without a pang. This Shakespeare was too much of an artist
to do—though even in this way he did something—and
without this device he could not succeed. As I said, in the
creation of Falstaff he overreached himself. He was caught
up on the wind of his own genius, and carried so far that
he could not descend to earth at the selected spot. It is not
a misfortune that happens to many authors, nor is it one we
can regret, for it costs us but a trifling inconvenience in one
scene, while we owe it to perhaps the greatest comic character in literature. For it is in this character, and not in the
judgment he brings upon Falstaff's head, that Shakespeare
asserts his supremacy. To show that Falstaff's freedom of
soul was in part illusory, and that the realities of life refused
to be conjured away by his humour—this was what we
might expect from Shakespeare's unfailing sanity, but it was
surely no achievement beyond the power of lesser men. The
achievement was Falstaff himself, and the conception of that
freedom of soul, a freedom illusory only in part, and attain-
able only by a mind which had received from Shakespeare's
own the inexplicable touch of infinity which he bestowed
on Hamlet and Macbeth and Cleopatra, but denied to Henry
the Fifth.

* * *

J. DOVER WILSON (1881–   )

Wilson is a graduate of Caius College of Cambridge University. He has long been Regius Professor of Rhetoric and English Literature at the University of Edinburgh. He is one of the keenest and most resourceful of contemporary critics of Shakespeare. His work is always brilliant and original and often controversial. Some of his best known works are *The Elizabethan Shakespeare* (1929), *The Essential Shakespeare* (1932), *What Happens in "Hamlet"* (1935), *The Meaning of "The Tempest"* (1939), and *The Fortunes of Falstaff* (1944).

FALSTAFF HIGH ON FORTUNE'S WHEEL
(from: *The Fortunes of Falstaff*, 1944)

. . . Consider first the situation in which the battle of Shrewsbury leaves the round knave [Falstaff]. His claim to the honours of the field, though jestingly phrased, is seriously advanced, and an ample reward demanded. "There is Percy!" he cries, pitching the body off his back at the feet of the amazed Prince, who having just breathed an epitaph over the prostrate form of his "old acquaintance," thinks for a moment that a ghost stands before him; "There is Percy! If your father will do me any honour, so; if not, let him kill the next Percy himself. I look to be either earl or duke, I can assure you." And having secured a promise of support from the good-humoured Prince, who then goes off with his brother John to survey the battlefield, Falstaff concludes the scene with this brief soliloquy, which forms his last words in Part I:

I'll follow, as they say, for reward. He that rewards me, God reward him! If I do grow great, I'll grow less, for I'll purge, and leave sack, and live cleanly as a nobleman should do.

As far as I am aware, no one has ever asked what reward, if any, he receives, or whether he ever attempts to make good this hint of adjusting his behaviour to his increased importance in the public eye. Yet Shakespeare develops both points in the very next Falstaff scene. Why have they been overlooked? Because that scene, being the second scene of

Part II, has been thought of as *belonging to another play*, only distantly connected with words and events at Shrewsbury, of which we read in the penultimate scene of Part I. On the other hand, once the connection is made, it becomes obvious that Falstaff's conduct at the beginning of Part II will be inexplicable to an audience, unless they have his exact situation and actual words at Shrewsbury fresh in mind. In short, Part II was written to be played immediately, or at not more than twenty-four hours' interval, after Part I. It is the most telling proof among many of the theatrical and dramatic unity of the two parts.

And when we turn to consider this second scene of Part II, we are met with a transformed Falstaff, a transformation which should, I believe, be marked in the way such things are apt to be marked in the theatre, by a startling change of costume. "Enter Sir John alone, with his page bearing his sword and buckler" is the stage-direction the Quarto gives for him. The diminutive page, probably played by the same boy who takes the part of tiny sprightly Maria in *Twelfth Night*, has, we shortly afterwards learn, been presented by the Prince to serve as squire to Falstaff's new-furbished knighthood; with an eye, as Falstaff himself points out, to the ludicrous contrast the pair will make, as the boy waits at his heels. The effect is all the more ludicrous that the little squire comes on carrying the immense sword and buckler which denote his master's knightly dignity. Falstaff does not carry his own sword for an excellent reason. He cannot, because he enters hobbling upon a stick; he is, in fact, playing the wounded hero, though we discover at the end of the scene that the true cause of his halting is gout, or pox, and that he is turning "diseases to commodity." And not being able to carry a sword, he is dressed, no longer as a soldier, but as Elizabethan gentlemen dressed in civil life. In short, I suggest, his first appearance on the stage since Shrewsbury shows him to us as the complete courtier, or as we should now put it, man about town; that is to say, fashionably, fantastically, hilariously decked out, according to the very latest and most foppish cut, yards and yards and yards of it, with some absurdity of a cap to crown the sartorial edifice. All his entries were, no doubt, the subject of much thought on the part of the presiding genius of the tiring-room, and such a costume would bring the house down before he opened his lips. It would carry important dramatic implications also, since it immediately apprises the audience, reminded of Shrewsbury by the wounded hero touch, of the changed status and social aspirations foreshadowed at the end of Part I, while it provides a visible focus for the hints of this change to be now dropped.

For, whatever be his costume, the dialogue shows without a doubt that he is cutting a figure in the world. The resolution to "purge," made on the battlefield, has developed: he has taken to consulting doctors and even to reading Galen on his own account. And to be a valetudinarian is to display the hall-mark of gentility, as we have already learnt from Hotspur's popinjay, if we need to be taught so persistent a fact of human nature. He has, also, a fashionable complaint, whichever of the two it may be he suffers from; and the evident irritability of his temper, with a visible twinge or two perhaps, should inform the audience, long before he names the alternative possibilities, that the bandages about the foot conceal an inflammation not caused by wounds. In a word, there is something of the gouty colonel of a later age in this old soldier and Shrewsbury champion. The Prince, he testily remarks, is almost out of his favour, which implies maybe that the "reward" hoped for in Part I has not come up to expectations. We are told towards the end of the scene that it is a "pension," and its inadequacy is revealed by the state of the pensioner's purse. Yet a pension, even if always spent before receipt, has its uses, at any rate as a basis for credit; and it is clear that he is busy equipping himself on the strength of it. The outburst against that "whoreson Achitophel" Master Dommelton, who refuses to accept Bardolph as a surety in the matter of a purchase of satin for a short cloak and slops—the first really ill-tempered speech we have had from the jovial knight—is an indication that he is furnishing himself with a wardrobe; and Mistress Quickly gives further hints of the same sort in his next scene when she speaks of his dining with Master Smooth, the silkman, and of his calling on the way thither at Pye Corner to buy a saddle, no doubt for the horse he has previously commissioned Bardolph to purchase in Smithfield. He even seems to be contemplating marriage, though apparently hesitating whether to bestow the style of "Lady Falstaff" on Mistress Quickly, old Mistress Ursula, whom he had weekly sworn to marry since he perceived the first white hair on his chin, or some proper gentlewoman from the stews. Here is a Falstaff moving in a very different element from that of highway robbery and purse-taking, to which he belongs in Part I.

"IF I DO GROW GREAT, I'LL GROW LESS"

He is different in other ways too. There is nothing in Part II to equal the sheer delight of the first Boar's Head scene. Yet he is no less brilliant or entertaining on the whole. But the entertainment has shifted its centre of gravity. We laugh as much as ever, but no longer in the heart, or with the thought "were't not for laughing, I should pity him." We find his wit no less fascinating, but he begins to inspire less affection. His impudence and effrontery increase: he remains as ever imperturbable, and the "gout" after doing duty in the first scene is heard of no more; but with our pleasure at his sallies and our admiration for his intellect there is mingled a spice, and presently more than a spice, of critical detachment. The difference, which is subtle but profound, felt only gradually but becoming more and more unmistakable, is best described by saying that he passes from the realm of the humorous into that of the comic.

Falstaff is his own chief theme throughout, and the change just noted is well exemplified by comparing his treatment of this theme in the two Parts. In Part I the staple of his jesting is his moral weaknesses and physical disabilities. He is ready with mock-apology for his sins and for his size, with affectations of holiness and patter about repentance. It is sighing and grief that has blown him up like a bladder; he has more flesh than another man and therefore more frailty; and if he has forgotten what the inside of a church is made of, it is company, villainous company, that has been the spoil of him. The appeal to our laughter is made in the name of helplessness, bodily and spiritual. We are asked to contemplate him staggering along life's way, with his broken wind, although eight yards of its uneven ground is to him what a pilgrimage of threescore and ten miles would be to anyone else; and which villain among us is stony-hearted enough to turn a deaf ear, sheer blarney as we know it all to be? And there is a subtler side to it, well brought out by John Bailey. "What specially wins our love" for Falstaff, he declares, is that he, "at his most triumphant times, is triumphant at his own expense. If he did not know that he was a gross tun of flesh, a drunkard, a coward, and a liar, we should know it much more and love him much less. Here, as in religion, the way of confession is the way of forgiveness. And forgiving is very near loving."

Both apology and confession belong to Part I; not a trace of either is to be found in Part II; even the plea of old age, which he turns to such eloquent account in the address "in the behalf of that Falstaff" at the Boar's Head, is disclaimed, except once in a tender moment with Doll. When Bradley writes, "Instead of being comic to you and serious to himself, he is more ludicrous to himself than to you; and he makes himself out more ludicrous than he is in order that he and others may laugh," he is speaking, as he usually is, of the Falstaff of Part I. Of him the words are true enough; but the Falstaff of Part II *is* more ludicrous to us than to himself, while the only sport he makes of his own person is the picture he evokes of himself walking before his page "like a sow that hath overwhelmed all her litter but one," and a couple of quibbling asides about his waist and his "gravy" in the first scene with the Lord Chief Justice. Instead of exploiting or lamenting his weakness, he proclaims his wit. The new note—may we not call it the note of comic hubris?—is heard in his first words:

Men of all sorts take a pride to gird at me: the brain of this foolish-compounded clay, man, is not able to invent anything that intends to laughter, more than I invent, or is invented on me: I am not only witty in myself, but the cause that wit is in other men.

How often is that quoted in the *laudes Falstaffii* which too many know better than Shakespeare's *Henry IV*! And no wonder, for we have only to change the first into the third person and it might have been written in Falstaff's honour by Morgann or Bradley. Yet self-praise, apart from tributes to his own valour, not intended seriously, is something we have not had from Falstaff before. And I feel sure that Shakespeare gives him this piece of complacency by way of throwing, as Meredith would say, the oblique light of the comic muse upon him. If not, why does the fat man continue in the same vein, with scornful and patronizing remarks about the Prince, the victor of Shrewsbury, who out of pure friendship and kindness of heart has resigned all claim to the overthrow of Hotspur and has countenanced the fraud which is the only basis of those present pretensions?

As to the pretensions themselves, listen to the old turkey-cock strutting and puffing before the Lord Chief Justice, who makes polite reference to his impending service under Prince John:

There is not a dangerous action can peep out his head but I am thrust upon it. Well, I cannot last for ever, but it was always yet the trick of our English nation, if they have a good thing, to make it too common. If ye will needs say I am an old man, you should give me rest: I would to God my name were not so terrible to the enemy as it is.

Only half of this, of course, is believed by the speaker; but that half is enough to set the comic muse smiling. The words might almost have been written by Bernard Shaw for one of his numskull Englishmen.

Falstaff, Bradley tells us again, is able to reduce "the would-be serious things of life" to nothing by means of his wit and his gaiety, and so "to walk about free and rejoicing." True enough in the first Boar's Head scene; but in the scenes of Part II he is no longer free, for the simple reason that now he has begun to take something seriously, namely his own career and ambitions. It is all intensely funny, of course, and the wit, I repeat, is as brilliant as ever. But the best joke of all, a joke altogether lost if Part II be not enjoyed as an immediate continuation of Part I, is that the old mock-maudlin highwayman should have blossomed out into this preposterous, self-satisfied, pink of gentility. And the joke is one which Falstaff, for the first time in the play, is himself unconscious of.

Yet we too remain unconscious of where Shakespeare is taking us, until well on in Part II. In Part I Falstaff is the great Boon Companion of modern literature; by the end of its sequel he is seen to be an impossible companion for a king of England. But he remains the same exceedingly entertaining person throughout, with a like genius at command; and though (prying into the secrets of Shakespeare's art, in order to clear it of misunderstanding) I have put my finger on the false claim to Hotspur's corpse as the point at which the change of emphasis begins, no watcher in the theatre, or reader following the play scene by scene for the mere enjoyment of it, will detect this, or even become aware except insensibly that a change in his attitude is taking place at all, so delicately and by such fine degrees are the readjustments made upon the scales. Let him pass straight from the tavern scene after Gad's Hill to the finale outside Westminster Abbey, which is virtually what Bradley and his followers do, and he will, like them, find the rejection an outrage; whereas the same rejection, taken at its right point of dramatic time, that is after the whole play has been experienced in the order and under the conditions Shakespeare intended, becomes unexceptionable, even a happy solution.

Bradley sees clearly what Shakespeare had to do. He even admits that in Part II it was his purpose "to work a gradual change in our feelings towards Falstaff, and to tinge the humorous atmosphere more and more deeply with seriousness," and he notes many of the later stages in the attempt to carry this purpose out. The attempt fails, however, in his opinion, because the dramatist found himself incapable of alienating our sympathies from a character, in the creation of which he had "overreached himself." "If," he declares,

as the Second Part of *Henry IV* advanced, he had clouded over Falstaff's humour so heavily that the man of genius turned into the Falstaff of *The Merry Wives*, we should have witnessed his rejection without pang. This Shakespeare was too much of an artist to do—though even in this way he did something—and without this device he could not succeed.

That the "gradual change in our feelings" is aesthetic as well as moral, comic before it becomes serious, altogether escapes him, since he fails to catch sight of the nimbus of ridicule that shines ever more brightly about the fat man's bald crown as Part II proceeds. It was not necessary to transform Falstaff into the fatuous laughing-stock of *The Merry Wives* in order to make a success of *Henry IV*. Shakespeare is a greater artist than Bradley takes him for, and knows subtler ways of regulating the sympathies of his audience. At the beginning of *Richard II* he presents us with the portrait of an insolent young tyrant; before the play is over he has us mourning the same man as St Richard, King and Martyr. With Falstaff the process is reversed: our sympathies, at their height in Part I, have largely ebbed away by the end of Part II. But, though a narrow examination can fix the turning-point at the passage from one to the other, it is, like the turn of the tides, invisible to the eye of a spectator.

In the theatre, which is the ultimate tribunal for matters of this kind, the question is how Falstaff should be acted, even what are to be the tones of his voice. Bradley implies that he should be played in Part II exactly as he was in Part I, since he draws the evidence upon which he builds up his conception of the character indiscriminately from both parts, without noticing traits which mark a change. Thus he refuses to see—or rather, to hear—his pettiness, his irascibility, his self-importance, and what Hudson well calls "the arrogance" of his "utter impunity." And his followers are equally blind or deaf to such tones. The issue must, I say, be left to the players in the last resort. But an encouraging feature of twentieth-century Shakespearian productions is that the players have begun to look for help to the scholars, while the scholars, on their side, are increasingly inclined to learn from the players. The present account of how one scholar believes Falstaff should be played in Part II is offered as a modest contribution to this symposium.

Before I continue, however, there are still one or two remarks of a sign-post character to be made. In the first place, as most critics have observed, whereas in Part I Falstaff is usually shown in the Prince's company, in Part II Shakespeare keeps their paths so far apart that they only meet once, before the final encounter outside the Abbey. This separation, dramatically accounted for as due to action by the King, taken at the suggestion of the Lord Chief Justice, is technically required for the presentation, not only, as we have seen, of the Prince's character, but also of Falstaff's. It is often remarked that the Prince's wit is at its best when Falstaff is there to bring it out; it is equally true that the presence of the Prince is the stimulus which transports Falstaff, and us with him, into that sphere where he moves as the happiest of jesters. He is, in short, at his most enchanting, when he is enchanting his patron. In Part II his intellectual powers are no less, but are devoted to other ends. In the second place, then, while we see a good deal more of him in Part II than in Part I, what we see may be called the normal Falstaff, the Falstaff who has to live by the clock, the Falstaff of mean shifts, who abuses the King's press more damnably than ever, who has all the tricks of the sharper or "cheater" at his fingers' ends. Thirdly, the touch of hubris already noted grows more marked as scene follows scene, until we become acutely conscious that the old scoundrel is riding for a fall. And, lastly, to underline all this, we find him brought into contact with the only man in England he really fears, the Lord Chief Justice.

THE LORD CHIEF JUSTICE AND MISTRESS DOROTHY TEARSHEET

The role of the Lord Chief Justice cannot, I think, be given its full dramatic weight by anyone who has not seen Part II in the theatre. Certainly, I had no notion of its importance until I witnessed a performance in April 1939 at the Schiller Theater, Berlin, with Heinrich George playing Falstaff, and playing him superbly. As far as my knowledge goes, the only writer hitherto to realize the significance of the Justice is Miss Muriel Bradbrook, who makes the interesting suggestion that "for the purposes of the stage" he "walked around in Cheapside in full robes of office" when the play was originally produced. Apart from his symbolical function in this Tudor morality, here for the first time in the drama is a personage whom Falstaff hates and detests. It takes him all he knows to keep his temper when they meet, and the urbane old gentleman crosses his path at awkward moments. The effect on the stage of this figure of majestic dignity and self-composure, and of Falstaff's unconcealed antagonism, is most striking. With those calm eyes upon him his "fool-born jests" seem to break and fall away, like spume beneath a rock; and we recognize that there is, after all, Law in England, and that Riot, for all his gaiety and impudence, has met his match. Speaking of the "comic world," with its "humorous atmosphere," in which he asserts Falstaff moves in both parts, Bradley writes: "The intervention of a serious spirit breaks up such a world, and would destroy our pleasure in Falstaff's company. Accordingly, through the greater part of these dramas Shakespeare carefully confines this spirit to the scenes of war and policy, and dismisses it entirely in the humorous parts." Had he ever seen the play upon the stage, he must, I think, have observed that, on the contrary, Shakespeare embodies this "serious spirit" in the person of the Lord Chief Justice, and that the character is made to intervene, solely in order to disturb, if not exactly to destroy, our pleasure in Falstaff's company. We begin to feel this at their first encounter.

Shakespeare often expresses in the words and actions of one character what he intends to make us feel, without intellectual formulation, about another. And by throwing Falstaff, at the opening of Part II, into the company of the Lord Chief Justice he brings him under the eyes of someone who sees him exactly as he is and will not hesitate to put it into words. The wicked old rascal does his best to avoid a meeting. Forgetting his gout, he bolts down a side-alley directly he catches sight of his enemy; he feigns deafness to his serving-man's calls, and when the "young knave" plucks him by the sleeve, pretends to take him for a beggar; lastly, finding he can no longer refuse to see the great man himself, he still keeps him at arm's length with talk of his lordship's health, of the King's return from Wales, of the royal apoplexy, of the nature of that disease, and so forth. Nor should the venom in his apparently innocent enquiries be overlooked: were the apoplexy he harps upon to prove fatal, the office, if not the life, of the judge might lie at the mercy of the heir apparent's favourite. For dexterous evasion and brilliant effrontery, Falstaff is at the very top of his form. Yet neither evasion nor effrontery will serve; in the end he is compelled to stand and listen.

My lord is courteous, for he is a great gentleman; on the whole, even lenient, since good soldiers are precious in times of danger, and this one is reputed to have done signal service at Shrewsbury; so that, in reply to the thrasonical brag already quoted, he dismisses him with the mild charge, "Well, be honest, and God bless your expedition." But he looks his man straight in the eyes, and is firm throughout, meeting the rogue's insolence with a sharp reminder that, while he holds his office, he has pains and penalties at his disposal. "This apoplexy," Falstaff insists, "as I take it, is a kind of lethargy, an't please your lordship," well knowing that nothing pleases his lordship less, "a kind of sleeping in blood, a whoreson tingling." Upon which follows this dialogue:

LORD CHIEF JUSTICE. What tell you me of it? be it as it is.

FALSTAFF. It hath it original from much grief, from study and perturbation of the brain. I have read the cause of his effects in Galen, it is a kind of deafness.

LORD CHIEF JUSTICE. I think you are fallen into the disease, for you hear not what I say to you.

FALSTAFF. Very well, my lord, very well—rather, an't please you, it is the disease of not listening, the malady of not marking, that I am troubled withal.

LORD CHIEF JUSTICE. To punish you by the heels would amend

the attention of your ears, and I care not if I do become your physician.

FALSTAFF. I am as poor as Job, my lord, but not so patient. Your lordship may minister the potion of imprisonment to me, in respect of poverty, but how I should be your patient to follow your prescriptions, the wise may make some dram of a scruple, or indeed a scruple itself.

LORD CHIEF JUSTICE. I sent for you, when there were matters against you for your life, to come and speak with me.

FALSTAFF. As I was then advised by my learned counsel in the laws of this land-service, I did not come.

This adroit use of the aegis of military service to ward off the arm of the civil law was a point which inns-of-court students would take with keen amusement; but what goes before is thrust and parry of naked steel, and those who claim the scene as a triumph for Falstaff, or as proof that "there is no gravity so firm but that he can thaw it into mirth," appear to miss Shakespeare's intentions entirely. The grave face smiles at times forbearingly, no doubt; but I can see no evidence of mirth. His quibbling "you are too impatient to bear crosses," uttered in reply to Falstaff's final fling, the pot-shot request for a loan of £1000, is sardonic pleasantry, implying that such an absurd demand is not to be taken seriously, nothing more. "Honours easy" should, I think, be the verdict upon this first round; and in the next the fat knight gets decidedly the worst of it.

This time the scene opens with a dialogue between Mistress Quickly and sheriff's officers, bearing the pleasing names Snare and Fang, from which it appears that she is about to have Falstaff arrested for debt. Her action is prompted, we may suppose, by the prospect of his departure for York. While he continued to use her house she might hope for small payments on account—I say hope, though there is no indication in either part that Falstaff ever pays down money for anything. She could reckon also on the custom of patrons like the Prince and Poins, whom he brought with him. But all this would come to an end with his leaving for the wars, while if he were killed she could look for nothing at all. It is not our first glimpse of the shifts by which he lives. In act 3, scene 3 of Part I she complains that he owes her £24, a debt which is now grown to over £65. Clearly he uses her as his banker, upon whom he overdraws to an unlimited extent, without troubling her with his newly won pension;

and yet, as we have seen, his purse is empty except for the seven groats and two pennies which the page turns out of it in scene 2. The arrest, with the scuffle between Bardolph and the officers, Mistress Quickly and the boy, provides plenty of stage-fun of the horse-play variety. It shows too a Falstaff ready for such emergencies; for no sooner does Fang pronounce the word "arrest" than he shouts, "Away, varlets! Draw, Bardolph, cut me off the villain's head, throw the quean into the channel," that is to say, into the gutter; cries, no doubt, which often resounded through the streets of Shakespeare's London, when catchpoles had desperadoes to deal with. A crowd hurries up, and the situation is just beginning to take on an ugly look, when "Enter the Lord Chief Justice and his men" to safeguard the King's peace; whereupon Quickly, called upon to explain the case, proceeds to do so after her rambling fashion.

Two facts emerge from this speech, of no relevance to her plea but of considerable dramatic interest: first, that Prince Hal had not long since found himself obliged to administer a thrashing to Falstaff "for liking his father to a singing-man of Windsor"; and second that, while his bruises were being tended on that occasion, Falstaff had sworn to make her his wife, borrowing thirty shillings at the same time. Equally revealing is the defendant's reply to these charges. "My lord," he explains, "this is a poor mad soul, and she says up and down the town that her eldest son is like you. She hath been in good case, and the truth is, poverty hath distracted her." This attempt to evade the issue, and alienate the sympathies of the Lord Chief Justice from her by suggesting that she claims him as the father of her child, is justly stigmatized by him as a "more than impudent sauciness" and countered in the stern summing-up:

You have, as it appears to me, practised upon the easy-yielding spirit of this woman, and made her serve your uses both in purse and person. . . . Pay her the debt you owe her, and unpay the villainy you have done with her. The one you may do with sterling money, and the other with current repentance.

The words are not the only hint in the play of intimate relations between Falstaff and Quickly, though (perhaps because the Folio text tones down the passage) no commentator seems to have noticed it, except Johnson, who reflects the episode in his description of Falstaff as "always ready to cheat the weak and prey upon the poor; to terrify the timorous and insult the defenceless." Thus long before we reach Doll Tearsheet, the seamy side of Falstaff's life is being exposed to our view. It is all implicit in Hal's summary of that life at their first meeting in Part I. But we may have forgotten about such matters in the bliss of Eastcheap; and in any case express particulars are far more telling, especially upon the stage, than general statement. That they are now being brought out is an indication that Shakespeare has begun to work upon our moral sensibilities.

While Falstaff, at his lordship's appeal to him as a man of "reputation," is patching it up with Quickly, Gower enters with letters containing more news of the King's return from Wales and of his sudden illness. After reading them, the Chief Justice questions Gower further on these grave matters. At which point, Falstaff, now disengaged, tries to thrust himself into the conversation. Three times he makes the attempt, and is ignored on each occasion by the preoccupied and anxious old statesman. Nettled at this supposed affront, he buttonholes Gower in his turn and stages a tit-for-tat by pretending to be totally deaf when the Chief Justice addresses remarks to him. It is a feeble revenge, and is dismissed by the intended victim, when he is able to grasp what it is all about, with the smiling but caustic words, "Now the Lord lighten thee! thou art a great fool." In the eyes of serious persons, and against a background of state affairs (which is to be the Prince's background when he becomes king), Falstaff is a very trivial sort of creature. And how absurd is Vanity, when it attempts to fence with Justice!

* * *

H. B. CHARLTON (1890–1960)

Charlton, for many years Professor of English at the University of Manchester, was a distinguished scholar, critic, and popular lecturer on Shakespeare and other dramatists of the English Renaissance. His method is to make shrewd comment on individual scenes and situations and to present searching analysis of the principal characters, notably of Falstaff. His principal works are *Senecan Tradition in Renaissance Tragedy* (1946), *Shakespearian Tragedy* (1949) and *Shakespearian Comedy*.

FALSTAFF'S TRIUMPH OVER THE TRADITIONAL ROLE OF
BRAGGART SOLDIER AND CLOWN
(from: *Shakespearian Comedy*, 1938)

Our argument is solely with true Jack Falstaff, old Jack
Falstaff, Shakespeare's Jack Falstaff; with his forbears, or indeed with his own pre-play proclivities, when he was not an
eagle's talon in the waist and could have crept into any alder-
man's thumb-ring, we have no concern whatever. Yet not
all his genealogists have had a limitedly historic object. Behind many of their attempts to trace his family tree, there
is a hope that a knowledge of his ancestry may help to
interpret the character of the man himself, and that in this
way, light may be thrown on what Shakespeare deliberately
or intuitively meant him to be. In particular, most of these
critics seeks to help criticism to extricate itself from a dilemma in which all who are attached both to Shakespeare
and to Falstaff find themselves involved, a dilemma which
reaches its climax in Henry V's callous rejection of the old
man who has been his intimate confederate in an incessant
round of escapades—

> the nimble-footed madcap Prince of Wales
> And his comrades, that daff'd the world aside,
> And bid it pass.

It is a scene which has aroused more repugnance than any
other in Shakespeare. Henry IV is dead, and Hal succeeds to
the Crown. In earlier days there had been much merry talk
between Falstaff and Hal, anticipating their gay doings
"when thou, sweet wag, art king." Falstaff is at Mr. Justice
Shallow's in Gloucestershire when Pistol brings news of
Henry IV's death. Falstaff sees all his dreams come true.
"Away, Bardolph! saddle my horse. Master Robert Shallow,
choose what office thou wilt in the land, 'tis thine. Pistol, I
will double-charge thee with dignities." "I know the young
king is sick for me. Let us take any man's horses; the laws
of England are at my commandment." He comes to London,
and without waiting to deck himself for court, puts himself
in Hal's way, "to stand stained with travel, and sweating
with desire to see him; thinking of nothing else, putting all
affairs else in oblivion, as if there were nothing else to be
done but to see him." The king and his train enter, to be

greeted rapturously by Falstaff. "God save thy grace, King Hal! my royal Hal! . . . God save thee, my sweet boy." But the king does not even speak to him; he commands the Lord Chief Justice, Falstaff's old enemy, to convey the royal message—"My lord chief-justice, speak to that vain man." Falstaff is completely nonplussed. "*My* king! my Jove! *I* speak to thee, my heart." Then he hears from Hal's own lips:

> I know thee not, old man: fall to thy prayers;
> How ill white hairs become a fool and jester!
> I have lond dream'd of such a kind of man,
> So surfeit-swell'd, so old and so profane;
> But, being awaked, I do despise my dream.

He hears himself banished in moral strains he has only once heard spoken by that voice before—and then it had been in open fooling:

> When thou dost hear I am as I have been,
> Approach me, and thou shalt be as thou wast,
> The tutor and the feeder of my riots:
> Till then, I banish thee, on pain of death,
> As I have done the rest of my misleaders,
> Not to come near our person by ten mile.

There is a faint speck of material consolation:

> For competence of life I will allow you,
> That lack of means enforce you not to evil:
> And as we hear you do reform yourselves,
> We will, according to your strengths and qualities,
> Give you advancement.

But even this appears in the immediate sequel as a further stroke of callous cruelty. For, at once, the Lord Chief Justice returns and orders his officers to carry Sir John to the Fleet prison. If anything further be needed to make this treatment odious, it is Lancaster's approval of it—"I like this fair proceeding of the King's!" for Lancaster has just previously performed a most opprobrious act of treachery, or rather of Bolingbrokian political strategy: he has deluded the rebels into accepting seemingly honourable terms, to find themselves haled off to execution. It appears indeed as if the family morals are in the blood of all of them, Henry IV, Henry V and Lancaster. Falstaff knew them for what they were. When Lancaster jibes at his capture of Colevile—"It was more of his courtesy than your deserving," Falstaff has the right rebuke ready. "I know not: here he is, and here I yield him: and I beseech your grace, let it be booked with the rest of this day's deeds; or, by the Lord, I will have it in a particular ballad else, with mine own picture on the top on't, Colevile kissing my foot: to the which course, if I be enforced, if you do not all show like gilt two-pences to me, and I in the clear sky of fame o'ershine you as much as the full moon doth the cinders of the element, which show like pin's heads to her, believe not the word of the noble: therefore let me have right, and let desert mount."

Yet he had thought that Hal was different from his family, as indeed Hal had so far been different. "Good faith, this same young sober-blooded boy [Lancaster] doth not love me; nor a man cannot make him laugh; but that's no marvel, he drinks no wine. . . . Hereof comes it that Prince Harry is valiant; for the cold blood he did naturally inherit of his father, he hath, like lean, sterile and bare land, manured, husbanded and tilled with excellent endeavour of drinking good and good store of fertile sherris that he is become very hot and valiant."

With hardly a dissentient voice, the later world has scorned Hal for his offence against humanity. Mr. Masefield lets it colour all Henry V's subsequent deeds, and writes him down for a heartless schemer. "Prince Henry is not a hero, he is not a thinker, he is not even a friend; he is a common man whose incapacity for feeling enables him to change his habits whenever interest bids him. Throughout the first acts he is careless and callous though he is breaking his father's heart and endangering his father's throne. He chooses to live in society as common as himself. He talks continually of guts as though a belly were a kind of wit. Even in the society of his choice his attitude is remote and cold-blooded. There is no good-fellowship in him, no sincerity, no wholeheartedness. He makes a mock of the drawer who gives him his whole little pennyworth of sugar. His jokes upon Falstaff are so little good-natured that he stands upon his princehood whenever the old man would retort upon him. He impresses one as quite common, quite selfish, quite without feeling. When he learns that his behaviour may have lost him his prospective crown he passes a sponge over his past, and fights like a wild cat for the right of not having to work for a living."

There is scarcely a reader who will not sympathise with Mr. Masefield's attitude, though perhaps few would press the case so far. It is indeed hardly thinkable that Shakespeare expected us to feel so bitterly against Prince Hal. Yet it is equally unthinkable that our feelings towards him can remain sympathetically genial.

Doubtless, Shakespeare's problem is inherent in his story. Legend and history affirmed that after a riotous youth, Prince Hal reformed himself into the noble Henry V. The old play of *The Famous Victories* chooses that as its main theme. It opens with the Prince and his associates, Ned and Tom, and, after a second's delay, Sir John Oldcastle also, rejoicing in the proceeds of a highway robbery by which they have relieved the King's Receivers of a thousand pounds. Hal invites them to adjourn to "the olde taverne in Eastcheape; there is good wine, and besides there is a pretie wench that can talke well." Later, we hear how they enjoyed themselves. "This night, about two houres ago, there came the young Prince, and three or foure more of his companions, and called for wine good store; and then they sent for a noyse of musitians, and were very merry for the space of an houre; then, whether their musicke liked them not, or whether they had drunke too much wine or no, I cannot tell, but our pots flue against the wals; and then they drew their swordes and went into the streete and fought, and some tooke one part and some tooke another; but for the space of halfe an houre there was such a bloodie fray as passeth." They are arrested and carried to the Counter prison. The King hears of his son's arrest, and forgives the officers for it, though he makes them put in a full plea in extenuation of their audacity—"Althogh he be a rude youth, and likely to give occasion, yet you might have considered that he is a prince, and my sonne, and not to be halled to prison by every subject." He has the roysterers released, after uttering a brief lament over his son: "thrice-accursed Harry, that hath gotten a sonne which with greefe will end his fathers dayes." In a short time, the Prince is bullying a judge who will not acquit one of the Prince's men; he ends by giving him the famous box on the ear, for which the judge has him haled off to the Fleet prison. Soon, however, he is out again, frolicking with his rowdy companions, and vowing what gay times they will have when he is king. He hears that his father "lies verie sicke," and sets off at once for the court, gleefully declaring that "the breath shal be no sooner out of his [father's] mouth but I wil clap the crowne on my head." Going out, he alludes for the first time in the play, to the reformation expected of his character, but does not for a moment countenance the notion; indeed, he roundly scoffs at it. "But thers som wil say the yoong Prince will be 'a well toward yoong man'— and all this geare, that I had as leeve they would breake my head with a pot as to say any such thing." At court, the sick King is lamenting his son's dissoluteness. "Oh my sonne! my sonne! no sooner out of one prison but into another? I had thought once-whiles I had lived to have seene this noble realme of England flourish by thee, my sonne; but now I see it goes to ruine and decaie." The reprobate prince enters his father's house, noisily, blusteringly, wearing a sort of motley and brandishing a dagger. Weeping, his father up-braids him for his deeds and for following this "wilde and reprobate company." In a flash, the prince repents: "my conscience accuseth me." "And those vilde and reprobate companions, I abandon and utterly abolish their company for ever! Pardon, sweete father! pardon!" When he is afraid that his father will not at once forgive him, he says, "I will go take me into some solitarie place, and there lament my sinfull life; and when I have done, I will laie me downe and die." His penitence is absolute, complete, and permanent. Approaching his sleeping father, and thinking him dead, he reverently carries away the crown, saying that he will weep day and night to atone for his former negli-gence. The King, however, is not really dead. Missing the crown, he suspects the prince, but is at once reassured of the latter's motives, and determines to crown him forth-with. Doing so, he dies. On the prince's succession, his old friends rush into his presence to secure the anticipated prizes. But it is now a new Henry. "Oh, how it did me good to see the King when he was crowned," says Oldcastle; "Me-thought his seate was like the figure of heaven, and his person like unto a god." But another of the gang suspects another sort of change; "who would have thought that the King would have changed his countenance so?" They soon know how different things now are—and forthwith are turned off. "I prethee, Ned, mend thy maners, and be more modester in thy tearmes. . . . Thou saist I am changed; so I am indeed. . . . Your former life greeves me, and makes me to abandon and abolish your company for ever. And therefore; not upon pain of death to approach my presence by ten miles space. Then, if I heare wel of you, it may be I wil do somewhat for you; otherwise looke for no more favour at my hands then at any other mans."

Such is the stuff of *The Famous Victories* where it is nearest to Shakespeare's material. But it will be seen that its anonymous author has not caught himself in Shakespeare's difficulties. He has simply taken successive episodes from the familiar tale and staged them. At its face value, the story was sufficiently amusing; he saw no need, and perhaps had no art, really to dramatise it. Hal's sudden and complete change of character would be accepted as a sort of Pauline conversion attested by history. There was no need to prepare for it; indeed, he could make Hal himself laugh at the mere thought of its possibility. Credible through legend, there was no obvious obligation to make it convincing by characterisation. But that was not Shakespeare's way. With him, the deed was always a trial of the man. Stage figures, driven hither and thither at the command of the plot, were almost as contemptible in his eyes as was a brewer's horse to Falstaff, a mere thing which at a tug of the rein suffers itself to pull away from the delectable and substantial stuff behind it and therefore always behind it. Shakespeare's characters are incessantly striving to break into life. Dramatically this lends a larger dare to his great enterprise. But it has its greater hazards. Hal's conversion must be grounded in character. To make it credible and consonant with Henry V, it must follow a deliberate motive or an unconscious but convincing prompting from the stuff of his nature. Hence the cumulative priggishness of the young roysterer. His attempts to salve in words the long-grown wounds of his intemperance, his plea that he is only upholding the unyoked humour of his idle confederates for a while, his admission that he is deliberately experimenting, toying with a political practice to falsify men's hopes, and, by reformation, ultimately to show more goodly—all this is an offence against humanity, and an offence which dramatically never becomes a skill. The noble change which he has so elaborately purposed is an unconscionable trick. Every time he invites us to weigh his follies with the purpose, he displays a revolting alacrity in sinking from our esteem. His grace is clearly saying that against which our flesh rebels. Retrospectively, even his follies lose something of their savour. To secure a charge of foot for Falstaff, for whom, afoot, "eight yards of uneven ground is three score and ten miles," is a rollicking but heartless joke, without the zest which was in the hiding of his horse when the job in hand was the highway robbery. It is easy for Hal on a plea that he is of all the humours that have showed themselves humours since the old days of goodman Adam, to demonstrate in act that the drawer is a fellow of fewer words than a parrot. But when triumph is so easily secured, onlookers may remember that the victim is yet the son of a woman, and that, as "his industry is upstairs and down-stairs," Hal is heartlessly endangering the poor drawer's means of subsistence. One prefers to cling to the figure which Vernon saw, the prince who acted with a restrained dignity

> which became him like a prince indeed;
> He made a blushing cital of himself;
> And chid his truant youth with such a grace
> As if he master'd there a double spirit
> Of teaching and of learning instantly.
> There did he pause: but let me tell the world,
> If he outlive the envy of this day,
> England did never owe so sweet a hope.

Or even more pleasantly, one chooses to recall his spontaneous offer to lie his hardest for Falstaff's sake:

> For my part, if a lie may do thee grace,
> I'll gild it with the happiest terms I have.

Perhaps it would have been better if Shakespeare had stinted preparation, letting the conversion come through the stress of present circumstance, almost indeed as it does come, when, in his new dignity as King, he swears to the Lord Chief Justice that the memory of the suffering he has caused his father shall instigate his own regeneration:

> My father is gone wild into his grave,
> For in his tomb lie my affections;
> ... The tide of blood in me
> Hath proudly flow'd in vanity till now:

> Now doth it turn and ebb back to the sea,
> Where it shall mingle with the state of floods
> And flow henceforth in formal majesty.

But, on his own plea, it is the end which tries the man. The end is his rejection of Falstaff. And after that, even the wicked will not readily fall in love with him. It seems a safe guess that such a Hal, so false to Falstaff, will of that seed grow to a greater falseness. If indeed, a greater falseness is within the scope of conjecture.

For Shakespeare's art could not use the semblance of flesh without vitalising it into life. Hal's reprobates would in their turn come nearer to humanity than is a shotten-herring or a stage-puppet. These rascals cannot be swept away to suit the plot, and one of them in particular, though he would be a fool and a coward but for inflammation, has pledged himself so deeply into our affections, that his fate angers us to the heart.

There appears to be no escape from the fact. This huge mass of flesh, this Sir John, has distorted the drift of the historic story and of the deliberate plan of Shakespeare's play. He has converted an intended hero into a heartless politician, and a happy ending into a revolting conclusion. How is such a critical predicament to be avoided?

The most specious way is Stoll's. He denies that there is a real predicament. We only think there is because we are merely amateur, not "professional," critics. We are ignorant of technique and of historic development; and, feeling the dilemma, we betray a total misapprehension of dramatic methods. Falstaff is a comic character, and nothing more; as good playgoers, we should imitate the Elizabethans and ask no more. Everything that Falstaff does or says is part of the type which Shakespeare is undertaking to exhibit (and presumably has so informed Mr. Stoll directly). It is all so simple, got with much ease. And Mr. Stoll seems impregnable in his panoply of illustrative foot-notes from plays of every age and every nation.

But, one feels prompted to ask, did Shakespeare only write for professional critics? And for those of his day, or those of ours? Is Falstaff a figure for the Elizabethans only, and for those rare people of our own day who have persuaded themselves that they are seeing him historically? And though admittedly the play's the thing, is it a critical sin, when one has seen it and been moved by it, to let the mind dwell on what has been seen? Moreover, even if one can be so certain of what the limits of a dramatic type are, are they so sacrosanct that the characterisation of one of them is merely the adoption of a tradition? Is a dramatist only a stage-carpenter, knocking a play together according to a convention, or is he a creative artist with his own apprehensions of life, and, so far as his material permits, with his own distinctive technique? And why indeed does Falstaff still abide with us of these later times? Why moreover, do we, taking Shakespeare as him to whom we owe our own deepest flashes of insight into human nature, why do we, here and now, protest that he has been untrue to posterity's sense of mortal values? Even to say that Falstaff is a "comic" character is to state a problem, not to give an answer. Wherein comic, and why one of the greatest of comic characters?

Other exponents of Falstaff, whilst not denying that his rejection is a real and legitimate problem for us, have sought to show that there could be no problem in him for Shakespeare's contemporaries. There is little harm, and little profit, in such demonstrations. It is certain that Mr. Spargo's attempt to explain Falstaff as a survival of the mediæval Vice whose rôle it was to be merry and in the end to be punished, involves a wild conjecture about Elizabethan audiences, and has no bearing whatever on the difficulties of a modern one. Mr. Tolman's is at least a more coherent and feasible proposal. Falstaff was created to make the reformed Hal an intelligible and dramatically satisfying figure. He fascinates Hal into evil and us into good humour. He is attractive enough to palliate Hal's roysterings and sufficiently repellent to justify the later Hal's break with him. There is nothing impossible in supposing this to have been Shakespeare's intention. But Mr. Tolman admits that if such was his intention, it went awry. Falstaff outgrew that function.

•   •   •   •   •   •   •   •   •   •   •   •

Being what he is, so gifted, so entirely and unswervingly devoted to his single purpose, Falstaff triumphs wherever he goes. Whatever the dilemma, whoever the opponent, Falstaff scores. He sees at a glance the stroke to play, half-sword or his old ward: but he has all strokes at command, and none can anticipate his rapid change from one to another. He never knows when he is beaten. He can wrench any true case the wrong way. He turns defence into attack, and at the end, by audacity and effrontery, he rises above his opponents with superb patronage and in complete victory. With a confident brow and a throng of words, or indeed, with but one word, he can reduce an opponent to abject insignificance, putting him in his proper place in a world of which Falstaff is natural king. "*I* call thee coward! I'll see thee damned ere I call thee coward; but I would give a thousand pound I could run as fast as thou canst." So much for Poins. A moment's notice is too much for Pistol. "Discharge yourself of our company, Pistol"; and when Pistol goes on brawling, Falstaff ignores him until, the noise becoming too uncomfortable, he rebukes him with Olympian brevity: "Pistol, I would be quiet." But Pistol is too far gone to heed. Bardolph is commanded to throw him out, but it soon appears that Falstaff himself will have to dispose of the roysterer. "Give me my rapier, boy," and then, to Pistol, "Get you downstairs." The ease and confidence of it is typical, and the economy. As with his capture of Coleville, there is marvellous thrift in his nice adaptation of means to the desired end: "Do ye yield, sir, or shall I sweat for you?"

A more sustained encounter is his play with the Lord Chief Justice: the pretended deafness; the impressively patriotic reproach to the servant; the strategic friendly concern for the justice's well-being; the deliberate mishearing, and then the bold confession of it; the polite hints that the Lord Chief Justice should ponder whether greater ones than he may not be implicated; then the bid for a sort of moral ascendancy in his own behalf; a patronising reference to the Justice's wisdom and the prince's rudeness; and, a last score, the recognised right of the soldier to round on the stay-at-home. The stupendous effrontery reaches its proper climax—"Will your lordship lend me a thousand pounds?"

Your Shallows, your hostesses, and your Dolls are easier victims. Falstaff merely shifts the responsibility for his debts on to the backs of his creditors; and, with an air of indefeasible righteousness, acts as if the size of his debt to it rendered him proprietor of the inn. "Shall I not take mine ease in mine inn but I shall have my pockets picked?" When Mrs. Quickly is competely exonerated from the charge he has brought against her, he reduces her to absolute subjection by forgiving her for the crime she has not committed. "Hostess, I forgive thee: go, make ready breakfast; love thy husband, look to thy servants, cherish thy guests: thou shalt find me tractable to any honest reason: thou seest I am pacified still." For such benign condescension, she will in the end pawn all she has, plate and gowns, to lend him money, and will commemorate the signal favour he is conferring on her in accepting it, by giving him a supper, and, at her own suggestion, inviting Doll, though she be a rival flame, to add to Sir John's joy at the feast.

. . . .

That is the way of Falstaff. He can wrest every circumstance to his own advantage.

. . . .

Yet in the end, Falstaff is rejected. Moreover, as Mr. Bradley has pointed out, though the rejection is devastatingly abrupt, yet, in retrospect, the Falstaff of the second part of *Henry IV* is somehow not the complete victor of the first part. His early frolics are the spontaneous and irrepressible exercise of his nature, scrapes and difficulties often sought for the zest of practising his genius for turning them to advantage. But the later escapades are schemes, deliberate plans forced on him by necessities as mean as any which drive a sharper living on his wits to exploit his sordid trickeries. Robbing the King's exchequer in Falstaff's early way is plainly his vocation; his thefts of later days are merely petty filching. The Gadshill robbery is "for sport's sake, to do the profession some grace." This is recreation. But practising upon the spineless spirit of Mrs. Quickly to make her purse serve his turn, is in another order of exploits. Indeed, after Shrewsbury, Falstaff is perpetually on the watch for gulls whom he can temper between his finger and his thumb and soften into disbursing. There may still be hints of former greatness in the economics of his recruiting scheme, though it is a damnable abuse of the King's press. But the pleasant Cotswold air and the inimitable foolery of Shallow are somewhat spoiled by the known intention to turn them to a thousand pounds loan. And when Falstaff, having cajoled and defrauded Mistress Quickly into abject subjugation, accepts her invitation to supper, his aside to Bardolph as she goes in glee to prepare the feast—"Go, with her; hook on, hook on," is a plot for more loot which is out of all grace.

The wit may be the same, and its agility. But the setting

is different. Throughout the second part of *Henry IV*, the Falstaff who hitherto had pitted himself against kings, princes, and gentlemen, is almost circumscribed to brushes with servants, inferior associates, hostesses, and the raggle-taggle who do a bum-bailiff's dirty work. Only once in this second part has he a real bout with the prince; and his sallies against the Lord Chief Justice are but reminders of his former triumphs. He does not so much fool Shallow as permit Shallow to fulfil his own destiny by proving himself naturally a fool. The earlier Falstaff would have despised the Shallows and the Slenders—except as Gadshill victims—as much as he despised the scarecrows he had pressed into his regiment: they would have been good enough to toss, yet not enough seriously to employ his wit. But now that he finds this consumption of the purse to be an uncurable disease, he is at the mercy of the meanest tradesmen. Without their favour, his life can be brought to a standstill: there will be no more satin for a short-cloak. With their talk of security they can withhold all Sir John's requirements, even as did Master Dombledon: "Let him be damned, like the glutton," says Falstaff of this unyielding shopkeeper, "pray God his tongue be hotter! A whoreson Achitophel! a rascally yea-forsooth knave! to bear a gentleman in hand, and then stand on security!" But the tradesman's counter is a barrier Falstaff cannot surmount.

When haberdashery has become an insuperable impediment to Falstaff's existence, his world is no longer what it was. Hitherto, that were all one; there was linen enough on every hedge. But now the low ebb of linen with him is a handicap: he may in a spurt of the old spirit pride himself that he takes but two shirts out with him; but shirts are no longer a superfluity to him in the perpetual motion of drinking of sack, unbuttoning after supper, sleeping upon benches after noon, and greeting fair hot wenches in flame-coloured taffeta. Yet this is only part, and a smaller part, of a sad change.

Falstaff knows that he is not what he was. "A pox of this gout! or, a gout of this pox! For the one or the other plays the rogue with my great toe." His diseases prove harder to turn to commodity. He had formerly revelled in his vast waist as no slight prompting to his wit. The discomfitures of his heavy going have been an unfailing spur to the quickness of his intellectual sallies. But now he is sensitive to jibes about his bulk. "Men of all sorts take a pride to gird at me." As fodder for their jests, he walks before his page "like a sow that hath overwhelmed all her litter but one," a sad way of causing wit in other men. He, who had once in his humour likened himself to an apple-john, can no longer tolerate the name of it, for the prince set "a dish of applejohns before him, and told him there were five more Sir Johns, and, putting off his hat, said, 'I will now take my leave of these six dry, round, old withered knights.'" Such affronts could only now be borne when, leaving fighting o' days and foining o' nights, though Doll be on his knee, he is beginning to patch up his old body for heaven. His bulk pathetically obstructs him: "an I had but a belly of any indifferency, I were simply the most active fellow in Europe: my womb, my womb, my womb, undoes me." And when Falstaff himself volunteers, as an explanation of comparative ineffectiveness, "I am old, I am old," it is indeed growing late. There may be a merry song or two before the end. But the man who was born about three of the clock in an afternoon, with a white head and a something round belly, and who has lost his voice with halloing and singing of anthems, will scarcely approve his youth much further.

Yet though Sir John's falling away is plain, no less plain is the suspicion of his author's grief at seeing it. Falstaff must still be allowed his supremacy, though it is superiority over meaner mortals than have formerly been his victims. Only comparatively speaking, and when Shallow is the object of comparison, is he still in good liking or does he bear his years very well. He yet may seem to play his old tricks and with the appearance of equal success. He can, for instance, still so far overcome his mountainous flesh to be—for Doll at all events, and though only for her—her "whoreson little valiant villain," a "sweet, little rogue." And shrunk though he be by such association—"You help to make the diseases, Doll; we catch of you, Doll, we catch of you"—it is still occasionally granted to his virtue to be as good a man as was Sir John. His genius can come to yet more proof for the world's ultimate good than can the specious supremacy of its Lord Johns of Lancaster: "I would you had but the wit: 'twere better than your dukedom." Nor does it need memory to call back the queer pity of his last moments in *Henry V* to feel the moving sadness of his latter end in the second part of *Henry IV*: "A' made a finer end and went away an' it had been any Christom child; a' parted even just between twelve and one, even at the turning of the tide; for after I saw him fumble with the sheets and play with flowers and smile upon his fingers' ends, I knew there was but one way; for his nose was as sharp as a pen, and a' babbled of green fields. 'How now, Sir John!' quoth I: 'what, man! be o' good cheer.' So a' cried out 'God, God, God!' three or four times. Now I, to comfort him, bid him a' should not think of God; I hoped there was no need to trouble himself with any such thoughts yet. So a' bade me lay more clothes on his feet: I put my hand into the bed and felt them, and they were as cold as any stone; then I felt to his knees . . . and all was as cold as any stone."

Though in the second *Henry IV*, the associates left to him now are bottle-ale rascals and wenches as common as the way between St. Albans and London, women related to him as the parish heifers are to the town bull, yet even over such a globe of sinful continents there is spread an air of inexplicable or at least of irrational pathos, in the simple recognition that Sir John, the great Sir John, draws near his end. When he is sent away first to the wars, a man of merit sought after to the last, his departure finds the good wenches so blubbered with tears that their hearts are ready to burst. Between memories of the twenty-nine years come peascod-time that they have known him as the best of honest and true-hearted men, and the fears that he may return no more, there is a weeping which nothing can assuage but such insensibility as comes from sack and still more sack. Doll's kisses may be bought, but her flattering busses for an old decrepit man with an empty purse are the pathetic pledges of a feeling that he is still far worthier than any scurvy boy of them all. The hope is indestructible that, if he have but a care of himself, he may yet fare well enough to give her the riotous joy of dressing herself handsome to celebrate his safe return from the wars. For Doll and such as knew him as she did, he is still "as valorous as Hector of Troy, worth five of Agamemnon and ten times better than the nine Worthies." Men, other men, all men, may die like dogs; but "well, sweet Jack, have a care of thyself." As he departs for the scene of battle, all grievances are forgotten: "Come, I'll be friends with thee, Jack; thou art going to the wars"; but there is the sorrow of happy though reprobate memories in the parting phrase—"and whether I shall ever see thee again or no, there is nobody cares."

This is the Falstaff who lives in the affections of Mistress Doll, of Mistress Quickly, and of the whole world of Shakespeare's readers, the Falstaff who survives in the memory of man. But he was ruthlessly trampled into extinction by Henry V: casting him off, the King killed his heart. Even more cruelly, so too did Shakespeare. It was murder in Hal; in Shakespeare, the crime worse than parricide—the slaughter of one's own offspring.

* * *

E. M. W. TILLYARD (1889–   )

Tillyard is a Fellow of Jesus College and University Lecturer in the University of Cambridge. He has written three important books on Shakespeare's work: *Shakespeare's Last Plays* (1938), *Shakespeare's Problem Plays* (1950), and *Shakespeare's History Plays* (1944).

Though in his volume on the histories he substitutes aesthetic criticism for historical approach, he gives major attention to Shakespeare's treatment of the Elizabethan attitude toward history. He divides Shakespeare's history plays into two tetralogies, the second of which is composed of *Richard II*, the two parts of *Henry IV*, and *Henry V*.

THE EPIC NATURE OF HENRY IV
(from: *Shakespeare's History Plays*, 1944)

It remains to support my assertion that in *Henry IV* Shakespeare gives his version of contemporary England, a version allying him to the writers of epic.

Now as the stylistic mark of tragedy is intensity, that of the epic, though tragic intensity may occur, is breadth or variety. And in *Henry IV* there is a variety of style, fully mastered, which is new in Shakespeare and which can hardly be matched even in his later work. This variety contrasts, and I believe was meant deliberately to contrast, with the comparative monotony of *Richard II*. I will mention a few of the styles which Shakespeare practised in these plays.

As a kind of backbone, and corresponding to the high political theme of the plays, is the stately but no longer stiff blank verse used to describe the great happenings which are the main nominal theme. It is the stylistic norm that Shakespeare inherited from the whole series of History Plays he had already written and it is now his absolute servant. One may still call it Shakespeare's official style, but there is not the slightest sense of his using it because he should, and not because he would. It is the perfect correlative of his sincere and solemn heed of the awful and exemplary unfolding of history. Take, for instance, the induction to Part Two, where Rumour tells of the false reports he has spread. It is high-sounding rhetoric; strongly, even violently, metaphorical: and it moves with a gait that is at once ceremonial and consummately athletic:

> Open your ears; for which of you will stop
> The vent of hearing when loud Rumour speaks?
> I, from the orient to the drooping west,
> Making the wind my post-horse, still unfold
> The acts commenced on this ball of earth.
> Upon my tongues continual slanders ride,
> The which in every language I pronounce,
> Stuffing the ears of men with false reports.
> I speak of peace, while covert enmity
> Under the smile of safety wounds the world.
> And who but Rumour, who but only I
> Make fearful musters and prepar'd defence,
> Whiles the big year, swoln with some other grief,
> Is thought with child by the stern tyrant war,
> And no such matter?

It is from this norm that many of the finer passages take their origin: for instance Northumberland's surmise of bad news when Morton enters after the Battle of Shrewsbury:

> How doth my son and brother?
> Thou tremblest; and the whitness in thy cheek
> Is apter than thy tongue to tell thy errand.
> Even such a man, so faint, so spiritless,
> So dull, so dead in look, so woe-begone,
> Drew Priam's curtain in the dead of night
> And would have told him half his Troy was burnt;
> But Priam found the fire ere he his tongue,
> And I my Percy's death ere thou report'st it—

or Henry V's smooth and Olympian, but powerfully felt, protest that from now on he is quite dedicated to his duty:

> The tide of blood in me
> Hath proudly flow'd in vanity till now:
> Now doth it turn and ebb back to the sea,
> Where it shall mingle with the state of floods

> And flow henceforth in formal majesty.
> Now call we our high court of parliament;
> And let us choose such limbs of noble counsel,
> That the great body of our state may go
> In equal rank with the best govern'd nation.

But there are many passages which depart from the norm and in so doing borrow and repay a virtue which in isolation they would not possess. Hotspur's hearty homeliness gains enormously by being set against Shakespeare's official style: think for instance of these lines side by side with the passage just quoted:

> Oh, he is as tedious
> As a tired horse, a railing wife;
> Worse than a smoky house. I had rather live
> With cheese and garlic in a windmill, far,
> Than feed on cates and have him talk to me
> In any summer-house in Christendom.

Moreover in everything Hotspur says there is a quicker speed and a more abrupt emphasis than in the plays' normal blank verse. Brilliantly set off by the norm, too, are some passages of lyrical beauty. Mortimer's words about his Welsh wife have a Keatsian mellifluousness:

> I understand thy kisses and thou mine,
> And that's a feeling disputation.
> But I will never be a truant, love,
> Till I have learn'd thy language; for thy tongue
> Makes Welsh as sweet as ditties highly penn'd,
> Sung by a fair queen in a summer's bower,
> With ravishing division, to her lute.

And when Lady Percy praises Hotspur, she speaks with a lyrical fervour that anticipates the praises of Antony in *Antony and Cleopatra*. Hotspur's honour, she says,

> stuck upon him as the sun
> In the grey vault of heaven, and by his light
> Did all the chivalry of England move
> To do brave acts. He was indeed the glass
> Wherein the noble youth did dress themselves;
> He had no legs that practised not his gait;
> And speaking thick, which nature made his blemish,
> Became the accents of the valiant,
> For those that could speak low and tardily

> Would turn their own perfection to abuse,
> To seem like him: so that in speech, in gait,
> In diet, in affections of delight,
> In military rules, humours of blood,
> He was the mark and glass, copy and book,
> That fashion'd others.

But it is through his use of prose, and of a varied prose, that Shakespeare creates the fullest range of contrast with his blank verse norm. Indeed, some of the prose has a perfect polish that may go beyond any similar quality in the verse. This prose is the property of the Prince and of Falstaff; it is derived from the best things in Lyly's plays; and it looks forward to the elegancies of Congreve. Like its original and its offspring it is founded on the normal speech-cadence of the most intelligent and highly-educated of the aristocracy. It is simple, but measured and deliberate; and so highly wrought that not a syllable can be altered with impunity. This, for instance, is how the Prince comments on the plan that he and Poins should disguise themselves as drawers to overhear Falstaff:

From a god to a bull: a heavy descension; it was Jove's case. From a prince to a prentice: a low transformation; that shall be mine. For in every thing the purpose must weigh with the folly. Follow me, Ned.

And these words of Falstaff have the same qualities:

But Hal, I prithee, trouble me no more with vanity. I would to God thou and I knew where a commodity of good names were to be bought. An old lord of the council rated me the other day in the street about you, sir, but I marked him not: and yet he talked very wisely, but I regarded him not; and yet he talked wisely, and in the street too.

Falstaff commands not only the most exquisite conversational vein, but the Euphuism, of Lyly; and his exhibition of it when he poses as the king reproving the Prince is satirical much in the manner of Congreve exhibiting the affectation of contemporary fashions of speech. But the prose ranges through most ranks of society, through the country gossiping of the two Justices and the plainness of Davy to the Dickensian ramblings of Mrs. Quickly. It embraces a large portion of English life. Taken together, the verse and prose of the play

are a stylistic exhibition of most phases of the commonwealth.

The theme of Respublica, now given a new turn and treating not merely the fortunes but the very nature of England,
what I am calling the epic theme, is subtly contrived. And
the contrivance depends on two conditions: first that the two
parts of the play are a single organism, and secondly that we
are assured from the start that the Prince will make a good
king. By itself the first part does not fulfil the theme of
England, which occurs only in hints or patches; by itself the
second part with so much business in Gloucestershire would
contain an overbalance of provincial England: but treat the
two parts as a single play, and the theme of England grows
naturally till its full compass is reached when Henry V, the
perfect English king, comes to the throne. If we were in
doubt about the Prince's decision, we should not have the
mental repose necessary for appreciating a static picture of
England: we should be obsessed, as we are in *Henry VI*,
with the events of civil war; and the troubles of Henry IV
would quench our interest in the drone of the Lincolnshire
bagpipes or the price of stock at Stamford Fair.

The idea of picturing all England occurred in embryo in
2 Henry VI, where Shakespeare brings in many social grades.
But any coherent picture was out of the question in a play
concerned with the progressive disintegration of society.
Henry IV shows a stable society and it is crowded, like no
other play of Shakespeare, with pictures of life as it was lived
in the age of Elizabeth. There is nothing archaistic about the
Eastcheap tavern and its hostess, about the two carriers in
the inn yard at Rochester, about the bill found in Falstaff's
pocket, about the satin ordered from Master Dombleton for
Falstaff's short cloak and slops, or about the life Shallow liked
to think he had led at the Inns of Court: they are all pure
Elizabethan. But opinions will differ on how they are to be
interpreted. The hard-boiled critics will see no more in them
than lively bits of local colour serving to make the heavy
historical stuff more diverting to a mixed audience. Those
who, like myself, believe that Shakespeare had a massively
reflective as well as a brilliantly opportunist brain will expect
these matters of Elizabethan life to serve more than one end
and will not be surprised if through them he expresses his
own feelings about his fatherland. It is also perfectly natural
that Shakespeare should have chosen this particular point in

the total stretch of history he covered, as suited to this expression. Henry V was traditionally not only the perfect king but a king after the Englishman's heart; one who added the quality of good mixer to the specifically regal virtues. The picture of England would fittingly be connected with the typical English monarch. The details of that picture bear out the notion that Shakespeare deliberately contrived such a connection.

First, it is difficult to deny a deliberate contrast between the play's first scene showing the remoteness of Henry IV from his own people, accentuated by his desire to leave his country for a crusade, and the second scene showing the Prince's easy mixing in the less reputable life of London. The audience would have jumped to it once that, as in Wilson's *Three Lords and three Ladies of London*, London was now the theme; and they would have identified the Prince with it. But even here Shakespeare will not allow London to usurp everything, witness these words:

FALSTAFF. 'Sblood, I am as melancholy as a gib cat or a lugged bear.

PRINCE. Or an old lion or a lover's lute.

FALSTAFF. Yea, or the drone of a Lincolnshire bagpipe.

PRINCE. What sayest thou to a hare or the melancholy of Moorditch?

And the Prince's soliloquy at the end of the scene, promising that he will exhibit all the proper regal virtues, reassures us that we have been justified, that we have been safe, in identifying the Prince with English life generally. And the process is repeated whenever the Prince condescends to take part in events, in Kent or London. Thus it is that when the Prince is crowned, and even though he is then in anything but a condescending mood, we identify him with the picture of England, then complete.

And there are many things, in which the Prince has no share, that make up this picture. How Hotspur helps in this has been described above; and nowhere more effectively than in the scene in Wales with Glendower and Mortimer. Indeed one of this whole scene's main functions is to create a sense of England through a contrast with Wales. Here not only is the bluff anglicism of Hotspur contrasted with Glendower's Welsh romanticism, but Lady Percy's school-girlish simplicities—"Go, ye giddy goose," and "Lie still, ye thief,

and hear the lady sing in Welsh"—are very English and contrast equally with Lady Mortimer's lyricism which Glendower interprets to her husband:

> She bids you on the wanton rushes lay you down
> And rest your gentle head upon her lap.

Thereafter in Part One the theme of England is not greatly
developed: it remains in suspense so that it may get full
expression in Part Two.

Here, Shakespeare introduces the theme of England just as
he did early in Part One: he puts a minutely circumstantiated
domestic scene after a scene dealing in a high manner with
civil war; political action in the historical past yields to a
picture of England to-day. I refer to the conspirators' discussion at York (I. 3) and Mrs. Quickly's attempt to arrest
Falstaff (II. 1). To illustrate the skill of Shakespeare's transition, here are some lines from the Archbishop's last speech in
I. 3, where the reference to London is both perfectly apt to
the business in hand and prepares us for the change to the
domestic intimacies of Eastcheap in the next scene:

> What trust is in these times?
> They that, when Richard liv'd, would have him die
> Are now become enamour'd of his grave:
> Thou that threw'st dust upon his goodly head,
> When through proud London he came sighing on
> After the admired heels of Bolingbroke,
> Criest now "O earth, yield us that king again,
> And take thou this." O thoughts of men accurst!
> Past and to come seems best; things present worst.

The next scene, and especially Mrs. Quickly, give the answer
to the Archbishop's first question and deny the sentiment of
the last line. There is something entirely reassuring in Mrs.
Quickly's good nature, in her muddled intellect and in her
photographic memory of detail. "Thou didst swear to me,"
she says to Falstaff,

upon a parcel-gilt goblet, sitting in my Dolphin-chamber, at the
round table, by a sea-coal fire, upon Wednesday in Wheeson
week, when the prince broke thy head for liking his father to a
singing-man of Windsor, thou didst swear to me then, as I was
washing thy wound, to marry me and make me my lady thy wife.

Hearing this, we answer that there is a great deal of trust in these times and we are glad to repose in the present. And we accept Mrs. Quickly as the type of all the stupid good-natured women in England. Just as Dogberry and his men reassure us that in *Much Ado* the tragic element will not be allowed to prevail, so Mrs. Quickly reassures us that civil war will yield, as the plays' main theme, to England.

It is in the scenes in Gloucestershire (III. 2; V. 1; V. 2) that the theme of England is completed. But here there is the question of interpretation. Dover Wilson considers these scenes "a studied burlesque of provincial life and manners for the hilarious contempt of London spectators," and if he is right they will be far from creating an epic picture of England. I think that he is wrong and that his opinion falsifies and impoverishes the scenes themselves and goes against the whole trend of Shakespeare's feelings about the country. Shallow and Silence may be ridiculous characters; some of the yokels gathered for recruiting may be pathetic: but these persons are no more a satire on country England than Nym and Bardolph are a satire on Elizabethan London. From first to last Shakespeare was loyal to the country life. He took it for granted as the norm, as the background before which the more formal or spectacular events were transacted. Shakespeare tells us this; when he slips in the spring and winter songs after the prolonged affectations in *Love's Labour's Lost*, or when he inserts the English realism of Petruchio's country house into the Italianate complexities of the *Taming of the Shrew*. And at the end of his career he made the wholesomeness of the pastoral life in the *Winter's Tale* redeem the barren and tortured jealousy of Leontes. Far from being a satire, the Gloucestershire scenes in *Henry IV* complete the picture of England and put the emphasis where Shakespeare meant it to be: on the life of the English countryside. And that emphasis is given precisely as the Prince becomes Henry V.

Shakespeare manipulates the matter so delicately that it is hard to bring forward any neatly tabulated evidence of his intentions. But it is worth noting two of the hints he gives us. First, the chief character of the scenes, Justic Shallow, however ridiculous he is and however much at sea when he leaves the things he understands, is a good countryman. He knows what he is doing when he tells Davy to sow the headland with red wheat; and when he offer Falstaff a pippin "of his own graffing," we do not question his horticultural skill. And if in the scene where he first appears he is ludicrous in thinking they still talk of him as "mad Shallow" at Clement's Inn, he is genuine enough when he asks the price of a yoke of bullocks at Stamford Fair. But the context of this question is so much to the point that it had better be quoted:

SHALLOW. Jesu, Jesu, the mad days that I have spent! and to see how many of my old acquaintance are dead!

SILENCE. We shall all follow, cousin.

SHALLOW. Certain, 'tis certain; very sure, very sure; death, as the Psalmist saith, is certain to all; all shall die. How a good yoke of bullocks at Stamford Fair?

Shallow's crass simplicity, his dense unawareness of how trite is his moralising and how steep the descent from it, is the most exquisite comedy. And yet Shakespeare uses this passage to express the way he sees life and to strengthen the pattern of the present plays. Shakespeare did indeed see life as a ridiculous but fascinating blend; a blend in the present scene of men dying and bullocks sold in the busy market; while, for the pattern of the play, Shallow speaks his words just after Henry IV has been brought to the point of death: it is in this context that he speaks generally of death and then turns to Stamford Fair, reminding us that it is still flourishing. He tells us what Hardy tells us in a more direct fashion:

> Only thin smoke without flame
> From the heaps of couch grass:
> Yet this will go onward the same
> Though Dynasties pass.

Secondly, there is Davy. The upset in Shallow's house caused by Falstaff's visit must have been great. But Davy is undefeated. Through all the turmoil of unusual hospitality he insists on seeing to the details of his job: the bucket must have a new link; and his friend William Visor of Woncot (though a knave) must not be allowed to suffer at the plea of Clement Perkes. Davy is both administrator and politician, perhaps in his little way the double of Henry IV, and certainly the symbol of the undefeated operating of the country life.

Taken all together, the scenes I have indicated as creating the picture of England (not to speak of the incidental references) include most phases of English life from high to low. The biggest gap is in the middle. Shakespeare says little of the merchant class, in which he had grown up. Perhaps it was this omission that prompted him, when ordered to write again on Falstaff, to choose a middle class setting. There is nothing epic about the *Merry Wives of Windsor;* yet its setting may derive from Shakespeare's epic intentions in *Henry IV.* This omission, however, with its possible result, is incidental. There is enough of England in *Henry IV* and enough confidence in England to make the two parts Shakespeare's ripe expression of what he felt about his country.

I have used the word epic to describe *Henry IV* but I do not mean that this epithet is merited simply through the English local colour. It is only the intense, the tragic, the agelong that can give the temporary and the local the necessary dignity. Without the eternal character of Achilles the mere life as lived in the *Iliad* would not be raised to epic height. In *Henry IV,* as I have remarked, there is nothing tragic, nothing to correspond to the greatest things in the *Iliad;* but there are other things that serve. First, there are the agelong types, the fool, the adventurer, the "unofficial self," assembled in the character of Falstaff. Secondly, there is the great contrast (typified in the lines of Hardy quoted above) between the theme of civil war, the terrible vicissitudes of high politics, and the theme of the perennial cycles of ordinary life and their persistent rhythms: the cycles of birth and death; and of the seasons with their appropriate tasks, without which man simply cannot exist. Thus it is that the great variety of *Henry IV,* unequalled in Shakespeare, is given a coherence very different indeed from the coherence of Shakespearean tragedy but in its own way not inferior.

* * *

MURIEL C. BRADBROOK (1909–   )

Miss Bradbrook, a lecturer at Girton College, belongs to the so-called skeptical school of Shakespeare criticism, in that she finds the essence of the poet's work in the literary and stage conventions he adopted. Some critics feel that she fails adequately to realize that the poet transformed all the stage devices which he borrowed into integral parts of the particular play that she is criticizing. Her principal works are

Growth and Structure of Elizabethan Comedy (1932); *Themes and Conventions of Elizabethan Tragedy* (1952); *Shakespeare and Elizabethan Poetry* (1951); and *The School of Night* (1936), containing an important chapter on *Love's Labour's Lost.*

FALSTAFF AND THE MORAL WORLD
(from: *Shakespeare and Elizabethan Poetry*, 1951)

The Falstaff of Part 2 is, I think, a rather different creature. Here he takes up much more of the action, but he is kept apart from Prince Hal. The Prince indeed appears only twice before the scene of his father's death, and in one of these scenes he is not with Falstaff. Instead of being contrasted with Chivalry and the forward child Understanding in the persons of Hotspur and Hal, Falstaff has a train of attendants who are his dupes and hangers-on: Pistol, Doll Tearsheet, Justice Shallow, Silence and the ragged regiment are provided for him to exercise his wits upon. In Part 2 he has a number of soliloquies—those on the page, on Shallow and on John of Lancaster—in which he speaks with a new tone, one of shrewd analysis, cool calculation and detached satiric observation. He speaks in the accents of Prince Hal's satiric portrait of Hotspur in Part 1. The Prince has indeed misled his old companion and infected him with the spirit of "policy." In Part 1 Falstaff's charm lies largely in his unpremeditated and extempore sallies, his brilliant improvising. He "does it all natural." But in Part 2, where he is no longer revelling with the Prince, but playing his dupes, like any coney-catcher, or mediating upon his next move, Falstaff becomes less of the clown and medieval grotesque, more of an observer and commentator. The narrative connexion between his wanderings and Prince John's mopping-up operation does not carry any significance. He is roving at large and, until the last scene, is given a large tether.

Nevertheless Hotspur being dead and Prince Hal kept off the stage, Falstaff has the scene to himself, except for his encounter with the Lord Chief Justice, who plainly tells him "The king hath severed you and Prince Harry" (1. 2. 231–232). Yet Falstaff is as confident as ever: he boasts to the Lord Chief Justice that he has "checked" the young prince for misbehaving in court—as if he would dare!—he gives an extremely cool little sketch of Hal and Poins to Doll Tearsheet, and in soliloquy for the first time he is shown calculating the effect of his mirth upon the prince:

> O I will divise matter enough out of this Shallow to keep prince Harry in continuall laughter, the wearing out of sixe fashions . . . O, it is much that a lie, with a slight oathe, and a jest, with a sad browe, will doe with a fellow that never had the ach in his shoulders.
>
> (5. 1. 86–93.)

This is Falstaff's own version of "I know you all." The Prince may think he has been making use of Falstaff: Falstaff thinks he has been making use of the Prince.

Whereas in Part 1 the relation of Falstaff and the Prince had been kept in revelry, parody and unembittered mirth, and had been counterweighted with the relations of each of them to Hotspur and to Bolingbroke, in Part 2 things are very different. The Prologue is spoken by Rumour, "Painted full of tongues," or as we might say, the Fairy Wish-Fulfilment, who sets the tone not only for the following scene but for the whole play. Hesitation, uncertainty and deception are the themes of the Second Part. It is in fact more symbolic than Part 1: instead of the quartet of fully-drawn characters, we have an open antagonism between Falstaff and the Law. The gorgeous figure of Justice in scarlet and ermine appears. We never see Hal opposed to Gascoigne as we see him opposed to Hotspur, and as a character the Lord Chief Justice cannot compare with the representative of Chivalry; he is symbol, not man. Yet though he and Falstaff part with sparring honours easy, the mere appearance of Justice in robes of office, and the sound of that cold legal voice which we realize Prince Henry had already once obeyed is a very *memento mori* to Sir John. When King Henry V openly adopts this unbending embodiment of Law—whose noble defence of his office has been cunningly reserved to this point—as "the Father to my youth" (5. 2. 118), the symbolic significance is plain. Justitia is in loco parentis. Falstaff's place is filled. Henry takes up the burden of Office, and Gascoigne symbolizes Office as well as the Rule of Law. It is in the next scene that Sir John, hearing of the old King's decease, cried: "The laws of England are at my commandment. Happy are they who have been my friends and woe unto my Lord Chief Justice" (5. 3. 143). Perhaps some of the audience would remember that among the crimes charged against Richard II at his deposition was that he had said the laws of England were whatever he declared them to be. The subjection of the King to the Rule of Law, which had been one of the main constitutional issues of the later Middle Ages, was perhaps a topic not to be handled other than circumspectly under the Tudors: the Stewarts however were to receive a lesson on the subject in the course of the next century.

The final rejection of Falstaff has caused many qualms for the manner in which King Henry speaks. It has been defended on the grounds that the King and Falstaff have both travelled a long way since the revels in Part 1. From one point of view Falstaff is here the cheater cheated. Throughout Part 2 he has been shown engaged in a series of confidence tricks, such as the ordinary coney-catcher of the time was accustomed to use: the last of his dupes is with him as the booty he hopes for—all but the thousand pounds—is snatched from under his nose. As Falstaff said to the Lord Chief Justice, it is "tit for tat."

But this is also the clash of two distinct and differing worlds. Professor Willard Farnham has spoken of the religious overtones of King Henry's words beginning:

> I know thee not old man, fall to thy praiers.
>
> (5. 5. 52.)

An anointed King was *persona mixta*, who had some of the functions of an ecclesiastic and when Professor Farnham compares this scene, the rejection of the world of the tavern with rejection of profane love at the end of *Troilus and Criseyde*, he seems to me to have hit on a particularly happy analogy. Chaucer was no more turning into a misogynist and a Desert Father than Hal is turning into a precisian. "Like Hal, Shakespeare can accept Falstaff and even love him but at the same time keep him in his place . . . Shakespeare never for a moment shows the irritation of the reformer-satirist that the world can produce such a creature as Falstaff. Nor does Shakespeare ever suggest in a modern fashion that Falstaff, by never allowing any of his desires to be repressed, really has a good answer to life."

I have said that Falstaff does not belong to a world in which moral judgments apply. Hence when he comes into contact with the world of morality, which is the real world, there is a direct clash. We have a creature of one sort of world, the hero of one literary "kind," coming up against another. Hal and Falstaff had revelled together, but, as in real life, the world of the Boar's Head—that emblem of Christmas misrule—had joined what the world outside would put asunder. A kindly dismissal in private such as Bradley would have wished for would be quite impossible; for when Henry says:

> Conceive not that I am the thing I was

he means it quite literally. Conversion, transformation, the power of holy oil, or what you will—man and office were now inseparably conjoined and even to his brothers, Henry is The King. It may even be that, in spite of the fact that he dominates Part 2 and that his rogueries seem to be the main reason for its existence, Falstaff's rejection was overshadowed for an Elizabethan audience by the scene of reconciliation with the Lord Chief Justice, and treated as a kind of anti-masque. Certainly, if his fall had to be shown, the more steep and grievous it could be made, the better; and I doubt if the high social standing of the Fleet Prison would provide much mitigation.

On the simplest level, the last act gives the audience the pleasure of a transformation scene, long anticipated, in which disguises are thrown off. The stage transformation of Henry's appearance in robes, crown and sceptre is one of the soundest dramatic cards to play; and Henry himself recalls the opening soliloquy of Part 1 in showing:

> th' incredulous world
> The noble change that I have purposed.
>
> (4. 5. 152–153.)

when he proclaims that he lives

> To mocke the expectation of the world,
> To frustrate prophecies, and to race out
> Rotten opinion, who hath writ me downe
> After my seeming.
>
> (5. 2. 126–129.)

Rumour, "rotten opinion," those who judge by the view are to be confounded: the disguise, or seeming, is triumphantly cast off, as in the older plays the King would cast off his physical disguise.

Though Henry may be allowed the final act, the previous ones have been Falstaff's. In terms of contemporary reference, he was more popular than any other character. It is Falstaff and Justice Shallow whose names fill pages of the Shakespeare Allusion Book: it is Hotspur's part that the stage-struck prentice quotes in *The Knight of the Burning Pestle*. Prince Hal, the student in the art of reading men, may have pleased the judicious, Bolingbroke provided some continuity with the themes of the moral history, but Hotspur and Falstaff, the Prince's two factors, outshone everyone else in popular esteem.

Hal robs Percy in the end, as he robs his own factors at Gadshill in the older account. He engrosses the glory by slaying his rival at Shrewsbury. But in the early part of the play Percy is the embodiment of military virtue and of all the more endearing military weaknesses. He is cheated by the politician Worcester, deserted by his friends, but his sheer courage carries the fight almost to a successful conclusion. Choler, recklessness and ungovernable persistence in his humour are his weaknesses, in which he seems almost a first study for Coriolanus: yet his mocking scepticism of Glendower's claims, his banter of the charming Kate, and his scorn of the mincing lord who met him at Holmedon are as shrewdly observed as they are mercilessly indulged. The magnificent praise of him in King Henry's second comparison of the two young men, added to the praise of Hal, and his heroic disregard of the odds against him make him a true shadow of the hero of Agincourt: so that when the Prince again insists that he will absorb all Percy's honours:

> Two stars keep not their motion in one sphere,
>   Nor can one England brooke a double raigne
> Of Harry Percy and the Prince of Wales
>
> (5. 4. 65–67.)

Percy is seen like one of the men whom King Henry has "marching in his coats," as Hal's understudy and deputy, a symbol of greatness to come.

Shakespeare may have felt a particular warmth for the Percy family through his connexion with Sir Charles Percy, Essex's friend. A letter of Sir Charles, written in 1600 from

his home in Gloucestershire, and comparing himself with
Justice Shallow, shows a most lively appreciation of the fun,
and it was Sir Charles who ordered the notorious performance of *Richard II* on the eve of the Essex rising.

At all events Hotspur does far more than is required of the
conventional rebel leader, and his character, which is perhaps an amplification of the Bastard Falconbridge, as well as
an anticipation of Coriolanus, is Shakespeare's own invention.
With such a pair to set him off, Prince Henry is in some
danger of being overshadowed. His principal moment is the
scene with his father in which the King compares his son
with Richard II and Percy with himself. The tragic echoes
back and forth are sounded less for their political implications
than to give depth and resonance to the deep personal emo-
tion that wells up between father and son. The King's tears
of "foolish tenderness," the deep tones of his distress, and
the personal nature of his appeal call out in Prince Hal as
moved a response:

> Do not thinke so, you shal not find it so. . . .
> . . . and in the closing of some glorious day
> Be bold to tell you that I am your sonne. . . .

The estrangement between Prince Henry and his father is
one between two whose likeness is so strong, and whose feelings are so deep-seated that only at such moment do they
betray themselves. This scene is anticipatory of the one at
the end of 2 *Henry IV*, and really forestalls it. For a reconciliation at this level cannot be undone, and it gives implicit
but sufficient measure of the relation between the Prince and
Falstaff.

The construction of 1 *Henry IV* is therefore built on a
fourfold contrast, the four "species" represented by the King,
the Prince, Falstaff and Hotspur, and the relationships between them. The method is that of shadowing or parody,
and of contrasts and opposition: heroics and clowning, robbing in sport and rebelling in earnest, the King of Misrule
versus the King of England, Harry Hotspur versus Harry
Monmouth.

Part 2 is constructed rather differently. Rebellion, a desper-
ate venture even with Hotspur, dwindles and diminishes and
splutters out without a fight. Lancaster's merciless duping
of the miserable remnant by something akin to a legal quibble

is a mere episode in the story, and the end of the great Northumberland is told in half a dozen lines by a messenger (2 *Henry IV*, 4. 4. 94–99). The chief effect of the wars is to furnish Falstaff with opportunities for recruiting.

Prince Hal, having nothing to do but hang about in the wings waiting for the end of the play, and being kept carefully away from his father and Falstaff, makes but a single appearance at the Boar's Head, where, however, the interest is less in his duel of wits with Falstaff than in the humours of Mistress Quickly, Doll Tearsheet and Pistol. The whole of the political theme is kept "marking time." It is true that Shakespeare tidied up the odds and ends left over from Part 1, but such an occupation cannot counterbalance the effect of Falstaff and his rout of gulls and disreputables. The counterbalance is left to the emblematic figures and the emblematic moments: to Rumour, the Lord Chief Justice, the taking of the crown by Hal and his final appearance as King. The low comedy on the other hand is more realistic, more directly a painting of contemporary manners than it was in Part 1. Justice Shallow and Mrs. Quickly are "humours" of the Dickensian sort: portraits, with notes of pathos such as are not heard in the comic revels of Part 1, but with a good deal of realistic writing in the "low style."

Except for the last act, Part 2 is Falstaff's play; and the play of a Falstaff who was almost as unlikely as the hero of *The Merry Wives of Windsor* to die of a heart fracted and corroborate, but had gained in malice, shrewdness and calculation. In *Henry IV*, Part 1, the delights of the characters were dolphin-like and showed above the element of revelry in which they lived and moved. The uncongealed flow of life sustained them. In Part 2 the characters have particular humours and whimsies, observances to be noted. They are more Jonsonian. The most penetrating annotation is King Henry's account of his son, given to the Duke of Clarence.

Notes

TEXT: If we are to judge from the few editions of the Second Part of *Henry IV*, it was nowhere so popular with the reading public as Part One. The only edition to appear before the Folio of 1623 was the Quarto of 1600. As usual, the title page plays up the features most likely to entice a buyer of the volume. Part of this advertisement reads:

> The Second part of Henrie the fourth, continuing to his death, and coronation of Henrie the fift. With the humours of Sir John Falstaff and swaggering Pistol.

This quarto text seems to have been based on a prompt copy. At least, it lacks 170 lines appearing in the folio, passages probably cut in the acting version. However, 40 lines not in the folio appear in the quarto, and most of these probably represent the author's emendations, though a few omissions may be attributed to the carelessness of the printer.

DATE: Henry IV, Part II was written immediately after the completion of the first part and probably reached the stage some time during 1598.

SOURCE: The sources of this play are the same as for *Part I:* Holinshed's *Chronicles* and *The Famous Victories of Henry V.* In the old play Shakespeare found the skeleton for the scene in which the Prince takes the crown from his father's deathbed, and also for the crude scene in which the new king banishes his old companions. But nearly all the scenes in which Falstaff appears in *Henry IV, Part II* are the product of Shakespeare's untrammeled invention.

A NOTE ON SHAKESPEARE'S GRAMMAR: In Shakespeare's day the syntax and other aspects of English grammar and vocabulary were in a state of transition from an earlier, highly inflected language. The loss of endings obscured the distinguishing marks of various parts of speech, and the result was not so much confusion as freedom. (A full exposition of the peculiarities of Elizabethan language may be found in Abbott's *A Shakespearian Grammar*, Third Edition, 1871.)

This note will reassure the reader that constructions which seem ungrammatical were justified according to the accepted canons of Elizabethan usage.

* * *

INDUCTION

1. Line 37
the posts come tiring on. The messengers arrive tired from their riding.

ACT I, SCENE 1

2. Line 72
Drew Priam's curtain. Priam in Greek legend was the King of Troy. He suffered many misfortunes during the Trojan War and was finally killed by Neoptolemus.

3. Lines 102–3
Sounds ever after as a sullen bell,
Remembered tolling a departing friend.
A church bell tolled during the passage of a funeral procession from the church to the graveyard.

4. Lines 127–30
The bloody Douglas, . . .
'Gan vail his stomach and did grace the shame
Of those that turned their backs.
Douglas began to lose courage and thus shared the shame of those who took to flight.

5. Line 182
That if we wrought out life 'twas ten to one. That the odds were ten to one against our survival.

6. Line 205
Of fair King Richard, scraped from Pomfret stones. King Richard II was murdered at Pomfret Castle. (*Richard II*, Act V, Scene 5, lines 108 ff.)

ACT I, SCENE 2

7. Line 16
Thou whoreson mandrake. Whoreson means bastard. The mandrake was a poisonous plant which, because of its forked root, was imagined to resemble a man. (See also Note 59.)

8. Line 19
I was never manned with an agate till now. Falstaff compares his diminutive page with an agate because the agate stone was often carved into tiny figures.

9. Line 27
his face is a face-royal. Falstaff is punning on "royal"—a coin with the king's head on its face.

10. Line 42
Achitophel. David's treacherous counselor, who aided David's son Absalom in his conspiracy against his father (2 Samuel 15:12 ff.).

11. Lines 44–5
The whoreson smooth pates do now wear nothing but high shoes. "Smooth pates" was a contemptuous allusion to short-haired city tradesmen. They were later called "roundheads." "Wear . . . high shoes" was a proverbial expression for pride.

12. Lines 53–5
for he hath the horn of abundance, and the lightness of his wife shines through it. Falstaff puns on three meanings of "horn": cornucopia; emblem of a cuckold; the glass of a lantern. Lightness here means unchasteness.

13. Line 58
I bought him in Paul's. St. Paul's Cathedral in Shakespeare's day was given over to various commercial and social activities. On one of its pillars, jobless men posted up lists of their qualifications for prospective employers.

14. Line 112
some relish of the saltness of time. Age is salty as opposed to the freshness of youth. Saltness also means lasciviousness.

15. Line 133
I have read the cause of his effects in Galen. Galen was a celebrated Greek physician (130 A.D.–C. 200 A.D.), who was still regarded as authoritative in Elizabethan times.

16. Line 149
some dram of a scruple. Trifle of a doubt. A pun on "dram" and "scruple," both very small units of weight.

17. Line 184
His effect of gravy, gravy, gravy. Falstaff is punning on the word "gravity," used by the Chief Justice in the preceding line. It is believed that the vowel *a* was pronounced alike in the two words.

18. Line 191
these costermonger times. A costermonger is a peddler of

costards—a variety of apples; costermonger times—a time
when a peddler's valuation is put on everything.

19. Line 255
three-man beetle. A rammer or mallet that requires three men
to wield it. The humor lies in the suggested use of a three-
man beetle to produce so insignificant an application of force.

ACT I, SCENE 3

20. Lines 36–41
Yes, if this present quality of war,
Indeed the instant action: a cause on foot
Lives so in hope as in an early spring
We see the appearing buds; which to prove fruit,
Hope gives not so much warrant as despair
That frosts will bite them.
Yes, the present cause, an action already started, lives in such
doubtful hope as do the buds in spring, for hope gives less
warrant that they will come to flower than despair gives war-
rant that they will be frostbitten.

21. Line 55
To weigh against his opposite. To serve as a counterpoise to
that which is opposed to it.

ACT II, SCENE 1

22. Lines 97–8
*the prince broke thy head for liking his father to a singing-
man of Windsor.* A singing-man was one of the professional
musicians—basses, tenors, and countertenors—who performed
in cathedrals and royal chapels. Comparison with them appears
to have been usually uncomplimentary. As Professor Ernest
Breneke of Columbia has pointed out, there may be an allusion
here to John Mandelin, a singer in King Richard II's chapel.
He resembled the dethroned king so closely that a group of
conspirators against Henry IV dressed him in royal robes and
sought to pass him off as King Richard, who was to organize a
tournament at which King Henry was to be murdered. The
conspiracy was exposed and Mandelin was captured and exe-
cuted.

ACT II, SCENE 2

23. Lines 20–29
*But that the tenniscourt-keeper knows better than I; for it is
a low ebb of linen with thee when thou keepest not racket*

there; as thou hast not done a great while, because the rest of thy low countries have made a shift to eat up thy holland: and God knows, whether those that bawl out the ruins of thy linen shall inherit his kingdom: but the midwives say the children are not in the fault. Interpretations of this passage vary a good deal. There is a possible pun on "racket" (tennis racket and noise); "low countries" may mean lower part of the body in general and posterior in particular, with a possible allusion to the Netherlands, which again may tie in with Holland; "to make shift" is to bestir oneself, with a pun on "shift"—shirt or undergarment; holland is linen or cotton cloth; and so on.

The general meaning seems clear enough: the Prince tells Poins that he has worn out his shirts as a result of sensual indulgence, and that only God knows whether the bastard children who do their bawling from the sorry remnants of his shirts in which they are wrapped will be allowed to enter the Kingdom of Heaven—though the midwives say that the offspring is not to blame for the sins of the fathers.

24. Line 92
you rascally Althæa's dream. Althea was a queen in Greek mythology. At her son's birth she dreamed that he would live only so long as a brand then in the fire would remain unconsumed. The dream that the Page in the lines following (90–95) mistakenly describes as Althea's is actually that ascribed to Hecuba, wife of Priam, King of Troy.

25. Line 110
how doth the martlemas, your master? Martlemas probably means Martinmas (Nov. 11), for it suggests a fatted ox.

26. Lines 127–8
Nay, they will be kin to us, or they will fetch it from Japhet. They will claim to be descended from royalty, or they will trace their ancestry all the way back to Japhet, the son of Noah, who was thought to be the ancestor of all Europeans.

27. Line 163
Ephesians, my lord, of the old church. "Ephesians" means boon companions. The old church is the ancient church of Ephesus, whose theories of church government the Puritans accepted as authoritative.

28. Line 192
God to a bull. A reference to the legend of Europa, a Phoenician maiden. When Zeus fell in love with her, he as-

sumed the form of a white bull and carried her on his back to Crete.

ACT II, Scene 4

29. Line 22
here will be old Utis. "Utis" was the eighth day after a church festival—that is, the last and so the merriest day of a celebration.

30. Lines 24 ff.
The hostess' speeches are crowded with malapropisms or quicklyisms. For example:
   line 25. "temperality" means a mixture of "temperature" and "temper."
   line 40: "calm" for "qualm."
   line 62: "rheumatic," perhaps, for "choleric."
   line 64: "confirmities" for "infirmities."
   line 87: "pacify" for "satisfy."
   line 92: "debuty" for "deputy."
   line 176: "aggravate" for "moderate."

31. Line 45
You make fat rascals. Falstaff puns on the word rascal, which in addition to its usual meaning of rogue also meant a lean deer.

32. Line 95
Master Dumbe, our minister. Ministers incapable of preaching original sermons were called "dumb."

33. Line 105
tame cheater. Gambler's decoy. Mistress Quickly in the lines following mistakes it for "escheater," an officer of the Treasury.

34. Stage directions (after line 118)
Pistol's speech throughout the play is a parody of the bombast that issued from the mouths of stage braggart captains in plays, almost contemporary, like Kyd's *The Spanish Tragedy*. It is intended to ridicule these earlier romantic plays and the taste of those who admired them.

35. Line 173
Have we not Hiren here? Hiren, for Irene, is perhaps a reference to one of George Peele's lost plays: *The Turkish Mahomet and Hyrin the Fair Greek.* (See Note 34.)

36. Lines 177–82
Shall pack-horses
And hollow pampered jades of Asia,
Which cannot go but thirty mile a-day,

> Compare with *Cæsars*, and with *Cannibals*,
> And *Trojan Greeks*? Nay, rather damn them with
> *King Cerberus*; and let the welkin roar.

These lines are a garbled passage from Marlowe's *Tamburlaine*, Part II. (See Note 34.)

37. Line 193
Then feed and be fat, my fair Calipolis. Burlesque of a line in George Peele's (1558–1597) *The Battle of Alcazar.* (See Note 34.)

38. Line 195
"*Si fortune me tormente, sperato me contento.*" If fortune torments me, hope contents me. Pistol's form of the widely current motto is neither Spanish nor Italian, but his own confused mixture. (See Note 34.)

39. Line 207
shove-groat shilling. Shove-groat was a game in which coins were shoved along a table into numbered spaces. It appears to have been known by many other names, of which the most familiar is Shuffleboard.

40. Line 211
Then death rock me asleep, abridge my doleful days! A quotation from a popular poem attributed to Anne Boleyn or her brother, written when they were awaiting execution.

41. Line 213
Untwine the Sisters Three! Come, Atropos, I say! The Sisters Three are the three Fates of Greek mythology. Atropos was the one who cut the threads of life spun by Clotho and drawn out by Lachesis. (See Note 34.)

42. Lines 238–9
ten times better than the Nine Worthies.
The Nine Worthies of popular tradition were three pagan champions: Hector, Alexander the Great, and Julius Caesar; three Jews: Joshua, David, and Judas Maccabeus; and three Christians: Arthur, Charlemagne, and Godfrey of Bouillon.

43. Line 262
as thick as Tewksbury mustard. Tewksbury is a town in Gloucestershire. It was noted for mustard balls manufactured there.

44. Lines 272–3
and breeds no bate with telling of discreet stories.
This is ironical. Falstaff says that the Prince excites no censure by telling proper stories—that is, the stories he tells are always improper and slanderous.

45. Lines 286-7

    Saturn and Venus this year in conjunction! What says the almanac to that? The prince identifies Falstaff with Saturn and Doll with Venus. In astrology, Saturn is said to be the planet that regulates old age; and heavenly bodies are in conjunction when they are visible at the same time.

46. Lines 288-90

    And, look, whether the fiery Trigon, his man, be not lisping to his master's old tables, his note-book, his counsel-keeper. The fiery Trigon is a meeting of Aries, Leo, and Sagittarius—three divisions of the zodiac—in a fiery sign. Poins is referring to Bardolph with his flaming countenance. "Tables" (memo book), "note-book," and "counsel-keeper" all refer to Mistress Quickly.

47. Line 320

    by this light flesh and corrupt blood. Falstaff refers to Doll, who then takes offense with "How, you fat fool! I scorn you." The Prince then defends her by calling her an "honest, virtuous, civil gentlewoman."   s.v.

48. Lines 372-3

    for suffering flesh to be eaten in thy house, contrary to the law. The reference is to the law forbidding the sale of meat during Lent.

    ACT III, SCENE 2

49. Line 24

    a cotswold man. Cotswold Hills in Gloucestershire, a region famous for its athletes.

50. Lines 52-3

    A' would have clapped i' the clout at twelve score; and carried you a forehand shaft a fourteen and fourteen and a half. Shallow means that old Double could hit the target at twelve score—that is, at 240 yards; and that he was so good that he could make the forehand shaft—used for point-blank shooting and heavier than the arrow customarily used for distance shooting—carry fourteen and a half—that is, 290 yards.

51. Line 121

    Prick him. To prick was to make a puncture opposite a name on a list—equivalent to the modern "Check him off."

52. Lines 145-6

    for we have a number of shadows to fill up the muster-book. These shadows were entries in the muster roll of the names of nonexistent men, whose pay the officer pocketed.

53. Lines 155–6
the whole frame stands upon pins. Falstaff appears to be punning on the phrase "Prick him down" in Shallow's preceding question, the pricking being done by means of a pin; and perhaps also on pins in the sense of legs.

54. Line 207
we lay all night in the windmill in Saint George's field. Windmills were apparently favorite places for assignations, and hence became a synonym for brothels.

55. Lines 236–7
and here's four Harry ten shillings in French crowns. Equivalent in French crowns of four shilling pieces first coined in Henry VII's reign. These coins in Shakespeare's days were current at only half of their face value.

56. Lines 279–82
a' shall charge you and discharge you with the motion of a pewterer's hammer, come off and on swifter than he that gibbets on the brewer's bucket. Falstaff says Wart shall load and fire with the speed of the motion of a metalsmith's hammer, and retreat and advance swifter than he who handles the yoke (or beam) used for transporting beer. This required quick movements, since two hooks had to be attached at the same time.

57. Line 300
I was then Sir Dagonet in Arthur's show. Arthur's show—the reference being to the fabled King Arthur of the Round Table—was an annual exhibition of archery at Mile-End Green in which each contestant took the name of an Arthurian character. Sir Dagonet was Arthur's fool.

58. Line 328
and the feats he hath done about Turnbull Street. This street was the center of brothels.

59. Line 339
and the whores called him mandrake. Because some mandrake roots were imagined to resemble the male sex organs, the mandrake was regarded as a symbol of lechery. (See Note 7.)

60. Line 343
And now is this Vice's dagger become a squire. The Vice, a comic character in the morality plays, carried a thin wooden dagger.

61. Line 355
I will make him a philosopher's two stones to me. A philosopher's stone was supposed to turn baser metals into gold.

Falstaff promises that he will endow Shallow with twice the worth of a single stone.

ACT IV, Scene 1

62. Lines 94–6
My brother general, the commonwealth,
To brother born an household cruelty,
I make my quarrel in particular.
This passage is obviously corrupt. Its meaning seems to be as follows: the reasons for my quarrel are both private and public. The Archbishop's brother, Lord Scroop, had been beheaded by King Henry.

63. Line 125
O, when the king did throw his warder down. The reference is to the armed contest between Henry Bolingbroke (who later became King Henry IV) and Thomas Mowbray, which King Richard II stopped at the last moment by throwing down his warder—that is, his staff. See *Richard II*, Act I, Scene 3, lines 1–118.

64. Line 206
As his misdoubts present occasion. As his suspicions give a reason for so doing.

ACT IV, Scene 3

65. Lines 20–3
I have a whole school of tongues in this belly of mine, and not a tongue of them all speaks any other word but my name. Falstaff means: I am known everywhere only for my belly.

66. Line 27
The heat is past; follow no further now. Heat in this passage means a single course in a contest, with a pun on the meaning "the height or stress of an action." Compare the modern "the heat is off."

67. Line 45
I may justly say, with the hook-nosed fellow of Rome. Falstaff refers to Caesar and his *veni, vidi, vici*—usually rendered, "I came, I saw, I conquered." "Hook-nosed" refers to the so-called Roman or aquiline nose.

68. Line 53
I will have it in a particular ballad else. By "particular ballad" Falstaff means "a ballad of mine own." By "ballad" he means a broadside ballad—that is, a narrative in doggerel celebrating

a recent event or martial exploit, printed on one side of a folio sheet. These ballads were often illustrated with crude woodcuts. Sometimes they were fitted to popular tunes.

69. Lines 99–100
a kind of male green-sickness. Greensickness is usually identified with chlorosis—an anemic ailment of young women.

ACT IV, Scene 4

70. This scene telescopes events that are in reality separated by five and eight years. It moves from the close of the Archbishop's rebellion in 1405 at Branham Moor to 1413, the year King Henry IV died.

71. Stage directions
Westminster. The Jerusalem Chamber.
The "Jerusalem Chamber" was in reality in Westminster Abbey, not in Westminster Palace. Yet the presence of the Prince and courtiers, the arrival of Prince Hal, and so forth, make it clear that the scene must take place in the palace.

72. Line 48
aconitum. This is wolf's bane, a poison supposed to be powerful enough to work a hole in the strongest vessel.

ACT IV, Scene 5

73. Lines 78–9
We bring it to the hive, and, like the bees,
Are murdered for our pains.
"As bees are murdered by those who wish to get the honey that the workers have brought to the hive, so am I murdered for the treasure I have accumulated." Shakespeare shows some confusion in the development of his figure, for it is not the workers, but the drones, who are murdered in the hive.

74. Lines 114–5
Let all the tears that should bedew my hearse
Be drops of balm to sanctify thy head.
Balm was the consecrated oil used by a high official of the Church to anoint an English king at his coronation.

75. Lines 139–77
O, pardon me, my liege! . . .
Many portions of this speech by the Prince seem like empty rhetoric to a modern reader. But to an Elizabethan audience the rhetoric added weight to the Prince's indignant disclaimer of his father's accusations.

76. Lines 162–3
   Other, less fine in carat, is more precious,
   Preserving life in medicine potable.
   An elixir made out of gold was thought to possess magical curative properties.

   ACT V, SCENE 1
77. Line 1
   By cock and pie, sir. This was a rustic half-humorous oath, mild and harmless. The origin is thought to be a perversion of the word "God" in "cock," and "pie," the book of rules used in the consecration of a bishop and the ordination of priests. In the popular mind the phrase came to be associated with the cock and the magpie.
78. Lines 15–6
   shall we sow the headland with wheat? The headland was a strip of plowed land at the end of furrows.
79. Lines 89–91
   the wearing out of six fashions, which is four terms, or two actions. "Four terms" means one year, because there were four terms in the legal year. "Action" means law suits, probably for debt.

   ACT V, SCENE 2
80. Line 18
   That must strike sail to spirits of vile sort. To strike sail is to lower sail as a sign of surrender in a naval battle.
81. Line 34
   Which swims against your stream of quality. This is about equivalent to "goes against the grain."
82. Line 38
   A raggèd and forestalled remission. A beggarly pardon, sure to be refused.
83. Line 48
   Not Amurath an Amurath succeeds. The Turkish Sultan Amurath IV, who in 1596 succeeded his father, after having had his five brothers strangled. Amurath became a by-word for tyranny.
84. Line 72
   May this be washed in Lethe and forgotten? According to Greek mythology, drinking of the waters of the river Lethe in Hades brought oblivion.

ACT V, SCENE 3

85. Line 3
with a dish of caraways. "Caraways" was a confection containing caraway seeds.

86. Lines 18–9
Do nothing but eat, and make good cheer,
And praise God for the merry year.
This carol, and the one beginning, "Be merry, be merry, my wife has all" (l. 35), are probably not traditional but written by Shakespeare himself.

87. Line 38
And welcome merry Shrove-tide. Shrove-tide was the name given to the days—usually three—immediately preceding Ash Wednesday. It was a time of great merrymaking. Shrove-tide was so called because it was a time for shriving, that is, for confession and absolution.

88. Lines 78–9
And dub me knight:
    Samingo.
"Samingo" is a corruption of Sir Mingo, the hero of a popular drinking song. It became the refrain of the song.

89. Lines 93–4
I think a' be, but goodman Puff of Barson. "Goodman" was a term prefixed to persons under the rank of gentlemen—that is, yeomen or farmers. Barcherton, locally pronounced Barson, is a village in Warwickshire.

90. Line 106
Let King Cophetua know the truth thereof. A meaningless allusion to the king in the then popular ballad "King Cophetua and the Beggar Maid."

91. Line 108
Shall dunghill curs confront the Helicons? Pistol evidently confuses Mount Helicon, the haunt of the Muses, with the Muses themselves. He clearly resents the introduction of Robin Hood and his fellows into his exalted text.

ACT V, SCENE 4

92. Lines 5–6
she shall have whipping-cheer enough.
She shall have a big enough meal of lashes. In Shakespeare's day, whores were whipped by the beadle.

93. Line 8
nut-hook. A hook used to pull down branches of trees. It became a nickname for a constable.

ACT V, SCENE 5

94. Lines 30–1
'Tis "semper idem," for "obsque hoc nihil est." It is "always the same," for "without this there is nothing."

95. Line 39
Rouse up revenge from ebon den with fell Alecto's snake. Alecto was one of the Furies, depicted with snakes for hair.

96. Line 91
This that you heard was but a color. "Color" here means pretext with a pun on collar meaning a halter; choler meaning anger; and colors, flags of the enemy.

Bibliography

I. REFERENCE

BARTLETT, JOHN. *Concordance to Shakespeare*. London: Macmillan Co., 1960. An invaluable reference book, containing a complete verbal index to words, phrases, and passages in all the plays and poems.

BROOKE, C. F. TUCKER. *Shakespeare of Stratford*. New York: 1926. This volume, a handbook for students, gives the reader a brief, scholarly survey of the essential facts about the dramatist and his work.

COLLIER, J. P. and W. C. HAZLITT. *Shakespeare's Library: A Collection of the Romances, Novels, Poems, and Histories Used by Shakespeare in the Composition of His Works*. 2nd ed. 6 vols. London: 1875.

HALLIDAY, FRANK E. *A Shakespeare Companion 1500–1950*. New York: Funk and Wagnalls Co., 1950. An alphabetized list of critics, actors, plays, etc., and their relation to Shakespeare: an indispensable reference book.

HOLINSHED. *Shakespeare's Holinshed: The Chronicle and the Historical Plays*. Compared by W. G. Boswell-Stone. rev. ed. London: 1907.

————. *Holinshed's Chronicle as Used in Shakespeare's Plays*. ed. Allardyce and Josephine Nicoll. New York: Everyman's Library, E. P. Dutton & Co., 1927.

INGLEBY, CLEMENT M. *Shakespeare's Century of Praise*. London: 1870. A history of opinion on Shakespeare and his work from 1591 to 1693. This contains a source of information about the contemporary and early reputation of the Bard.

————. *Shakespeare Allusion Book: A Collection of Allusions to Shakespeare*. Rev., re-ed., rearranged. 2 vols. New York: Oxford University Press, 1932. These volumes bring the reputation of Shakespeare first reported in *Shakespeare's Century of Praise* down to the year 1932.

KÖKERITZ, HELGE. *Shakespeare's Pronunciation*. New Haven: Yale University Press, 1953. The latest authoritative work on this important subject.

KÖKERITZ, HELGE, and CHARLES TYLER PROUTY (eds.). *Shakespeare, William. Shakespeare's First Folio*. Facsimile ed. New Haven: Yale University Press, 1954. A photographic facsimile of the First Folio edition of Shakespeare's plays. An introduction on the printing of the Folio, playwriting, and the printing practices of Shakespeare's day prepared by Mr. Prouty.

SCHMIDT, ALEXANDER. *Shakespeare Lexicon*. 3rd ed. 2 vols. Berlin: 1902. The only complete dictionary of the English words, phrases and constructions occurring in all the Poet's works.

II. SHAKESPEARE'S LIFE

ALEXANDER, PETER. *Shakespeare's Life and Art*. London: James Nisbet & Co., Ltd., 1939. Many important and new insights into the relation of Shakespeare's life to his art.

BRANDES, GEORG M. C. *William Shakespeare: A Critical Study*. Translated by William Archer. London: William Heinemann Ltd., 1902. A "life" by one of the most famous literary critics of the nineteenth century.

CHAMBERS, SIR EDMUND K. *William Shakespeare: A Study of Facts and Problems*. 2 vols. New York: Oxford University Press, 1930. A thorough assemblage of all the important facts of Shakespeare's life by the most rigorous scholar in the field.

CHUTE, MARCHETTE. *Shakespeare of London*. New York: E. P. Dutton & Co., 1949. An excellent biography of Shakespeare. It contains a bibliography.

LEE, SIR SIDNEY. *A Life of William Shakespeare*. 4th ed. New York: Macmillan Co., 1929. For years the most authoritative account of the Poet's life.

VAN DOREN, MARK. *Shakespeare*. New York: Doubleday and Co., Inc., 1953. This is an appreciation, particularly of the poetry in all Shakespeare's plays, by a sensitive critic, who is himself a poet.

III. SHAKESPEARE'S TIMES

JENKINS, ELIZABETH. *Elizabeth the Great*. New York: Coward-McCann, Inc., 1959. The most recent American biography, a distinguished piece of scholarship and literary skill.

NEALE, JOHN E. *Queen Elizabeth*. New York: Harcourt, Brace and Co., Inc., 1934. The authoritative biography.

RALEIGH, SIR WALTER. *Shakespeare's England: An Account of the Life and Manners of His Age*. 2 vols. Oxford: 1917. A complete account of the habits, interests and activities of the people during Shakespeare's lifetime.

STEEHOLM, CLARA and HARDY. *James I of England*. New York: Crown Publishers, Inc., 1938. A lively and acute account of James's personal life and kingship.

TILLYARD, E. M. W. *The Elizabethan World Picture*. New York: Macmillan Co., 1944. The authoritative account of the geography—celestial and earthly—and the organization of the world as the Elizabethan pictured it.

IV. SHAKESPEARE'S THEATRE

ADAMS, JOHN C. *The Globe Playhouse: Its Design and Equipment*. Rev. ed. New York: Barnes & Noble, 1961. A widely approved description of the theatre for which most of Shakespeare's plays were written.

BECKERMAN, BERNARD. *Shakespeare at the Globe (1599–1609)*. New York: The Macmillan Co., 1962. An excellent recent study of all the elements of the production of Shakespeare's plays by his company at the Globe Theatre. By the Director of the Theatre at Hofstra College.

CHAMBERS, SIR EDMUND K. *The Elizabethan Stage*. 4 vols. Oxford: 1923. A complete account of the subject.

HARBAGE, ALFRED. *Shakespeare's Audience*. New York: Columbia University Press, 1941. An important account of the size and character of the typical audience when Shakespeare's plays were mounted at the Globe.

HOTSON, LESLIE. *Shakespeare's Wooden O*. New York: Macmillan Co., 1960.

JOSEPH, BERTRAM L. *Elizabethan Acting*. New York: Oxford University Press, 1951. The best book on the subject. The author's thesis is that the performance of the Elizabethan actor was the same as that of the orator in the uses of voice, face, body, hands and feet.

NICOLL, ALLARDYCE. "Studies in the Elizabethan Stage since 1900." *Shakespeare Studies* 1 (1948), pp. 1-16.

SPRAGUE, ARTHUR C. *Shakespeare and the Actor's Stage Business in His Plays (1660-1905)*. Cambridge: Harvard University Press, 1944. Expertly selected examples of the "business" of famous actors in crucial scenes of the plays. *Hamlet, Macbeth, Julius Caesar* and *Romeo and Juliet* are all treated.

STOPES, CHARLOTTE C. *Burbage and Shakespeare's Stage*. London: 1913. The most thorough account of the Poet's relation to James, Richard and Cuthbert Burbage and the theatres in which Shakespeare's plays were acted.

V. GENERAL CRITICISM

BRADBY, ANNE (ed.). *Shakespeare Criticism 1919–1935.* New York: Oxford University Press, 1936.

BRADLEY, A. C. *Shakespearean Tragedy.* London: Macmillan Co., 1904; New York: St. Martin's Press, Inc., 1955. The author gives memorable expression to the essential features of nineteenth-century criticism, i.e., the emphasis on the characters. An indispensable volume for understanding this one aspect of Shakespeare's work. It deals with *Hamlet, Othello, King Lear* and *Macbeth.*

CAMPBELL, LILY B. *Shakespeare's Tragic Heroes.* New York: Cambridge University Press, 1930. This excellent study interprets the tragedies as expressions of Elizabethan psychology. Each one dramatizes a sickness of the soul: *Hamlet,* grief; *Othello,* jealousy; *King Lear,* wrath in old age.

CHARLTON, H. B. *Shakespearian Comedy.* New York: Macmillan Co., 1938.

———. *Shakespearian Tragedy.* New York: Cambridge University Press, 1949.

GRANVILLE-BARKER, H. *Prefaces to Shakespeare.* 2 vols. Princeton: University Press, 1946. The author explains his ideas of the proper staging and acting of *Hamlet, King Lear, The Merchant of Venice, Antony and Cleopatra* and *Cymbeline.*

MOULTON, RICHARD G. *Shakespeare as a Dramatic Artist.* 3rd ed. New York: Oxford University Press, 1929. This book is one of the best accounts of Shakespeare's methods in constructing his plays.

SMITH, D. N. (ed.). *Shakespeare Criticism: A Selection.* New York: Oxford University Press, 1916.

SPURGEON, CAROLINE F. E. *Shakespeare's Imagery and What It Tells Us.* New York: Cambridge University Press, 1935.

STAUFFER, DONALD. *Shakespeare's World of Images.* New York: W. W. Norton and Co., 1949. This book is a study of Shakespeare's formulation of ideas and moral attitudes in a single character, or in the tension established among two or more characters.

THORNDIKE, ASHLEY H. *English Comedy.* New York: Macmillan Co., 1929. A substantial part of this book is devoted to Shakespeare's comedies and their relation to other plays.

WHITMORE, C. E. *The Supernatural in Tragedy.* New York: 1915. The author treats the passage of the Senecan ghost into Elizabethan tragedy where it underwent a remarkable development, of which the ghost in *Hamlet* is the most famous example.

VI. HENRY IV, PART II

BAILEY, JOHN. *Shakespeare*. London: Longmans, Green, 1929.

BETHEL, S. L. *Shakespeare and the Popular Dramatic Tradition.* Durham, N. C.: Duke University Press, 1944. In his treatment of convention, Bethel follows Schücking. His book also contains a thorough analysis of the psychology of a popular audience. He draws some of his evidence from audiences of the current cinema.

CAIN, H. E. "Further Light on the Relation of 1 and 2 Henry 4." *Shakespeare Quarterly*, III (1952), 21–38.

CLEMEN, WOLFGANG. *The Development of Shakespeare's Imagery.* Cambridge: Harvard University Press, 1951.

GODDARD, H. C. *The Meaning of Shakespeare*. Chicago: University of Chicago Press, 1951.

HARRISON, G. B. *Shakespeare at Work, 1592–1603*. London: Routledge & Kegan Paul, 1933.

LEVIN, HARRY. "Falstaff Uncolted." *Modern Language Notes*, LXI (1946), 305–310.

NICOLL, ALLARDYCE. *An Introduction to Dramatic Theory.* London: Harrap, 1923. Nicoll holds that Shakespeare treats the rejection of Falstaff as though he were a mere dramatic type, whereas the poet had made him grow into an individual who steps out of the bounds of comedy into those of serious drama.

———. *Shakespeare*. London: Oxford University Press, 1952.

O'CONNOR, FRANK. *The Road to Stratford*. London: Methuen, 1948.

PRIESTLEY, J. B. *The English Comic Characters*. London: John Lane, 1925. The prolific English novelist rejects the prevalent critical notion that Falstaff outgrows the positions in the action that Shakespeare intended him to occupy.

RIDLEY, M. R. *William Shakespeare: A Commentary*. New York: E. P. Dutton, 1938.

SCHÜCKING, LEVIN L. *Character Problems in Shakespeare's Plays.* London: Harrap, 1922. Schücking's view is that Shakespeare's theatre was primitive. The characters explain themselves directly to the audience and we must take seriously what they say about themselves. Falstaff, for example, explains that he is a clown whose business is to be witty and to stimulate laughter in others.

SHAABER, M. A. "The Unity of 'Henry IV.'" *Adam Memorial Studies*. Washington, D. C., 1948, pp. 217–227. The author takes the view that *Henry IV, Part II* was an unplanned encore of *Henry IV, Part I.*

SPARGO, J. W. "An Interpretation of Falstaff." Washington University Studies, 1922. Spargo attempts to explain Falstaff as a survival of the mediaeval Vice, whose function was to entertain and, in the end, to be punished.

STEWART, J. I. M. *Character and Motive in Shakespeare.* New York: Longmans, Green, 1949. The author believes that psychoanalysis shows that Shakespeare gained insight into the obscure regions of his characters' minds, where motive is often born.

TOLMAN, A. H. *Falstaff and Other Shakespearian Topics.* New York: The Macmillan Company, 1925.